CHAPTERS

ON

SOCIAL SCIENCE

AS CONNECTED WITH

THE ADMINISTRATION

OF

STATE CHARITIES.

GEORGE L. HARRISON.

PRIVATELY PRINTED.

PHILADELPHIA:

1877.

Printed by
ALLEN, LANE & SCOTT,
No. 233 South Fifth Street,
Philadelphia.

PREFACE.

The following pages are selected from papers originally contributed to the annual reports of the Board of Public Charities of the State of Pennsylvania by the president of the Board. They appeared in those reports as published by order of the legislature in the years 1870 to 1874, inclusive. The writer has deemed it advisable to collect them into one volume for his own gratification and that of his friends, venturing to think that thus they may not be without some further utility.

It might have seemed desirable to recast and rewrite the whole, digesting what pertains to each of the subjects discussed into one consistent and continuous treatise adjusted to the present time. But this would have cost much labor, and would have been, in fact, the production of an entirely new work, and, especially, would have defeated a leading design of the writer in having this volume printed,—which was, to keep the whole in its original association with the past. It has been thought best, therefore, to leave the several chapters in their historical character, each with its proper date, appending such notes and explanations as may seem required by the state of the several questions at the present time.

The original form, therefore, remains, as addressed to the legislature under the circumstances then existing. There have been some slight omissions, but no additions in the text, and no modifications either in the sentiments or the expression, of sufficient importance to be mentioned.

The whole is dedicated to my family and friends and those who come after me, as a memorial of labors which have been for many years among the most cherished and most absorbing objects of my life.

The volume does not seek the public eye, but, while it does not challenge, it does not shun either perusal or criticism.

May, 1877.

G. L. H.

CONTENTS.

EDUCATION.

PRISON ECONOMY.

CARE OF THE INSANE.

EDUCATION.

COMPULSORY EDUCATION.

In the report of this board for 1870, the last topic presented was that of neglected children. The legislature was then appealed to, by the highest considerations of the interests and duty of the State, to make provision for their care and education. "The average of social virtue, dignity, and wealth," it was then said, "is much reduced by the presence of this debased and debasing ingredient. And it is a problem well worthy of the gravest and most patient thought of philanthropic political economists, whether anything, and (if anything) what can be done for the rescue of these unfortunates from their ill-starred condition, for the protection of the community which they deteriorate, and for the purity, welfare, and honor of the State, the mother of them all."

This evil exists in all parts of the country, but is most patent and pressing in large cities and crowded communities. The remedy—what it shall be, and how it shall be applied—is a subject beset with grave difficulties; but they are difficulties which must be sooner or later manfully met and grappled with. The stability and welfare of the State and its free institutions, the interests and safety of every citizen, and the weal or woe of the thousands of innocent and helpless victims, are involved in the question and wait upon your solution.

This is an eminently proper subject for this board to bring to your attention, both as a "Board of Public Charities," and as being required by law to report on the causes and remedies of vice and crime.

No almshouse, no hospital, no asylum or refuge for the poor, the diseased, the insane, the imbecile, the inebriate, or the juvenile offender, is more a work of charity, than would be a provision for the care and education of these neglected children. No courts of justice, no prisons or penitentiaries, or houses of correction, or reformatory schools, can tend more directly or powerfully to the diminution of vice and crime, than schools and homes for these poor unfortunates, ever growing up in ignorance and pernicious habits, preparing to leaven our whole social condition, and to assist in making our laws.

According to the census of 1860 (the data of that for 1870 are not accessible), the number of adults who could not read was :—

In the United States, of the whole adult population,	20	per cent.
" " of the white adult population,	9	"
" " of the native white adult population, ...	7½	"
In New York, of the whole adult population, ...	6	"
" of the native white adult population, . .	1½	"
In Massachusetts, of the whole adult population, . . .	7	"
" of the native white adult population,	¼	"
In Maine, of the whole adult population, ...	3	"
" of the native white adult population, . . .	¾	"

In Pennsylvania,	of the whole adult population, . .	6 per cent.
"	of the native white adult population,	3¼ "

It is to be observed that only the number of the adult population is here referred to in each case.

Of the native white population (adult) the number of illiterate adults, less their proportion of adults who were idiotic, insane, deaf-mutes, and blind, was:—

In Massachusetts, ...	—230
In Maine, ...	1,507
In Pennsylvania, ...	34,470

Thus the number in Pennsylvania was five to one of that in Maine, in proportion to the native white population of the respective States; while in Massachusetts, the result shows, if the returns are correct, that more than two hundred and thirty of the idiotic, insane, deaf-mute, and blind adults must have been taught to read, which is undoubtedly the fact. Since 1860, great improvements have been made in the constitution and working of the school system in Pennsylvania, and it is to be presumed that the proportion of illiteracy among her native white population has greatly diminished. Under such circumstances, the much greater proportion of illiteracy among the foreign-born population, though a great, is but a temporary, evil.

In reckoning the twenty per cent. of illiteracy in 1860, in the whole adult population of the United States, it is to be observed that the slaves were set down, according to their legal status, as all untaught to read, which was then not far from the fact.

NON-ATTENDANCE OF CHILDREN AT SCHOOL.

The number of children of the school age (from five to fifteen), not attending the public schools at all, was :—

In Massachusetts,	in 1869 and 1870, ...	9	per cent.
"	average absence of pupils, ...	19	"
In Pennsylvania,	in 1869 and 1870, ...	6	"
"	average absence of pupils, ...	33	"
In Philadelphia,	in 1869 and 1870, ...	12	"
"	average absence of pupils, ...	46	"
In New York (school age five to twenty-one),	in 1869,	24	"

The number of pupils in academies and private schools, in Massachusetts and Pennsylvania, may about balance the number in the public schools, of pupils under five and over fifteen years of age.

If, then, we make due allowance for the number of imbecile, insane, deaf-mute, and blind, for those taught to read at home, for those detained from school by chronic sickness, for those (particularly between the ages of five and eight) not yet sent to school, but who will attend hereafter, and for those (particularly between the ages of twelve and fifteen) not attending school in the given year, but who had already learned to read in former years, the percentage of absolute non-attendance in these two States will be reduced to a very low figure, probably to not more than one or two per cent., which is quite enough. And the apparent advantage of Pennsylvania over Massachusetts, in the percentage, may, it is not unlikely, arise from some difference in the manner of making the returns.

In Pennsylvania, the whole number of pupils registered in the public schools, *during the whole year*, are reported. In Massachusetts, the highest number attending for any time, that is, in the winter schools, is given. In other words, in Massachusetts the highest number attending the summer schools is returned, and the highest number attending the winter schools ; but though many pupils attend in summer and not in winter, and conversely, no attempt is made to give the full number of different names registered at both seasons of the year. However this point of comparison may be settled, any doubtful advantage in this respect is more than balanced by our manifest disadvantage in the average absenteeism of those actually registered as pupils.

If due allowance is made for the longer period of school age in New York, it will probably be found that, at least outside of the city of New York, the school system of that State is quite as effective in reaching the whole population as that of either Massachusetts or Pennsylvania.

It is in the large cities, as is shown by the statistics of Philadelphia, Pittsburg, Reading, and other large cities, that the greatest proportion of neglected and uninstructed children is found ; and in such communities the proportion is appalling. It cannot be less in Philadelphia, after all such allowances as those before referred to are made, than about six per cent. of the whole number of children of the school age—that is to say, about ten or eleven thousand. And the huge and unparalleled proportion of absence to attendance of the pupils themselves, viz., forty-six to fifty-four, is scarcely less appalling.

IGNORANCE AND CRIME.

Ignorance not only entails vice and wretchedness upon the individual, and loss and expense upon the State, but it is a fruitful source of crime. This might be presumed from the nature of the case, without facts; but facts establish it.

The percentage of convicts in State prisons, who were unable to read on admission, as reported in 1868, was:—

In the whole United States,	28 per cent.
In New York,	15 "
In Pennsylvania,	16 "
In Maine,	10 "

How far the result in the nation, as a whole, may have been influenced by the presence of the freedmen, it is not possible for us, at present, to determine; but it appears that, even assuming all the freedmen to be illiterate, the number of uninstructed convicts was nearly three to two of what it should have been in proportion to the whole number of the illiterate population of the United States.

To the percentage of illiterate of the whole adult population, and of the adult native white population, respectively, the percentage of illiterate *convicts* was:—

In New York,	as 2½ and 10 to 1.
In Pennsylvania,	as 2¾ and 5 to 1.
In Maine,	as 3⅓ and 13 to 1.

And, after making the proper comparisons, it will appear that, if all the people in these States had learned to read, the number of State prison convicts would probably have been diminished just about ten per cent.

DUTY OF THE STATE.

To furnish the needful education, therefore, to her neglected children, is what the State owes to them— is what the State owes to herself. Charity requires it; prudence and statesmanship command it. And, accordingly, we shall not hesitate to proceed to consider the subject in both these relations.

But when we propose to bring our schools to bear especially on this unfortunate class, we are met, *in limine*, with the objection that our present school system already provides for the whole case; that it offers the means of an elementary education to all who choose to avail themselves of its benefits. This may, in a certain sense, be true; but there are children, too young to be qualified or permitted to choose for themselves, and yet the choice made for them determines, it may be, the happiness or misery of their whole lives; determines whether they are to be useful or pernicious members of society; and shall that choice be permitted which imperils not only their happiness, but the welfare and existence of the State?

It is precisely those children, whose parents or guardians are unable or indisposed to provide them with an education; it is precisely those, for whom the State is most interested to provide and secure it; for other children would, probably, be educated, if the State did not intervene. And as for the children, so far as they choose for themselves, those who neglect the education offered them in the free schools, preferring the pleasures and license of vagabondage and truancy, are precisely those for whom such education is most needed; for a desire for education is next to education itself in its good effects, and those who determine to have it would probably obtain it, whether the State offered it to them or not.

Clearly it is the duty—that is, it is the highest interest of the State, to secure the education of these "neglected children," *if possible;* and the only questions are: Is it possible? and, if so, How can it be done?

To attain the end will, of course, involve something like what is called "Compulsory Education;" and, against such a scheme, there is started at once a great variety of objections and difficulties. Are these insuperable? Without argument, it might be assumed that they are not; for, "where there is a will there is a way." Moreover, it is demonstrated by fact, that they are not insuperable; for the thing has been done; and where it has been done, it has never yet been undone or repented of. It is a notable fact, that no country or community that has adopted either the system of public schools for all, or that has gone so far as to add to it that of compulsory education, has ever retraced its steps.

THE SYSTEM OF COMPULSORY EDUCATION HAS BEEN LONG AND SUCCESSFULLY TRIED.

This system has been long established in Norway. During the four hundred years of the subjection of this country to Denmark, it may be said that education was much neglected, and ignorance threatened to become universal. The law rendering education compulsory was passed in 1827, the agitation of which was begun in 1814, soon after the independence of the country was secured; and the enactments have been, since that time, rendered more complete, particularly by the law of 1860. The consequence is, that almost every Norwegian can read and write. The school age of compulsory attendance is, for children in the country, from eight to fifteen years, and in the towns, from seven to fifteen. Regular attendance upon the common schools is enforced by fines imposed upon the parents. If they persist in negiecting the training of their children, the law steps in, removes the children from their guardianship, and places them in families, where they will be conscientiously taught, the expenses being collected from those who should have cared for them. In Norway, compulsory education was the immediate result of political freedom.

In Sweden it was an agitation of ten years in the House of Peasants that finally constrained the government to take up the subject. Then there arose a remarkable and unanimous opposition from the bishops. Some held the matter to be absolutely local, and one with which the State should not meddle; others declared that, if schools were established, the people were too poor to send their children properly clad; others maintained that the education of the peasantry should be of a limited character. The bishop of Lund, that seat of the ancient university, maintained that popular education could not and should not be introduced. The reply of the celebrated poet Tegner, then bishop of the diocese of Wexjö, was similar in spirit. To the question, what should the folk-schools teach? he answered, "The culture of the laboring classes ought, principally, to be religious; this, if rightly impârted, includes morality; all other is to be regarded as not only needless but more hurtful than beneficial." Tegner was at that time fifty-seven years of age, and had been a bishop about twelve years. Notwithstanding the opposition of the established church, in three years from the time these answers were given, the present system of folk-schools had its foundation in an act of the Diet. By the law of 1842, one such school was required to be maintained in each socken, both in the city and in the country. [See the report of the United States Minister at Stockholm.] The result has been that in 1868 ninety-seven per cent. of all the children in Sweden were actually attending the folk or higher schools, or were receiving certified instruction elsewhere. Compulsory education in Sweden may be carried by law to the separation of children from parents; but this has been resorted to in but few instances, and only where the poverty of the parent rendered it necessary for the parish to support the child.

There is in Sweden a growing sentiment in favor of enforcing universal attendance, avoiding, if possible, the separation of parent and child. Instruction in the folk-schools is practically gratuitous.

In Prussia, also, as is well known, the system of compulsory education has been established long enough to have had its effect upon the training of a whole generation; and it is perhaps the best educated generation that has ever lived, or that is anywhere to be found. No other people have been so universally trained in the elements of learning and useful knowledge. This is the people that has revolutionized Europe on the fields of Sadowa and Sedan; and the success of Prussia in her great contests with Austria and with France, has resulted far more from this educated intelligence of her people than from any warlike arm, or any strategy or military science of her generals.

Austria has been wise enough to take a lesson from her defeat, and imitating the policy of the victor, she has entered upon a course of political and popular improvement, upon a system of liberality and progress, which, if persevered in, will render her a greater nation than she has ever been. One of the greatest benefits yet conferred upon the working classes of Austria, is the general school bill of 14th May, 1869, which makes national education compulsory, and greatly elevates the standard of it. In accordance with the law, compulsory attendance at school begins with every child at the age of six, and is continued uninterruptedly until the age of fourteen. But even then, the child is only allowed to leave school on production of certified proof that he has thoroughly acquired the full amount of information which this great law fixes as the absolute minimum of education for every Austrian citizen. Nor are any private schools tolerated by the government which do not efficiently provide the prescribed amount of secular instruction; although so long as this condition is fulfilled, the law imposes no limit to private educational establishments.

The misfortunes and miseries of France have taught

her the same lesson; and it is now stated, on good authority, that the French republican government has it in contemplation to establish for that country a thorough system of universal compulsory education. Had she established such a system thirty years ago the name of Sedan would have remained in comparative obscurity; the myriads of her soldiers would have acquired their knowledge of German geography in a more satisfactory way than that in which it was actually forced upon them, and the Paris commune would either have never existed, or would not have found the ignorant mob of idlers and vagabonds that were ready to execute its savage decrees of vandalism and murder.

England, too, has been roused at length from her lethargy. Her elementary education act was passed August 9th, 1870. This act of a liberal progressive administration, has made a step towards the thorough instruction and education of the masses of the English people, which an established church and an aristocratic State, with all the wealth of the richest country in the world at their command for centuries, had neglected or failed to accomplish or even to undertake. This education act includes the compulsory feature, and its detailed provisions, the result of a most exhaustive investigation and discussion, may be referred to as embodying an eminently practical effort towards solving and removing the difficulties which embarrass the subject.

Thus, in Europe, the system of compulsory education has been established in countries chiefly agricultural, and in others largely commercial and manufacturing; in countries with a scattered rural population, and in others with cities as large as our own; in countries comparatively poor and peaceful, and in others of the greatest wealth and warlike spirit; in countries where the distribution of wealth is most equal, and in others where it is most unequal. And, wherever it has been tried, it has proved successful and satisfactory; no retrograde step has been taken or even thought of.

Nor is it in Europe only that the system has been introduced. Massachusetts has, for several years, been trying it with some limitations, but with a constant and increasing tendency towards a more stringent and absolute enforcement of the rule, and with eminently satisfactory results. Not only Massachusetts, one of our oldest States, and, side by side with our own Pennsylvania, the very cradle of American freedom, and where the ancient fires of liberty still burn as brightly as anywhere else in our independent country; not only old Massachusetts in the east, but Nebraska in the west,—one of the most youthful States in the Union, where the life-blood of liberty and progress is throbbing with fresh and buoyant energy,—Nebraska has, by the framers of her constitution, sought to engraft this feature upon her school system in her fundamental law; a provision, however, which has been rendered prospective, in consequence of the rejection of the constitution because of an objectionable feature in the article on taxation.

The superintendent of public schools in Massachusetts reports, in 1870, that the law for the suppression of "truancy," as applied in Boston, is working satisfactorily. The city is divided into ten truant districts, one truant officer being assigned to each district.

These officers are expected to give their whole time to the investigation of cases of truancy, reported to them by the teachers of their respective districts, and in securing the attendance of absentees—that is, of children whose names are not enrolled in the schools, and who are, therefore, not known, technically, as "truants." Massachusetts, also, requires a certificate of a certain number of months attendance in school, as a condition of the employment of children in any manufactory.

The Massachusetts Board of Education, in their report of 1871, say:—

"By the present law, attendance at school for three months in each year is rendered compulsory for every child between the ages of eight and fourteen, except in certain special cases, while the towns are required to maintain their schools at least six months in each year.

"The board recommend that the statute be changed, so as to require attendance for the whole period, at least, during which schools are required to be maintained, believing that attendance upon the schools should be compulsory for the child for the same term in which the maintenance of the school is compulsory for the tax-payers. Since the only hope of security and prosperity for a republic rests in the virtuous intelligence of its citizens, the rightfulness of compulsory education is generally admitted. *Salus populi suprema lex.* The necessity of enforcing this right arises from the existence in our community of a large and growing class of persons, not only ignorant themselves, but only too willing to keep their children in ignorance for the sake of the pittance which may be earned by unskilled juvenile labor."

From New York comes the voice in regard to the crying evil of absenteeism: "There is no remedy that I know of but compulsory attendance." The superintendent of public schools declares that "the primary object of the State, in bestowing free education upon its citizens, is not to benefit individuals as such, but to qualify them properly for their relations and duties to each other as members of the same community." The superintendent of the schools in Maine has put the argument into this form: "The power which compels the citizen to pay his annual tax for the support of schools should, in like manner, fill the schools with all of those for whose benefit that contribution was made. It is in the light of a solemn compact between the citizen and the State community. The private citizen contributes of his means, under the established rule of the State, for the education of the youth, with a view to protection of person and security to property; the State, compelling such contributions, is under reciprocal obligation to provide and secure the complete education for which the contribution has been made. This implies the exercise of State power, and involves compulsory education as a duty to the tax-payer. The State builds prisons and penitentiaries for the protection of society, and taxes society for the same. But does she stop here, leaving him who has violated the law to be pursued by the community in a mass—to be apprehended by a crowd and borne by a throng to the place of incarceration? No; she pursues the criminal through legitimate instrumentalities, ferrets him out by the sharpest means of detection, and eventually secures that safety and protection to society for which society has been taxed. Now, to prevent crime—to anticipate and shut it off by proper compulsory efforts in the school-room, working with and moulding early childhood and youth 'to the principles of morality and justice, and a sacred regard for truth, love of country, humanity, and a universal benevolence, sobriety, industry, and frugality, chastity, moderation, and temperance, and all other virtues which are the ornaments of society' [cited from the Constitution of Maine], the State not only has the right to inaugurate such methods as may be deemed best, but is under strict obligation to do so by all the means in her power."

The world is moving! Shall Pennsylvania remain behind?

CLASSIFICATION OF THE EVIL.

The evil to be remedied is multiform. The absentees from the schools may be distributed into various classes. There are absentees from the public schools who are provided at least with an elementary education at home, or in private or charitable institutions. Of these nothing further is required but the ascertainment of this fact; and their case is then to be entirely set aside from any idea of compulsion or control.

For the rest, among the absentees from the schools are:—

1. Children living in the streets, without guardianship or supervision, and without employment, except such as they may choose or chance to pick up for themselves.

2. Children employed in manufacturing drudgery, not only in great cotton or woolen manufactories, but who are crowded into cellars and garrets and cramped and comfortless rooms—working, for example, in manipulating tobacco, and in all sorts of simple drudgery.

3. Children, in the city, kept at home by their parents to run errands or help them in their daily toil, trade, or business; as about grocers' shops or butchers' stalls, or other purely unimproving occupations, equivalent to idleness at home.

4. Children in the country, kept, from their earliest years, constantly employed in agricultural labors.

OUTLINES OF THE REMEDY PROPOSED.

It is necessary for the best interests of the State, and of the children themselves, that at least an elementary education should be secured to all these classes; but it is not equally necessary for all. For the first class it is most necessary, and its importance diminishes in the order of the enumeration, until the last class, in which it is least important. For, *any* honest employment, consistent with health, is better than idle vagabondage; and the knowledge of some trade, or of agriculture (which is the healthiest employment of all for a child, both morally and physically), is even more important towards making a good citizen than a knowledge of reading, writing, or arithmetic.

The truant and employment laws of Massachusetts, with some fuller provisions, might answer, for the remedy, in case of the first and second classes. Of the first class, the attendance at school should be required and secured absolutely; and for those among them entirely destitute of homes and means of support, proper refuges, maintenance and guardianship should be provided at the public expense. The safety of the community demands it; the economy of the tax-payer requires it; for it is, in the end, the cheapest way by which the case can be disposed of, and the only way to make the tax already paid effectual to accomplish its object.

And it is to be remembered that, though this form of the evil may be largely local, its dangerous consequences and the interest in having it remedied are not local. The character of great cities exerts a powerful, and often a sadly controlling, influence on the country, near and remote. They may be fountains of blessing to a State, or they may be sources of wide-spread corruption, nests of iniquity, festering sores upon the body politic. The children that grow up neglected in the city do not always remain there. They may carry the pestilential influence of their vices all over the State. While, if they were rescued from ruin, trained up in useful knowledge and moral habits, they would almost certainly be found in large proportion distributed over the whole area of the State, rendering efficient assistance in the development of its resources and the elevation of its character. Their education, therefore, concerns not only the city wherein they are found, but the whole Commonwealth.

The safety of the State may not be so much imperilled by the neglect of the second class as of the first; but, in point of fact, an almost equal positive loss of wealth, *i. e.*, of productive labor, is incurred. Besides, it is permitting outrageous cruelty to the children; and if the State, by solemn enactment, may provide for the prevention of cruelty to animals, though inflicted by the poorest man in the very act of earning his daily bread, will she not provide for the prevention of cruelty to her own children, however the necessities of the parents may seem to justify or excuse it? In these cases, the parents or employés should be absolutely required, under appropriate penalties, to send the children to school a certain portion of the year, until they have acquired at least those rudiments of knowledge which should be adjudged by statute to constitute the minimum of an elementary education. If obedience to such a law is refused, and if, from the poverty of the parties or from whatever cause, the penalties cannot be enforced, then, as in the former case, the State should interpose, and take the care and maintenance of the children into its own hands. To provide for their maintenance, by compelling them to devote to manual and exhausting labor that childhood which should be devoted to the studies and recreations of school, is, in the end, the most expensive way to the State in which it could be provided for.

Of the third and fourth classes, the attendance at school might be required by a similar process with similar provisions, and for similar, though, at least in the fourth class, not equally imperative reasons. Such is a general outline of a remedy proposed for the great evil in question. But it meets with many

OBJECTIONS.

1. "It would interfere with personal liberty." So does the imposition of military service or training. So does the requisition to serve on juries or to aid the sheriff in the *posse comitatus.* So does the law abating nuisances, or making it penal to sell certain articles without a license. If the safety and welfare of the State are sufficient reasons for those interferences with personal liberty, why should not the same be sufficient reasons in the other and more urgent case? Indeed, we might as well admit it to be a part of the personal liberty of the citizen to get drunk or go naked in the streets, or set fire to his house, or starve his family, as to have children, and, that he may use them only for his own accommodation, or in mere wantonness to cast them upon the community in vicious ignorance and sottish imbecility. If the law may restrain a man from cruelly beating his horse or his mule, shall it be considered an insufferable interference with his personal liberty to forbid his dwarfing the minds, debasing the morals, stunting the bodies, and enfeebling the constitutions of his children? Is the State more interested in the care of oxen than of men?

2. "It would be an interference with the rights of conscience."

So may be the imposition of military service, or the requisition of personal aid to the sheriff; but this case need involve no such interference at all, unless men have a conscientious repugnance to children being taught to read and write, and to lead moral and virtuous lives, instead of being left to grow up in ignorance and vice. And, even as for religious instruction, it would be to assume a strange position to say, "the instructor may teach the child that 'twice two are four;' he may even say, 'be temperate and chaste,' but I have conscientious scruples against his saying, 'obey the commandments of Almighty God.'" Still, all formal religious instruction or exercises in the schools that children are required to attend, including, under that category, even the reading of the Holy Scriptures, *if so it is insisted upon*,* may be confined to certain prescribed periods at the opening or close of the school-day; and all children may be excused from attendance at those periods, whose parents or guardians should expressly desire it.

3. "The State is not a benevolent institution, or an association for moral reform."

---

*And who will insist upon it? The opposition to the reading of the Holy Scriptures in the common schools, coming from professed infidels, Mohammedans, Jews, or Chinese, is scarcely of sufficient account, in this Christian country, to overrule the wishes of all other parties. The real brunt of the opposition comes from a professed Christian body—the Roman Catholic Church; and it should be distinctly understood, once for all, that if the Bible is banished from our public schools it is because that body of Christians demands its banishment. And then let it be considered with what force and fairness that church can turn around and raise the cry of "godless schools." By whose fault are they godless? Let the responsibility rest where it belongs. Let it be remembered that the same people who cry out most lustily against the "godless schools" are the people who have insisted upon utterly banishing from the schools the very reading of the Holy Scriptures. As for the different *versions* of the Bible, that, except with bigots, could not be a matter of essential moment, and it might easily be arranged that the question, whether the Protestant or the Douay version should be read, should be determined by the majority in each school division or school board.

But the State has its almshouses; it aids in the support of institutions for the deaf and dumb, the blind, the feeble-minded; it aids in establishing and in sustaining houses of refuge and schools of reform for the youthful victims of neglect, incorrigibility, or vice. Its legislature has its standing committee on vice and immorality, and has constituted this commission as its "Board of Public Charities." Surely it will hardly be urged as a proper reason against a legal enactment, that it will do some good,—that it will tend to accomplish even the highest ends of benevolence and morality. But here it is the very safety and welfare of the State that is appealed to, as the proper object of the proposed legislation. To prevent vice and crime by removing their causes, and thus to prevent their consequences of poverty and misery and shame, of injury and loss to society, is quite as consistent with the proper functions of the State, as to punish them after they have borne their fruits.

4. "It would vastly increase the cost and burden of the public schools."

If it should do so, it would still be only as the necessary means of securing for all the education which it is the constitutional duty of the legislature to provide. But it would probably not increase the cost of the schools nearly so much as it might be supposed or apprehended, while it might be made greatly to increase their general efficiency. It is to be assumed that school accommodations are already provided sufficient for all the children of school age in the Commonwealth. But even if it were necessary to reserve or supply separate schools for those whose children do not now attend school at all, and if to these were added the incorrigibly truant and the unreasonably absent from the other schools, together with those who for misbehavior or negligence are expelled from them, it would only leave more room in the other schools for the wants of an increasing population, and would, in the long run, involve only a change in the *distribution* of the whole number of children. The result would, in fact, be that the average attendance in the other schools would be much raised; the conduct and industry of the pupils would be improved, and in the end the number to be provided for in the separate school would be very small indeed. And as to the meagre remnant of extremely destitute children which would be, we believe, continually reduced under the system we propose, for whom maintenance as well as instruction would have to be provided, it is not easy to see how the State can decline the duty of making the provision, or why, while it has its numerous asylums of kindred character, it should *seek* to decline it. We think, therefore, that the expense would not be "vastly" increased; but whatever the cost would be, it ought to be cheerfully met.

5. "It would encourage reckless marriages, and the reckless idleness and wastefulness of parents."

This is the sort of objection that has been made, and may continue to be made against all relief afforded to the poor and wretched. There is an abuse to be guarded against, but it is not to be guarded against by leaving the destitute and miserable to rot and perish; but only by giving the relief in such judicious ways and degrees as to avoid abuses as far as possible. The same good judgment should be exercised in this case. But the objection is the less applicable here, because the natural and proper effect of the legislation proposed would be, on the whole, to diminish poverty and wretchedness, as well as ignorance, vice, and crime. Meantime it does not appear that the evil consequence alleged has actually followed where education has been made universally compulsory, whether in Sweden, in Norway, or in Germany.

6. "Merely to learn to read and write will not make better citizens or diminish crime."

Here it is to be observed, first of all, that the practical alternative is not, as is often invidiously suggested, between a knowledge of reading and writing on the one hand, and habits of morality and religion or a knowledge of a trade on the other; but between so much knowledge as is involved in reading and writing and no education at all; between so much knowledge as that or blank ignorance or a training only in habits of vice and crime.

In the second place, so far from its being true that such a modicum of learning, or any amount of knowledge, is naturally associated with immorality, the plain fact is that there is a natural affinity between knowledge and good morals; between the normal culture of the intellect and of the heart; between truth and rectitude; and that a knowledge of reading and writing increases both the means and the tendency to acquire both the knowledge and the habits of virtue and good morals. This is the general law, and the dissociation of knowledge from virtue, the perversion of knowledge to the aid and development of vice and iniquity, which, it is true, may sometimes happen, and which has happened in some notorious and terrible examples, is one of the most monstrous abuses known in human experience.

But, in the third place, it is not proposed that these children should be taught to read and write to the exclusion of all moral or religious instruction. The public schools of Pennsylvania are neither immoral nor godless schools. Ninety-nine in a hundred of the teachers are, and would continue to be, moral, and nine-tenths of them religious persons. Moral and religious instruction and training would be given, radiating constantly in an unconscious influence from the person, bearing, and example of the teacher; from the very air and order of the school-room; and in formal lessons, too, and special exercises, with such rare exceptions for weak consciences as have been before referred to. Moreover, we here add, that all the time, if any, besides Sundays and Saturdays, which any parents may require for their children to receive actual religious instruction from their own religious teachers, would be freely accorded to them. The church or the churches, and any benevolent, moral, and religious associations or persons, are, and will be, of course, at perfect liberty to give to these neglected children now in question, not only moral and religious instruction, but as full an education, in all respects, as they please. The State will not interfere with them. The State, in her school system, does not interfere with the church at all. The church is, and always has been, and always will be, while the fundamental principles of our civil and social polity remain what they are, at perfect liberty to educate in religion, morals, and every kind of learning, all the children in the State, if she will, and if she can induce them to receive her instructions. Of course the State will not, and cannot consistently, compel the attendance of the children upon such schools. The church is at as full liberty to do all she will and can *with* the State system of public schools, even including in that system the feature of compulsory attendance (for this feature is never to be applied to children who receive sufficient instruction elsewhere); the church has, and will have, *with all this*, just as full and free scope for all her benevolent activities as she ever had or could have with no State schools whatever. The church has had her opportunity, without these latter schools, falsely and slanderously styled "godless," and with immense revenues and means in her hands,—means and revenues, in many cases, bestowed upon her for this very purpose,—in Spain, in Italy, in Portugal, in the states of South America, and even in England; and what has been the result as to the education of the masses of the poorer and of the so-called lower classes of the community? In many cases, as in Sweden, she seems to have been positively principled against their education. The "church" has reason to hide her head in silent shame or humble confession at her own neglect, rather than to carp at the state for its imperfect efforts to supply her lack of service to remedy, as it may, the consequences of her unfaithfulness. Meanwhile, the state not only leaves the church at liberty to act for herself and in her own way, but invites her, and invites all good men, to render their aid in this work so fraught with beneficence towards its particular objects, as well as interwoven with the necessary conditions of the public welfare. And it is no small encouragement to the efforts of the state in this direction, to believe and expect, as we have good reason to do, that those efforts will be seconded, and their expense greatly curtailed, not only by the spontaneous favor of public opinion, but by the systematic aid of Christian benevolence, in furnishing homes and refuges, as well as a good training, to many of these children of neglect and want.*

*After so many repeated and complete explanations and refutations as have been made, the persistent efforts to hold up the system of secular education in common schools to obloquy, as being hostile, in any sense or degree, to the religious education of the young, is one of the most astonishing and inexplicable instances of an inveterate and perverse misunderstanding, or of obstinate and unreasoning misrepresentation, to be found in the history of human thought and human controversy. There is absolutely not the slightest antithesis or interference between the two. The church is left just as free as she ever was or could be to give all the religious education she can or will to any and all children, and all other education, too, if she chooses. The common-school system leaves her entirely untrammeled to discharge her whole duty in the training of the young; for as to the assertion, sometimes made, that a merely secular education is in itself worse than absolute ignorance, it scarely deserves the honor of a refutation. And yet, from the persistent tone and reiterated assertions of certain ecclesiastical opponents of the common schools, one would suppose the church was, by this system, absolutely stripped of her rights of training her children in religious culture at all, and that all the children taught in the common schools were actually deprived of a religious education, which they would otherwise receive, and positively condemned to sheer godlessness, irreligion, and immorality. On the contrary, the point is just this: the state, from the nature of the case, cannot and will not give a religious education to her children,—though she will have the Bible read in her schools until the church forbids it;—but she will give a secular education to all her children, unless the church herself or some other party chooses to give such an education to any or all, with or without a religious training. In carrying out

In the fourth place, if by "good citizens" is meant useful, productive members of society, it is not pretended that *all* which is of importance to make men such, is, to teach them to read and write; and if the state is disposed and can afford to secure to these children the knowledge of some trade or handicraft *also*, so much the better. Meantime, the mere knowing how to read and write tends, and powerfully tends, in the right direction; tends towards making men useful and productive citizens; tends, therefore, to increase the wealth and prosperity of the State, and thus to repay, and more than repay, all that it may have cost. Abundant evidence on this head has been collected by the United States Commissioner of Education, and published in his report for 1870, pages 439–467. The following questions were submitted to a great number and variety of competent witnesses:—

1. Have you observed a difference in skill, aptitude, and amount of work executed by persons you have

---

this plan, the state is not, here with us, hampered or hindered by those complications which exist in most European countries, where they have an established or state religion, side by side with dissenting religious bodies; and where an outcry is naturally created, whether in the state schools the religious instruction of the established church is given or not given. Especially is this outcry occasioned, and justly, if the funds of the established church are diverted by the state to the maintenance of a system of merely secular instruction. There is also equal reason for complaint, when the law of compulsory education absolutely requires that all children shall receive their education in the state schools, whether religious instruction is given in them or not; so that, even if the church or private schools furnish an equally good secular education, no such substitution is accepted for that given in the state schools. This may well be considered as interfering with the right of conscience and with personal and religious liberty. But nobody proposes that compulsory education, with us, should assume this form. Only a certain training in the public schools is to be required of all children of a certain age, *or its equivalent elsewhere.*

employed, arising from a difference in their education, and independent of natural abilities?

2. Do those who can *merely* read and write, and who merely possess those rudiments of an education, other things being equal, show any greater skill and fidelity as laborers, skilled or unskilled, or as artisans, than do those who are not able to read and write? and, if so, how much would such additional skill, &c. tend to increase the productiveness of their services, and, consequently, their wages?

The answers to these questions all tend to establish the point that the mere ability to read and write, by even an unskilled laborer, adds, on an average, from twenty-five to fifty per cent. to his value and efficiency.

Similar questions were propounded to large numbers of intelligent workmen, and of observers, who were neither employers nor workmen, and all with the same result.

It cannot be doubted, therefore, that the wealth of the State would be greatly promoted by giving at least a rudimentary education to those thousands of her children who are now suffered to grow up in ignorance and neglect.

In the fifth place, that the merely knowing how to read and write is to some extent a preservative from crime, is evident from the State prison statistics already given, from which it appears that if all in the State were taught to read and write, the number of criminals would be diminished nearly ten per cent. The consequence would be a great pecuniary saving; though one can hardly bring himself to mention this by the side of the immense moral gain.

7. "The evil complained of is very slight in the rural portions of the State."

If so, then all the other objections, for this case, proportionally lose their weight; then, its remedy could interfere but little with personal liberty or the rights of conscience; it could subject the State in but a slight degree to the charge of philanthropy; it could cost but little, and could not much encourage reckless marriages or extravagant living, nor could it much increase the exposure of the State schools to the charge of immorality and ungodliness, or inutility and impotence.

The remedy is, doubtless, more needed in cities and crowded communities than it is in sparsely settled and agricultural portions of the country; but we think that we have shown that its beneficial influences would not be confined to these districts of dense population, but that they would be widespread and general, and that we have also demonstrated that in the less thickly settled districts it is not impracticable, nor likely to work any evil, but rather that it will be productive of good and only good, as is proved by the experience of Prussia and Sweden and Norway, in which latter country it has been in full operation for more than forty years.

From a review, therefore, of the whole case, the board cannot but earnestly recommend as a remedy for this—one of the greatest, most painful, and most threatening evils that exist among us—the enactment of a general law of *compulsory education*, or as near an approximation to it as the legislature, in its wisdom, shall deem expedient and practicable; any necessary increase of expenditure to be met either by appropriations from the State treasury or by local taxation, or by both.

NOTE.

Since the foregoing was written, several European countries, such as England, France, Austria, and others, have made great progress towards the adoption of the principle of not only affording a certain amount of elementary education to all the children of the state, but of requiring they should actually receive it.

In New England, compulsory education has substantially existed for upwards of two centuries, under the old law of Massachusetts, of 1642. That law enacted that "Forasmuch as the good education of children is of singular behoof and benefit to any commonwealth, and whereas, many parents and masters are too indulgent and negligent of their duty in that kind, it is ordered that the chosen men appointed for managing the prudential affairs in the several precincts and quarters where they dwell shall have a vigilant eye over their neighbors, to see, first, that none of them shall suffer so much barbarism in any of their families as not to endeavor to teach by themselves and others their children and apprentices so much learning as may enable them to read perfectly the English tongue, and to get knowledge of the capital laws, upon penalty of twenty shillings for each neglect therein."

It was in the exercise of this same authoritative parental oversight that Massachusetts again, in 1836, forbade the employment of children under fifteen in factories, unless such children should have attended school for three months in the preceding year. Such an ordinance was a virtual compulsion of attendance for at least that period in each year, on the part of all children for whom employment was desired, since without the attendance the employment could not lawfully be given. The provision, slightly modified, still exists in that State, and has been put also on the statute books of other States.

So much for original American ideas as to compulsion.

Turning to laws directly compulsory, we go a little back of the date of the above report, in 1871, to make sure of giving a full history of progress in this direction.

Vermont, November 21st, 1867, passed, and November 23d, 1870, amended, a law requiring every child of good health and sound mind, between eight and fourteen years of age, to attend a public school at least three months in each year, unless otherwise furnished with the means of education for a like period, or unless such child should have already acquired the branches of learning usually taught in public schools. No child of this age to be employed in mill or factory without attendance upon school for three months of the year preceding. Penalty, in either case, ten dollars to twenty dollars.

Michigan, April 15th, 1871, passed "An act to compel children to attend school"—*i. e.*, all of good health and sound mind, between eight and fourteen—for at least twelve weeks in each school year, of which at least six weeks must be consecutive. Penalty for first offense, five dollars to ten dollars ; for subsequent ones, ten dollars to twenty dollars.

Texas, April 24th, of the same year, put on her statute book a law requiring the attendance of all her scholastic population on the public schools of their respective districts for at least four months of every year. Penalty, up to twenty-five dollars. The law, however, was dropped in the revision of 1876.

New Hampshire, July 14th, 1871, enacted that every person having charge of any child between eight and fourteen, residing in a district where a public school is taught, for an annual period of twelve weeks or more, within two miles of his residence by the nearest traveled road, must cause such child to attend such school for at least twelve weeks in every year, six weeks at least to be consecutive, unless excused for reasons specified. Penalty for first offense, ten dollars ; for any subsequent one, twenty dollars.

Connecticut, in 1872, amended her truant laws of 1865 and 1869, authorizing cities and towns to make all needful regulations concerning truants and vagrant children, to arrest them by the hands of the police, and to commit them, after a third arrest, to a house of correction or reformation for a period not over three years.

Massachusetts, also, in 1873 and 1874, amended her truant law, making it require every person having under his control a child between eight and fourteen, to send such child to public day-school for at least twenty weeks in each year, divided into two terms of ten consecutive weeks each, unless the child has attended a private day-school approved by the school committee for a like period, or is regularly attending a half-time school so approved, or has been otherwise furnished with the means of education for a like period, &c., &c.*

Nevada, February 25th, 1873, passed "An act to compel children to attend school,"—ages eight to fourteen; term of attendance at least sixteen weeks in each school year, eight of which to be consecutive. Penalty for first offense, fifty to one hundred dollars; for second, &c., one hundred to two hundred dollars.

Kansas moved in the same direction in 1874, by passing, March 9th, "An act requiring the education of all healthy children;" *i. e.*, all between eight and fourteen to be sent to school for at least twelve weeks in each year, six of which must be consecutive. Penalty, ten to twenty dollars.

New Jersey came next, with a law passed March 27th, 1874, and amended April 9th, 1875, requiring parents and guardians having charge of children between eight and fourteen, to cause them to attend some school at least twelve weeks in each year, six of which must be consecutive; or to be instructed at home for the same period in the branches commonly taught in the public schools, unless excused for cause. Penalty, three dollars for every week during which, after notice from the district clerk, there has been a failure to comply with the provisions of the law.

California followed closely after New Jersey, passing, March 28th, 1874, "An act to enforce the educational rights of children." All between eight and

* See several reports of the Hon. J. D. Philbrick, of Boston, on this subject.

fourteen to be sent to a public school two-thirds of the time for which said school shall be taught in the place of the children's residence, twelve weeks of the time to be consecutive, unless excused by the school board for reasons specified. Penalty for first offense, twenty dollars; second and so on, twenty to fifty dollars.

New York, May 11th of the same year (1874), passed, and in 1876 amended, an act with almost as pleasant a title as that of California, calling it "An act to secure to children the benefits of elementary education." Provisions as to age, eight to fourteen; term of attendance for each year, fourteen weeks, eight of which must be consecutive. Alternative of school attendance, instruction at home for at least fourteen weeks each year in spelling, reading, writing, English grammar, geography, and arithmetic. None under fourteen to be employed in any business during the school hours of any school day in which a public school is taught in the place of the child's residence. Penalty, fifty dollars.

Laws kindred to these have been passed in Maine and Arizona, and one is said to have been passed recently in Ohio. But as copies of them have not been yet received, the precise date of their passage and the precise conditions they impose cannot be now given.*

Unfortunately, it must be acknowledged that the success of the efforts thus made to secure the universal education of the children in these States has not, in all cases, been altogether satisfactory; but has varied

* The foregoing statistics have just been obtained from the Bureau of Education, at Washington.

according to the wisdom and thoroughness of the legal provisions, and especially according to the stimulus afforded by popular sympathy to their energetic and faithful execution.

It is to be particularly regretted that Pennsylvania has not been found prepared to place herself among the progressive States on this question. A better public sentiment among us needs to be aroused, shaped, and concentrated, before we can have a compulsory law, and still more, before such a law can be effectually enforced. The popular mind must be brought to a clearer apprehension of the appalling magnitude of the evil which such a law alone will remedy; to a clearer apprehension of the absolute necessity of universal education to the safety and perpetuity of republican institutions based upon universal suffrage. The suggestion that the popular mind cannot be so trained, is the suggestion of apathy or of desperation. The stale objection that compulsory education is inconsistent with democratic or republican or American ideas, is a mere prejudice or a downright impertinence. It is to be presumed that democratic, republican, and American ideas are not suicidal; are not inconsistent with what can be shown to be required by the public good and the very safety of the Commonwealth; and so the only proper and pertinent question in this case is, whether compulsory educaton *is* so required. But is it verily a democratic and American idea that, while universal popular education may be a good thing in a monarchy or despotism, there is no need of it in a free State? Besides, there is a class of men in society who should remember that it is their office to bestir themselves to lead public sentiment, instead of being idly and passively led by it. If the efforts of the Board of Public Charities on this subject had been zealously seconded by other parties who have had it in their power to exert an effective if not a controlling influence in the case; if they had exerted such an influence in accordance with their own personal convictions of what was demanded by the public good; if they had boldly and manfully stemmed the opposing current of misguided popular prejudice; it is confidently believed that, before this time, public sentiment in Pennsylvania would have been brought to such a pitch that we should not only have a law of compulsory education upon our statute book, but such a law carried into actual, thorough, and beneficent execution.

SCHOOLS OF REFORM.

DESTITUTE AND DELINQUENT CHILDREN.

In the annual report of this board for 1871, we endeavored to show that vice and crime were largely the offspring of ignorance, and we recommended a system of universal education, which would certainly embrace those classes of the youth of the State who were most exposed, through the far-reaching influences of "illiteracy," to a violation of law and order; and in our report for the following year, we reiterated the same view, and have shown by reliable statistics, *First*, that one-third of all prisoners are totally uneducated, and four-fifths are practically uneducated; and *Second*, that the proportion of prisoners from the illiterate classes is at least ten-fold as great as the proportion of those having some education. This is no longer an idea or speculation; it is a well-recognized truth, and has been so accepted by the more cautious and reflecting communities, both at home and abroad. Prussia has acted upon it with the most marked and beneficial results, and has been emulated by other continental powers, as we have already shown. The statesmen of France are co-laborers with her philanthropists in the endeavor to solve the problem of their nation's fluctuating political embarrassments, and believe they will find its solution in the state's neglect of the education of the people. They find unquestionably there that the crime of the country is largely the result of ignorance and mental impotence, and this fact is most strikingly confirmed by the following statement of the illiteracy which prevailed in the French prisons in the years 1867 to 1869, given in the report of the International Penitentiary Congress:—

Whole number of arrests,	444,133
Number unable to read,	442,194
Or 95.63 per cent.	
Whole number of convicts,	18,643
Number unable to read,	16,015
Or 87.28 per cent.	
Average number of juvenile prisoners,	8,139
Number unable to read,	6,607
Or 81.14 per cent.	

In Great Britain no measure of public policy is so much relied on for the elevation and amelioration of the condition of the people, and the firm prosperity of the state, as common-school education. It has been well said, that "education is a force restraining vice and crime." Where it is purely intellectual, it restrains by teaching the truth that "honesty is the best policy." Where it rises to the dignity of a Christian education, it includes, also, the higher restraint of the conscience. It may be safely stated as an irrefutable proposition, that the state which neglects the education of her youth, prepares them for vicious, degraded, and criminal lives, which are spent in depredating upon society, and in infecting by example, by contaminating and debasing influence, the lives of others, which would otherwise prove exemplary and useful.

The United States Commissioner of Education presents the following results of an examination of the statistics of pauperism in the three States of Pennsylvania, Ohio, and Illinois,—States not inferior to any in popular education. Take one million of persons from the population of these three States, in numbers proportioned to their population respectively, and the conclusion will be nearly as follows:—

Population,	1,000,000
Paupers,	8,000
Illiterate paupers (totally),	45,000
Illiterate paupers,	4,800

Thus of the whole population, there are illiterate between four and five per cent.; of paupers, illiterate, sixty per cent. These results clearly demonstrate that the want of education is the want of facilities to acquire employments, and to work profitably in them.

The evil, therefore, which society suffers from illiteracy in its relation to crime and pauperism, has not been exaggerated in our reports, and its influence upon common labor is not less prejudicial, and presents the most surprising and suggestive lesson. This is so well presented by Dr. Edward Jarvis in his contribution to the recent report of the National Bureau of Education, that we shall adopt his clear statements and their practical application to almost every department of industry.

Dr. Jarvis says:—"Beyond the mere knowledge of facts and principles, there are other advantages equally important and valuable, that grow out of the process of study and acquisition. The training and discipline of the school quicken and energize the mind, and give it a facility of applying itself and its varied faculties to manifold purposes."

"Thus boys and girls who are educated and trained to reflect by the studies of the school, carry their power and habit of mental action with them to whatever pursuit they may address themselves. In the various employments of their maturer life, whether they are laborers, farmers, mechanics, or workers in any other sphere, whatever may be the material on which they operate, whatever may be the transformation they may desire to effect, or results they may attempt to produce, they enlist the co-operation of their sharpened perceptions and disciplined reason in the plan and performance of their undertakings."

"Muscular force alone is not sufficient to fulfill the just demands of labor. It needs to be directed and measured, so that a blow shall be given, aimed aright in the proper direction, reach the intended point, and produce the desired effect. The hammer must hit the head of the nail, the axe the place where the wood is to be divided. The blow must not be so strong as to crush and injure, nor so weak as to fail of effect and be lost." These principles are applied in an analysis of various processes of labor, from the sawing of wood and the weaving of cloth to the most delicate operations of the skilled mechanic and the plain artist; and the conclusion is reached, that education is the economy of force, and gives it a greater power to create value. It creates skillfulness which has the ability to add to the value of material, which cannot be attained by ignorance.

"The cost of educating a laborer—of setting him to think and fitting him to expend his forces to advantage—is very small. The few years of youth, when the body is comparatively weak, the expense of teachers, books, &c., are but small expenditures compared with the gain. The return in increased productive power is great and permanent. It is the difference between the large and certain and the small and uncertain produce."

It is clear, then, that the interests of the State are promoted by the education of the people, and that no class can be safely excluded from its beneficial influences. But are the provisions which the legislature has heretofore made, or will be allowed to make under the amended Constitution, sufficiently comprehensive to embrace all ranks and conditions, or rather, will not those who most need the wholesome discipline and the enabling influences of education be practically excluded?

The meeting of the Constitutional Convention during the past year, has been an occasion of especial interest to this board; for wise and prudent as are many of the measures it has offered in amendment of the late Constitution, it has, we think, greatly embarrassed a question, in whose solution lies one of the highest interest to every community, and of the State herself, in a most eminent degree.

We refer to certain provisions which passed that body, restrictive upon the education of the poor children of the State. While the animus of the Convention seemed more favorable to universal education, and some of its acts afford a larger opportunity for certain classes of youth of the Commonwealth to enjoy more securely, and perhaps more largely than in the past, the advantages of education, it practically overturned both the injunction and spirit of the late Constitution, in curtailing the rights of the poor to the enjoyment of State aid in their education; and in positively forbidding it on the part of the several municipalities of the Commonwealth in combination with the aid of any private agency. The education of the most ignorant of the children of the State has been practically cut off, unless a more liberal action on the part of the legislature shall counteract the ill effects of the constitutional provision in this behalf.

If education is needed, it is needed by the illiterate. It was the prime object of the convention which framed the late constitution to provide an education for the poor gratis. The well-to-do will effect this in some respectable manner, whether the State helps them or not. But the destitute child of the State cannot obtain it without the State's aid, or the aid of the particular municipality which owns it. Such child is most significantly a ward, and to the ward of the State or the municipality, as the case may variously be considered, has the convention denied all practical relief from the evils of ignorance. We say, "practical relief," for that relief cannot be given effectually without combining with the provision made by the public the aid of private efforts and private benefactions. This, the nature of the case, and all experience, combine to demonstrate.

This board took an early interest in this matter as it came before the convention, and we are entirely convinced that its action in relation to it was caused by an inadequate consideration of the subject.

The idea that "charity" must attend upon any proceeding or device to draw the destitute and neglected children of the State out of the abyss of ignorance, and consequently of uselessness, and of vice and crime, for which they furnish the main material, seemed to be the effectual motive in inducing the passage of the restrictive measures referred to. By the provision of section seventh of the article on taxation and finance, municipalities are forbidden to appropriate money for any corporation, association, institution, or individual. None of the cities or counties of the State may aid private effort in the rescue and amendment and instruction of the debased and ignorant and vagrant children within their borders; and they are precluded, also, by the same provision, from contributing to the education of the blind and the deaf mute and the imbecile; or to appropriate money to the houses of refuge or schools of reform, because they are private corporations. This is the plain and obvious construction of the section referred to.

By section eighteen of the article on "legislation," the legislature is forbidden to make any State grant to any charitable or educational institution conducted by religious bodies, and by section seventeenth it is forbidden to aid any charitable and educational work conducted in any institution which is not "absolutely under State control," excepting by a vote of two-thirds of all the members elected to the legislature; so that in case of every grant to either of what are called the State institutions, excepting the two penitentiaries and the hospitals for the insane at Harrisburg and Danville, an overwhelming majority must always be secured in order to obtain support to the institutions, or for their extension, if desirable. And, as respects the destitute and orphan children of the Commonwealth, a like restriction is placed upon the State's affording aid in their education, although private beneficence may be offered to feed and clothe them, while pursuing an educational and industrial training. Is it probable that the State will expend the millions of money necessary to purchase these "private corporations," or establish State schools for vagrant children? Or, even if she should do so, would she not fail in their administration? Has it ever occurred that the defective classes were effectually benefited, without the co-operation of that warm humanity which stimulates private zeal and benevolence?

The subject of the training and education of the

destitute and neglected children of the State has been presented to the legislature very fully in our previous reports.

Its importance is not less grave than that of the most momentous questions of state concern, which can engage your attention. There is absolutely no provision made for the "education" of this class by the legislature or by any municipality within the bounds of the Commonwealth. The almshouses are of course open to them, and such education as is found in them, but they would go there only by constraint, and neither themselves nor the community would be the gainers by their residence in such refuges. Still the fact that the various municipalities of the State make certain provision for the needs of their indigent population, is an argument with many legislators, that the State is not called upon to provide for the education of this destitute class of the youth of the Commonwealth, who can never avail themselves of her legislation and her bounty in behalf of universal education. That this class of children is not reached by the public schools is undeniable. It is manifest wherever free schools exist, and wherever even "compulsory education" obtains. The Prussian system, it is true, has become so thoroughly established by long usage, and its influences have so permeated all ranks and conditions of the people, that it has made the most salutary inroads upon the habits of the debased and vagrant population of youth, and large accessions of this low element have in a course of years become prepared for reception into the common schools. In England the elementary education act of 1870, which is of a compulsory character, has been found entirely ineffective in reaching the destitute children of the land. Like the blind and the deaf mute, they remain "outside" because of some *deficiency*, which is as despotic and restraining as the want of speech or sight is to the former.

It is the deficiency of home care and guardianship, and for this they are no more responsible than are other defectives. To this class they belong. They are of the "unfortunates" of the State, wherever the State exists, in Europe or America, in New York, New England, or Pennsylvania; and they must have some kind of substitution for the lost parent or the abandoned parent or the degraded parent, as the raised letter must be resorted to in the instruction of the blind, and the manual alphabet for the deaf mute, in order to make it possible for them to receive the benefit of school education. Thus their destitution may be cared for by private benevolence, and thus they may be prepared to receive from the State the educational advantages which more favored youth obtain without such supplementary aid.

If private bounty will feed and clothe them, shall not the State aid in their education? If the poor should be taught gratis, shall these, the poorest of the poor, be excluded? If neither private bounty nor public aid relieve them, they must beg or steal or do some uncertain or degrading work, in order to obtain the food whereby to live and the clothing to cover their nakedness, for they must be fed and clothed, however meanly, whether they are taught or not. Must they starve or go naked in order that they may avail themselves of the educational provisions of the law? We say emphatically, No! and take the ground that where this want of parental guardianship is supplied by private effort and private benevolence, the State should do her part in their educational work, by making moderate *per capita* allowances to schools or homes established by private and philanthropic enterprise, wherever they are needed, for the industrial training and education of the class referred to. The State should, as a matter of course, exercise a right of inspection, and see that the money she grants is not squandered or misapplied, and should reserve the power of revoking its sanction and withholding its aid, whenever she judges that there is occasion for such course.

This fundamental evil, which, if not met and overcome, will render abortive all attempts at an appreciable reduction of crime and pauperism, and all efforts towards an increasing and healthy amendment of the morals of the lower classes, has been appreciated in many of our American communities, and in countries where the necessity is less paramount than it is in a democratic land. The system above recommended for its abatement and suppression has received in England a recognized status from the government, and the schools established by it are aided by government grants, and are practically employed as a part of the machinery of the educational work of the state. By this course of procedure (which, it is true, was long denied by the authorities and adopted only after it had been commended to their favor by the surest evidences of its efficiency in aiding the government to fulfill its desire and its duty), it was made manifest at the late International Congress, by indisputable testimony, namely, by authenticated returns from prisons and reformatories, that the condition of the whole juvenile population of England has been changed; and, in the language of a distinguished member of that body, "the system has cut up juvenile vagrancy by the roots, and has almost destroyed juvenile crime in many localities." It surely cannot be said that in such a work as that referred to, the utilization of private benevolence and economy for the public good, in the manner suggested, need compromise any doctrine or principle of any citizen or any party in the State, or excite the antagonism of any person or community whatever. But, looking from the standpoint from which this board is bound to survey the subject, namely, in its relations to human degradation, pauperism, and crime, it is believed that great danger is threatened to the State, in denying opportunites of education and improvement to the neglected classes of her children, and that a wrong is inflicted upon them and will be perpetuated until full and practical legislation is effected to rescue them from the fetters which restrain their mental and moral improvement. *Charity* is not involved at all in the measure proposed to your honorable bodies. It is only a right which is commended to your protection and vindication.

In a communication to your honorable bodies, made last year, which accompanied our report on the applications for State aid, we proposed to submit a scheme to the present legislature, which should present a uniform system of State policy and State aid to a class of institutions which might be beneficially encouraged by moderate *per capita* grants towards the education of the class of children who should be received into them.

This subject has been thoughtfully considered by us, in the interval, and we have exhausted, as we believe, the field of investigation and of thought, which is attainable. We have reached the conclusion, which we have set forth and recommended in this report, and present a scheme to your honorable bodies, of an impartial and general character, which is intended simply to place a class of children, whose condition needs the strengthening and ameliorating influences of education more than that of any other class, upon a like, though by no means an equal, footing with the less dependent children of the State.

We perfectly understand that it will require a fuller vote to accomplish the aid we seek for these abandoned children, but we trust that the apparent disfavor which the Constitutional Convention has seemed to cast upon this just and rightful work, will not be responded to by your honorable bodies, but will rather stimulate you to more earnest desire and effort to do justice to those whose neglect will assuredly be avenged upon the honor, the purity, and also the material wealth of the community.

The board submitted a memorial on this subject to the convention, while in session, and by resolution ordered it to be incorporated in this report, as completely expressing their views, and sustaining them by arguments, which they think should have been conclusive with the convention. The following letters from Mary Carpenter, the noble gentlewoman and distinguished philanthropist, and from Dr. Wines, well known for his labors in measures for the prevention of crime; who, expert themselves in questions of reformatory discipline, have also witnessed the practical operation and have seen the demonstrated results of such a scheme for the education of neglected and abandoned children as we now recommend; give unsolicited expression to the views of strangers to our borders; views which we happen to know are fully endorsed by many statesmen and philanthropists, who have known of the efforts of the Board of Public Charities in favor of the measure of public policy proposed. The letters are as follows:—

Geo. L. Harrison, Esq.,
President of the Board of State Charities,

MY DEAR SIR:—I thank you most sincerely for the copy of your memorial in behalf of the education of neglected and destitute children, lately submitted to the Constitutional Convention of Pennsylvania. I cannot but hope that an argument so cogent, so thoroughly unanswerable indeed, as your paper embodies, will have its effect upon the enlightened body to which it is addressed. It is only to-day that I received a letter from Mr. E. Carleton Tuffnell, inspector of the *pauper schools of England, in which he speaks of the excellent fruits of these institutions.

Among other things, he says, "there are in the pauper schools of London alone eight thousand children, all of the lowest class, who, under the system now pursued, are not only saved from a life of vice and

* One branch of the system of industrial schools of Great Britain.

crime, but turn out among the most valuable and productive members of society." These schools are all strictly industrial, and under the supervision of the "local government board." To me it seems the most natural thing in the world that your Constitutional Convention should not only encourage but welcome the co-operation, and especially the initiative of private benevolence, in the work of removing from the body politic the terrible plague-spot which you have so clearly and forcibly called to its notice and recommended to its consideration. If the convention fail to take the action recommended by your board, or some action equivalent, such failure can, it seems to me, be attributed only to the want of a thorough grasp and comprehension of the question. It is really a question of the healthy and vigorous action, if not indeed in the end of the very existence, of republican institutions. The instinct of self-preservation, it would seem, should lead the convention in the direction indicated by your memorial.

That God may help you in this work is the wish and prayer of

Yours, truly and faithfully,

E. C. WINES.

320 BROADWAY, NEW YORK, October 20th, 1873.

RED LODGE HOUSE,
BRISTOL, ENGLAND, November 17th, 1873.

Geo. L. Harrison, Esq., President, &c.,

DEAR SIR:—I have just completed the perusal of the very important documents which you have just sent me, respecting the course taken by the convention, concerning neglected and destitute children. I am perfectly astonished at the *retrograde* proceedings adopted by that body, in obstructing or almost preventing the past course of voluntary benevolence, and absolutely ignoring the *just claims* of the children of your Commonwealth, every one of whom has an absolute right to justice and equal advantage with every other. Your arguments are admirably developed; they are virtually the same as those which we have been bringing before the Committee of Council on Education for a quarter of a century, with respect to the same neglected class; and our appeal has not been unheeded.

I trust that you will rouse public opinion to support you. It will be a great misfortune to your State to pass laws so contrary to the spirit of the age. I rejoice to see the tone of the public press, and hope you will kindly keep me informed of progress.

Respectfully, yours,

MARY CARPENTER.

There are two classes of these vagrant and abandoned children which demand the educational care and training claimed for them; otherwise they become the enemies of order and good government. One of these classes is perpetually replenished from the other, as it, in turn, swells the ranks of maturer vice and crime. Those who have absolutely fallen into crime may be suitably provided for in our houses of refuge, especially if they be made less like juvenile jails, and be administered by a less repressive and penal system of government. But amongst these criminal youth, many of them graduates in wickedness, there are numbers whose faults are slight and venial, and whose transgressions have occurred solely through parental neglect or orphanage, and multitudes of these throng the alleys and courts and streets of all our larger communities, and become tenants, at length, of the hospitals and poor-houses and jails of every portion of the State. This is the class of children which is not reached by the State provision for universal education, and which that system never will or can reach. They do not need the exacting and constraining discipline which is necessary in houses of refuge, but they need to be touched and impressed by a guardianship assimilated to proper home training, and strengthened by the discipline of school and industrial education to resist temptations and learn to realize the enjoyment of earning a support by honorable employments.

The system which has been successfully adopted in Great Britain has proved itself adequate to this end. It is the system of day industrial schools, into which certain classes of children are received, either voluntarily or by commitment, if they will not or cannot attend the ordinary elementary schools. These classes embrace, first, children found begging, receiving alms habitually, living in the streets or about public places; second, those found in vagrancy having no home, nor fixed dwelling-place, nor guardianship; third, the destitute, either who are orphans or whose surviving parent is in prison, or who will not submit to parental or other authority; fourth, children under twelve years of age, accused of crime, but who have never been convicted of a felony.

These schools are all conducted on the family system, and are in all respects schools and do not at all resemble penal establishments. They give elementary instruction and industrial training, the object being to provide for the children an education which will enable them to earn for themselves a living, and become useful members of society. The school boards have power to establish these day industrial schools, and to certify them as fit and proper, when established by voluntary effort, and also to make certain *per capita* allowances to the managers. The English law has decided that education should be compulsory, but *not in all cases* gratuitous, and power is given to recover from the parent, when he can afford it, the whole or part of the cost of the education of the child; and from the guardians of the poor the whole expense of food and education, if the child is chargeable. The religious question is not involved at all in the case of these schools. Where the entrance is voluntary they can choose the schools conducted by managers of their own religious creed; and when sent by the magistrates the child's "religion" is first ascertained, and he is sent to a school of the same persuasion.

Such is the outline of the British method of accomplishing the education and industrial training of the neglected and destitute children, and, as already shown, it has been eminently successful. We recommend the adoption of a similar system for this Commonwealth. We shall not err in following any good example. It would be folly to reject a scheme because it has been projected and carried to success by strangers. We therefore ask legislation which shall establish a plan, kindred to what we have described, for the education and industrial training of our own vagrant and abandoned children, which shall prove effectual in preventing the crime and the pauperism that result from ignorance and idleness. As the maintenance of a convict costs, upon an average, $200 a year, and as he generally remains a criminal, it is clearly the part of true wisdom to adopt the more economical method of a preventive measure, which will save the State's money, and reduce its proportion of crime.

At the session of the British Local Science Association, recently convened in England, Miss Carpenter proposed the subject, "How can education be brought to bear on the hitherto untouched portion of the population." It was demonstrated that notwithstanding all the provisions made by the government and by private individuals, interested for the protection and education of young offenders and destitute children in reformatories, in certified industrial schools (which are private reformatories, accepted as such by the government), and in workhouse schools, a large residuum remained, who are untouched by any educational institutions, and who furnish a constant supply to these expensive boarding-schools. These neglected children still remained, although the school board had for three years endeavored to reach all. Such has been our own experience. It is clear and indisputable, then, that a fresh agency is needed. These children are half-civilized and half-fed. They cannot be admitted into the common schools. They require special schools where they will be taught industry as well as learning, and where they will receive some food which will enable them to remain the greater part of the day. These schools can be maintained at a very moderate cost to the State,—probably not over twenty dollars a year for each child; and they would extend the benefits of a suitable education and training to the lowest in the Commonwealth; from whom prisons and workhouses and reformatories are constantly recruited at a great loss to the State.

MEMORIAL

From the President of the Board of Public Charities to the Constitutional Convention of Pennsylvania.

On behalf of the Board of Public Charities, the undersigned begs to present to the Constitutional Convention some considerations bearing upon the seventeenth and eighteenth sections of the proposed article on "legislation," containing certain restrictions upon legislative appropriations. These sections, it is understood, have already been passed to a third reading, but were so passed before the article on education had been definitely acted upon.

The attention of the convention is, in the first place, respectfully invited to the present state of its constitutional provisions in reference to popular education. (1) The constitution is to require in general the maintenance of a thorough and efficient system of public schools, offering the opportunity of an elementary education to all the children of the State. (2) A constitutional provision for compulsory education has been rejected by the convention. (3) A provision for the establishment by the legislature of special schools for "neglected children" has also been rejected. (4) The municipalities as well as the legislature are to be forbidden to aid such private institutions as now exist for that purpose (section seven, taxation and finance).* That is to say, with the exception of this last restrictive provision, the common-school system of the State will be left substantially as it was before, the legislature being required to continue without diminution its annual appropriations.

In the second place the attention of the convention is respectfully recalled to a few of the simple facts of the case:—

1. According to the returns of the census of 1870, there are within the Commonwealth of Pennsylvania more than two hundred and twenty-two thousand persons above ten years of age unable to read or write, and probably the true number of such is not less than three hundred thousand or four hundred thousand, of which from seventy-five thousand to one hundred thousand are under the age of twenty-one, and of these last, twenty thousand or more are congregated in the single city of Philadelphia.

---

* SEC. 7. The General Assembly shall not authorize any county, city, borough, township, or incorporated district to become a stockholder in any company, association, or corporation, or to obtain or *appropriate* money for, or to loan its credit to, *any* corporation, association, institution, or individual.

2. This large army of neglected children, growing up in idleness, ignorance, vice, and crime, who are not only destined to increase our taxes, to endanger our property, and disturb our peace, to infest our highways and streets with mendicancy, pillage, and violence, to crowd the docks of our court-rooms and fill our alms-houses, jails, and penitentiaries, but who are soon to exercise with us and over us the sovereignty of the elective franchise, marching up to the polls with added thousands of new recruits every year—*these* are the cancerous source of what is probably the greatest peril to which our Commonwealth and free institutions are exposed.

3. This evil the common-school system, as at present organized, can never reach and remedy. It is to be understood that under the description of "neglected children" are meant to be included not only those who lose the benefit of the free public schools from the carelessness or willfulness of parents, but those also—and theirs is the greater number—who are deprived of those benefits in consequence of their destitution of any parental guardianship; of their vagabond lives, and their want of the very means of subsistence if they should go to school; of their ragged and filthy condi-dition, or their depraved and vicious habits, or their intractable characters, rendering them unfit to be received at school with the other children, or making it improper or impossible for them to be retained there. The reclaiming and education of these children could not be secured even by any law of compulsory attendance at school merely, but means must also be

provided to supply them with food and clothing and proper domestic guardianship while they may be receiving their education at school. If compulsion is needed elsewhere, charity also is needed here. Our schools may be ever so open and free, and sufficient for all, but these children will still remain outside. This is the lesson not only of our own past experience, but wherever the system of free schools has been tried —whether in Europe or America, in Old England or in New England, in New York or any other of our sister States. It has been found necessary to supplement the system either by private benefactions or public appropriations for the care and support of this class of destitute and neglected children. It is clear that they have not yet been reached by our system of public schools, admirable and thorough as has been its management for several years past. Nor are they likely to be reached by it, for it would seem by the superintendent's last report that the chronic evil of absenteeism from the schools has of late increased rather than diminished. Unless some modification or enlargement of the present instrumentalities is adopted, there is no reason to hope that the public schools will ever remedy the evil.

4. But to reach and remedy this evil is precisely the chief end of the common-school system. These children are precisely those whose education the State needs to care for. Most of the children of well-to-do parents, and who have good domestic care and training, will be tolerably well educated whether the State provide schools for them or not. It must not be

supposed, therefore, that the public schools have very nearly accomplished their purpose, while only this residuum remains unaffected by them. Rather we must remember that while this remains—and remains in its present enormous proportions—they have entirely failed of attaining their principal object.

Now the legislature *may do* either or both of those things which the convention has refused to require or recommend. (1) It may adopt the principle of compulsory education for the whole Commonwealth, or may authorize its local adoption. (2) It may establish either directly or indirectly, through the local authorities, special schools for neglected children. *Otherwise*, under the proposed section seventen,* if adopted, such children must be left to be cared for, if cared for at all, exclusively by private agencies, without any aid, encouragement, or co-operation whatever from the State in any case, or from the local authorities, unless such agencies should be organized outside of the influence and control of all religious bodies. So that, in this case, the State would either have to do the whole work, at the public expense, or would have no guarantee that such children would be cared for at all; for the aid of religion is not invoked, and private benevolence, unprompted and unsustained by the religious sentiment, even though receiving a questionable and precarious support from municipal bounty, can hardly be sufficient for the whole reliance.

* SEC. 17. No appropriation shall be made to any charitable or educational institution not under the absolute control of the Commonwealth, other than normal schools established by law for the professional training of teachers for the public schools of the State, except by a vote of two-thirds of all the members elected to each house.

Under such circumstances, what is the wisest course to take? Shall the legislature, by the adoption of this section seventeen, be practically required to do the whole work or nothing? Or, by a modification of this section, shall it be left untrammeled to adopt the intermediate course of encouraging the partial efforts of private benevolence by its fostering aid? This is the question.

But is the legislature, in any event, likely to undertake the whole work? Is there not reason to fear that should the convention finally adopt this section seventeen, as it is proposed, they will, under all the circumstances, practically give the full weight of their authority and influence in favor of leaving these neglected children absolutely to their fate, without the slightest effort to help or save them, and thus suffer this plague-spot of the body politic to grow and fester, and spread its pestilential infection without restraint or remedy? Is it said that the legislature will still have the power to introduce the system of compulsory education, either universally or partially, and thus to reach and remove the evil? But by this course, by this means alone, the whole evil cannot be reached and remedied; and besides, the convention has solemnly refused to require or recommend such a course, stamping it with its implied disapproval. Is it said that the legislature may establish or authorize the particular municipalities to establish special schools for the care and instruction of this class of children? But the convention has positively frowned upon such a plan. Is it said that the local civil authorities may aid the efforts of private benevolence in supporting such schools? But the convention has sternly forbidden them to aid any such institutions as now exist for that purpose, and has not proposed the establishment of any others. Is it said that at least the State itself may afford such aid by direct appropriations? The convention will have forbidden it unless a full vote of two-thirds can be obtained for it.

That is to say, even though a large majority of the people, through their chosen representatives, may for years and years seek to do it, they shall not, so long as one-third remain opposed; in other words, the antecedent probability that it is wrong or unwise to do it, is held to be as two to one; so that to effect it shall require that sort of earnest zeal and public agitation, and that overwhelming majority which might be required to change the fundamental law or revolutionize the form of government. But is it said that, at all events, the convention will not have forbidden private benevolence to exert itself to any extent, and under the impulse of any motives whatever, for the rescue and amendment of these poor, neglected outcasts? This is true; but then the convention had no power to make such a formal prohibition. And yet it may seriously be asked whether, if section seventeen be adopted with the rest, it will not appear that the whole moral influence of the action of the convention will tend to dampen any sympathy that might be felt for this class of children, and to paralyze any efforts that might be made in their behalf in any quarter or in any form. But be this as it may, there seems, as a matter of fact, but little reason to expect that for some time to come, and until a great pressure of public opinion can be concentrated on the subject, the legislature will be induced to adopt a thorough system of compulsory education or to establish special schools for this class of neglected children, to be exclusively supported at the public expense. The undersigned, as is well understood, is in favor of both of these plans, and for himself knows of no sufficient reason against them; but the reasons, whatever they may be, which have weighed with the convention against them, and have led to a decision which precludes their further discussion here, will be likely, it is presumed, to weigh with a majority of the legislature, backed up, as they may seem to be, by the authority of the convention itself. And may it not pertinently be asked, why it is that while both of these plans of doing the whole work by State authority and at the public expense—though liable to such objections that they are not likely soon to command the support of a majority of the legislature—are nevertheless left untrammeled to the discretion of that body; yet this other plan of encouraging and supplementing private efforts by State aid, not being liable to the same objections, and being at any time likely, it may be presumed, to have a majority of the legislature in its favor, should be absolutely forbidden, or compelled to secure the support of full two-thirds of all the members of both houses? Why not trust a majority of the people and their representatives in one of these cases as well as in the other? Why not allow them, if they will, in order to abate an enormous and crying evil, and to accomplish a great public good, to adopt a course which is felt to be less liable to popular objection, as well as another which is felt to be more so?

Is it said that special restriction is required in this case, because such legislative action is liable to abuse? But all legislative power is liable to be abused or exercised unwisely, and we must take this risk or abolish government altogether. The true questions are, first, is the proposed action, in matter and form, a proper subject of State legislation? and, second, is it demanded for the public welfare? As to the former question, that this is a proper subject of legislation is indirectly admitted by its being allowed on a two-thirds vote; and as to the latter question, it is admitted on all sides that the rescue and education of these neglected children would be a great public benefit; many of us think it essential to the very existence and permanence of our free institutions. Shall we then commit political suicide lest the legislature should make a political blunder? Shall we abdicate the very power of promoting the public weal because that power may be abused? Shall the public good be neglected or even put under the ban, because the legislature cannot always be trusted to do what is best? Shall the people not be allowed to manage their own affairs according to their own discretion, because, through their representatives, they may not always manage them wisely? Shall we once for all acknowledge the experiment of representative self-government a failure?

But perhaps this particular form of legislative action is thought to be specially liable to abuse. Is it so? Has such a disposition been shown by the Legislature of Pennsylvania or of other States to squander the public money in educating or aiding to educate destitute children, that it should need to be specially guarded against in the very constitution? Even if religious or ecclesiastical bodies should come forward and offer to establish schools for the education of such children, adding moral and religious instruction, it is difficult to see why that *in itself* should be a bar to the bestowment of State aid towards the support of such schools; and probably if there was but one form of religious belief and profession in the State, it would not be so considered. But where there is a variety of religious creeds among us—while there are several sects and denominations in earnest rivalry and conflict with one another, and while religious partisanship remains so strong as it is—so strong as often to override all other motives and considerations—it may freely be admitted that for the legislature to make appropriations from the public funds in aid of sectarian institutions, however excellent their general objects and tendencies, would be an exercise of power *especially* liable to abuse. But this form of abuse being effectually guarded against in this section eighteen as well as in section two of the article on education,* is there any such special liability to abuse in making the appropriations contemplated in section seventeen as should require the special prevention of the two-thirds vote? The institutions to be aided will not be sectarian, not under the control of any religious denomination, not

* SECTION 18. No appropriations, except for pensions or gratuities for military services, shall be made for charitable, educational, or benevolent purposes, to any person or community, nor to any denominational or sectarian institution, corporation, or association.

SEC. 2. No money raised for the support of the public schools of this Commonwealth shall be appropriated to or used for the support of any sectarian school.

for private gain or emolument, not addressed to the special interests of any party, ecclesiastical or political; they will simply aim, by private efforts and benefactions, to accomplish some of those charitable and educational purposes in which the highest interests of the State are most deeply involved, and for which the State makes no adequate provision by her general system of public schools. Shall the legislature be permitted freely to aid such institutions?

If attention is called to the great cost of the institutions, whether schools, refuges, or homes, here contemplated, and if the danger of their demanding exorbitant drafts from the public treasury is urged in favor of a restriction of appropriations in their behalf, the answer is, those institutions will not hold the purse-strings, and those who do hold them are not likely to give more than, in their judgment, the public good requires. The question is, shall they be restrained from giving as much? For the State to impose such restraint upon itself seems little short of absurdity. Indeed, this is the last of all directions in which to limit the public expenditure. Economy here is eventual extravagance, and extravagance the surest economy. The public benefit resulting from a removal of the evil in question would abundantly repay all the cost, even though the whole were drawn from the public treasury. But it is to be especially noted that the plan here in view is one which is contrived to relieve the public treasury instead of burdening it, always presuming one thing, that the end contemplated is acknowledged to be demanded by the general good, and that the State recognizes her interest in the removal of so great an evil. The State might justly and wisely assume the whole expense, but the present suggestion is, that, in case the establishment and support of the remedial institutions be thrown, in the first instance, on private benevolence, the legislature, without being hampered by any special restrictions, should then be permitted to make, from time to time, such appropriations in encouragement and aid of such institutions as should be deemed wise and reasonable, and consistent with the most rigid economy of the public funds. And it is respectfully suggested that the same economical motives which weigh in the minds of the members of the convention may be confidently counted upon to weigh in the legislature with quite sufficient force to keep its appropriations for such objects, and under such circumstances, within due bounds.* At all events, the State would pay but a *part* of the price for the benefit which it would receive.

If it be objected that the evil is local, and that the whole State ought not to be taxed for the relief or benefit of certain particular communities, the answer is three-fold:—

1. Then surely those communities should be allowed to tax themselves for the removal of the evil, and to economize in that taxation, by availing themselves, as far as they should see fit, of all the aid they could obtain from private sources.

---

* The total sum appropriated by the Legislature of Pennsylvania to local charities, embracing hospitals, homes, dispensaries, asylums, &c., &c., from 1752 to 1872, exclusive, a period of one hundred and twenty years, amounts to $377,000, including the sum of $70,000 granted by the Provincial Assembly to the Pennsylvania Hospital, during the latter half of the last century.

2. By far the greater part of all taxation is for the *direct* benefit of others than those who pay the taxes. The very idea of a state involves the principle of mutual protection and helpfulness, in which, after the analogy of a mutual insurance, the stronger parts give the weaker more than they receive. The state is built upon a community, a solidarity, but not a perfect equality of individual interests. When the different parts, instead of consenting in mutual co-operation, fall into dissensions, and jealousies of section with section, marshaling east and west, or city and country, or agriculturist and manufacturer, or rich and poor, against each other, the very existence of the state is endangered, and its proper purpose and object are annulled. But if the State is not to be taxed for the removal of the evil *because it is local*, how large a community is to be taxed for that purpose—a county, a whole city, a ward, a precinct, or each individual on his own account? The evil is not equally distributed over any area, however small, short of each individual's domicile; and when that is reached it is precisely some other individual or individuals that must be taxed for its removal. Besides, the whole common-school system is especially liable to the objection in question. Here the rich are taxed for the education of the poor; those who have no children for the education of the children of others; and the State taxes herself by the million to distribute her aid to the different localities and communities, giving most to those places where the most children are found to need the appropriation.

But the evil is, after all, by no means so purely local as seems to be generally assumed. It exists and is formidable in all the counties of the State. If the evil is greater in one part of the State than in another, it cannot be confined to that portion, but will spread its effects far and wide. And if one portion of the State remedies the evil within itself, the beneficial consequences of such remedy will be shared by all the other parts of the State. This dangerous element is, of course, found mainly in the thickly-settled communities, and there it must be encountered and dealt with. Eventually it is found in maturity all over the State, spreading its corrupting influences, filling our prisons and almshouses, and festering with disease in the hospitals. Under proper State inspection, surely the legislature should be allowed to aid, say *by a per capita allowance*, industrial and other schools, conducted by private individuals for the rescue of such children from the ruin which, in nine cases out of ten, is sure otherwise to overtake them and the State, from the blighting influences of their degraded and criminal lives. If, for example, there are twenty thousand neglected children in Philadelphia, and if, in the rest of the State, there are fifty or sixty thousand instead of the more exact proportion of seventy or eighty thousand, is this a reason for regarding the evil as in such sense local, that the State has no common interest in it? It is undoubtedly more concentrated where the population is more concentrated, and there, from its very concentration, it becomes not only more conspicuous, but more fearfully dangerous. But are not the safety and prosperity of the State largely bound up in the safety and prosperity of the city? May not the corruptions of the city spread their contaminating influences into the State? May not the accumulation of ignorant and unprincipled voters in the city control the elections and revolutionize the political character of the State? Does not the State assume to govern the city and bind it by the constitution and laws which it makes? And would the State allow the city to protect itself, for instance, from the increase of this dangerous element, by prohibiting the ingress into its limits of the families of ignorant and destitute foreigners? If the city should remedy this evil within its own boundaries, would not the State reap a double benefit, in the first place, so far as the city is a part and a large part of the State, and secondly, by the distribution from the city into other parts of the State of great numbers of industrious and well-educated and respectable, instead of idle and ignorant people? And will the State refuse to pay anything for the common benefit? For it is again to be observed that, on the plan now proposed, the city, through its private benefactions, together, perhaps, with its municipal appropriations, would assume the principal weight of the burden, and the State would come in with only such aid and encouragement as it might see fit to bestow. Shall all such appropriations by the State be forbidden or hampered with such restrictions as may practically amount to a prohibition?

The legislature, it may be finally said, cannot be trusted with an arbitrary control of the people's treasury; the people cannot be sure of having honest and intelligent legislators. What, then, is the true remedy? Will you, by constitutional provisions, secure as far as possible the thorough education of all the people in knowledge and virtue, and guard with every possible barrier the purity of elections? Or will you leave thousands and tens of thousands of children to grow up in ignorance and vice and thus assume the elective franchise, only providing constitutional barriers against any aid being given to the State for their education; and then proceed to restrain the legislature and strip it of its accustomed powers, and thus and so far deprive the very people of the functions of self-government? That the legislature cannot be trusted means that the people cannot be trusted. To restrain the legislature is to restrain the people. If the legislature may not make laws, the people cannot make them; for the people have no other organ than the legislature whereby to perform that function. Is it not inverting the order of things to leave the people in ignorance, and then restrain their legislature? Would it not be better to secure the intelligence of the people and the purity of their elections, and then trust their chosen representatives? It is true that the legislature may be once for all constitutionally restrained from meddling with matters where experience has shown that their interference is productive of more harm than good to the State. But the education of the people—the thorough education of all the people—is admitted on all hands to be pre-eminently a matter of high public concern, and a proper subject of State legislation. It is submitted, therefore, that this is a case in which, beyond all others, the legislature should be left free.

A draft of section seventeen, modified in accordance with the views thus imperfectly expressed, is with great diffidence herewith submitted. To require the *inspection* of the institutions in question, and the special recommendation of aid to them, by a board of commissioners appointed for the purpose by the governor, the legislature, or the department of the interior, if such a department should be created, is thought to furnish a sufficient guarantee against improper or wasteful appropriations. It is presumed that the wisdom of the legislature could easily frame a law, by which private beneficence, municipal co-operation, and State aid, might all be combined and concentrated upon the same great end, leaving the institutions in question, so far as they should require no compulsory or penal action, to the simpler or cheaper methods of private management; thus utilizing private benevolence and economy for the public good. Shall the Constitution of Pennsylvania, instead of encouraging and facilitating such a result, only throw obstacles in the way of its accomplishment?

A modified draft of section eighteen is also appended, in which the prohibition of appropriations to sectarian institutions is made absolute, the clause for charitable, educational, or benevolent purposes being omitted. It is not perceived why *against just those purposes* there should be an expression of such special antipathy. Shall the legislature be allowed to make appropriations *to* anything and *for* anything, provided only that it should not propose thereby to aid any charitable, educational, or benevolent purposes? May the legislature make appropriations, for example, for a peculiarly ecclesiastical or religious purpose, for building a church, or paying the salary of a clergyman of any denomination; and yet shall it be forbidden to aid in the education of its own outcast children in a school established and supported by such a denomination? It is not supposed that such a distinction was intended. It is therefore suggested, as most consonant with the presumed purpose of the section, and the prohibition against all such appropriations be made once for all absolute and universal.

It may be well to mention here—for the fact is not generally known even to legislators—that but four of what are called "State institutions," of a permanent character, are "absolutely" under "State control." These are the Eastern and Western Penitentiaries, the Pennsylvania State Lunatic Hospital, at Harrisburg, and the Hospital for the Insane of the Northern District of Pennsylvania, at Danville. *All* the others are private charitable corporations, to which the legislature has been in the habit of granting State aid at each session, in the same manner precisely as it has done to the former. Shall the education of the blind and the deaf and dumb be restricted by a two-thirds rule, because private beneficence originally founded these institutions and continues to share the expense of maintaining them? Is it well to curtail the opportunities of the insane poor to admission into that noble asylum at Dixmont, because it exists under the same conditions? or to prejudice the claims of delinquent children to the reforming influences of the refuges of Allegheny and Philadelphia counties, or feeble-minded children to education and maintenance in that model training-school of Delaware county? The supposed impolicy of encouraging and aiding private zeal and benevolence, in the work of the education and reform of neglected children, has long been practically disavowed by those enlightened governments of Europe which have shown any interest in the improvement of this juvenile class as a measure of philanthropy or political concern. More especially has this been the case in Great Britain, which has given all such schools a recognized status, supports them largely, and allows, in the case of the private reformatories, the magistrates to send children for detention in them. The government accepted this policy, however, only after it had been incontestibly shown that reformatory schools could be thus established and their objects most successfully attained. It had been found there, as it is most lamentably the case in this State, that the refuges or reform schools, which maintain the unelastic character of State establishments, and which mingle together, as they must, the highly criminal youth with the barely offending ones, guarding them all as criminals by strict surveillance and within high walls, take more or less the form and complexion of prisons, and that the children discharged therefrom are regarded with some such distrust as attaches to discharged convicts, and the disposal of the inmates to eligible situations is exceedingly difficult—as a rule, almost impossible. "The results of this (the later) system," writes the Rev. Sydney Turner, inspector of the reformatory and industrial schools of England, "have been very encouraging," In many schools of either class, eighty per cent. and upwards have turned out well after their discharge; *and these results are taken from the returns which the managers of each school have to make for the three years succeed-*

ing each inmate's discharge, of his character and circumstances. The results are seen still more decidedly in the diminution of the numbers of the younger class of criminals, and the lighter character of the crimes of which our juvenile offenders are now more commonly found guilty.

"In the year 1856, when this system began to be in more active operation, the number of juvenile offenders committed for one year was 13,981; in 1858, when the system had spread and taken root, the number sank to 7622; and in 1870, in spite of the very large increase of our population, the number of young offenders committed was but 9998."

Submitted with great respect by your memorialist and humble servant,

GEO. L. HARRISON,
President.

PHILADELPHIA; September 15th, 1873.

SECTIONS 17 AND 18 MODIFIED.

SECTION 17. The legislature may make appropriations to such normal schools as may be established by law, for the professional training of teachers for the public schools of the State; and in aid of schools or homes which may be established under provisions of a general statute for the care and education of such vagrant or abandoned or destitute and neglected children as cannot be gathered into the public schools; but no appropriations shall be made to any charitable or educational institution not under the absolute control of the Commonwealth, except upon the special recommendation of a board of commissioners appointed by law to visit and inspect such institutions.

SEC. 18. No appropriation shall ever be made to any ecclesiastical, denominational, or sectarian institution, corporation, or association, nor shall any appropriation (except for pensions or bounties for military service) be made by way of gratuity to any person or community whatever.

REFORMATION OF NEGLECTED, DESTITUTE, AND VICIOUS CHILDREN.

Our suggestions hitherto have related only to the amelioration of poverty and the cure of crime in the community. We have reached now the more important and hopeful subject of the prevention and final eradication of both; vice and misery are not limited to the adult classes who fill our prisons and almshouses; if they were, the certainty of their extirpation would be but a matter of time. But behind these poor wretches range their children, line after line, from youth to infancy, the "serried ranks of woe," with the sign of their heritage of want and guilt upon their faces, pressing forward to take their turn in the prisoner's dock, the poor-house, or the jail cell.

Common sense tells us every day that each of the hungry, vicious, filthy children, that we pass in our streets or alleys, is driven inexorably by want and ignorance, year by year, nearer to one or the other of the dead-locks in life; driven there to become not only a burden upon the State, but an active evil influence in it; and, more than this, the most tragical of all spectacles the world can offer, a depraved human soul, charging before God its loss and ruin upon society. To busy ourselves alone with mature and developed crime, and to ignore the breeding mass of embryo vice beneath, from which it is steadily supplied, is to attempt to dam the river at its mouth when it has grown into an irresistible torrent, which but a trifling effort would have dried up at the fountain.

The present generation is learning wisdom slowly in this matter. In England, Germany, France, and in the local and private efforts for their instruction and reform in this country, the weight of influence is brought to bear upon the children rather than the adults of our dangerous classes. The reform of the hardened convict, weighted with the habits and associations of half a life-time, will usually do no more than make him passive in either good or evil, while the education and moral training of a child gives us an active element of good in the State.

Such efforts for prevention of crime among us are, as we stated, but local or private. The Commonwealth of Pennsylvania has been especially tardy and languid in her recognition of their utility. Her total contribution to the homes, asylums, hospitals, &c., through which these lowest classes of the poor are reached, has been, for the one hundred and twenty years ending in 1871, but $377,000, while the first cost of one of her penitentiaries for crime exceeded a million and a half. Nor is the interior machinery of government in the Commonwealth employed as yet in the rooting out of this quick-growing crop of crime. Vice matured is cherished and cared for, with so little attempt at reform, that it would seem as if its generation rather than regeneration were the object to be attained. Every county has its jail and poor-house filled with idle paupers and prisoners, a dead weight on the working, honest tax-payer, while there are but two schools of reform in the State where the immature pauper or prisoner can be stopped short in his career, taught habits of thrift and industry, and given a handicraft which will enable him to become a useful and self-supporting citizen.

The blind folly of this preference for the punishment rather than the prevention of crime is equaled only by that of the farmer, who should expend his time and strength, year after year, in cutting down perpetually renewed crops of weeds, instead of occupying his ground with wholesome grain, which would yield him fair and abundant harvests.

What, then, is the first step in the prevention of crime? We answer, education! The statistics of every country prove the large proportion which the illiterate bear to the whole number of criminals.

It is estimated that in the sixteen Southern States two-thirds of the prisoners are illiterate, while in the rest of the Union more than one-third are so; which gives us about one-half the whole number of prisoners as without education. In the prison statistics of New York City (where crime, its causes and results are condensed with photographic clearness for the expert) it is reported that in 1871, in a population of 942,242, there were 62,238 persons unable to read and write; but of 51,466 prisoners in that year 19,160 were illiterate, showing that, of the ignorant class, one in three committed crimes, while of those who could read or write the proportion of offenders was as one in twenty-seven.

There is no need, however, to multiply such statistics as these; the experience of every man tells him that the ignorant are weak and fall stupidly and easily into error.

In Massachusetts, in the same year, out of 97,742 illiterate, 4791 were criminals—that is, one in twenty, while the proportion of criminals in the class who had received a primary education was as 1 to 126½. In the penitentiaries and county jails of our own State, practically one-half of the inmates are illiterate.

We are aware that it is often declared that "merely to read and write will not diminish crime or make better citizens." But the practical alternative is not between a knowledge of reading and writing on the one hand, and habits of morality and religion on the other; but between so much knowledge as is involved in reading and writing and no education at all; between so much knowledge as that or blank ignorance or a training only in habits of vice and crime.

But we believe that there is a natural affinity between knowledge and good morals; between the normal culture of the intellect and of the heart; between truth and rectitude; and that even the mere knowledge of reading and writing increases both the means and the tendency to acquire both the knowledge and the habits of virtue and good morals. And, besides, such instruction is not obtained to the exclusion of moral and even religious training. Ninety-nine in a hundred of the teachers in the public schools of Pennsylvania are and will continue to be moral, and nine-tenths are religious persons. Such instruction and training radiate constantly, in an unconscious influence, from the person, bearing, and example of the teacher, even where formal lessons and special exercises are not employed to promote them.

Any scheme for the redemption of neglected and vicious children, however, is incomplete which simply aims to quicken their brains; the habits of thought must be made wholesome and pure, just as cleanly habits of body are inculcated; their moral sense must be awakened, and self-respect cherished; and their conceptions of God elevated and vitalized by being brought to bear on their daily life.

There is a vague belief in the public mind (and a consequent apathy thereon) that this moral training ought to reach a child through domestic influences, and that the State is only responsible for the intellectual instruction which the public schools supply. These schools, it is argued, are amply sufficient to educate the eighty thousand to one hundred thousand persons in the State under the age of twenty-one who are unable to read and write. Acting under this conviction, the constitutional convention refused to extend to them any other relief, and hindered the action of the legislature by requiring a two-thirds vote before further aid from the State could be extended to them. The argument appears plausible. The State provides a costly machinery of education, and if certain classes will not avail themselves of it the loss and punishment must be theirs.

We present the plain facts of the case. The schools are, as a rule, so admirable that they are used not only by the working but wealthier classes. Rules of cleanliness, neatness in dress, &c., are established which effectually exclude the ragged, filthy hordes who need this training most; and the demands upon the intellectual exertions of the children in the schools of the large cities are so great, and the display at the "exhibitions" so costly, that it requires the most wholesome and plentiful food to enable a child to bear the physical strain of the one, and no small expenditure of money to meet the demand of the other. It sounds well in theory to point to our school-houses as a gift of the State to the poor, but the actual fact is that the hungry little beggar at their doors has no more chance of admission than Lazarus into the gates of Dives.

Of this class there are some twenty thousand in the city of Philadelphia alone, and a like proportion in the other large cities. Even if they were accepted they would not enter the schools, as they are either utterly homeless or the children of parents unable to feed and clothe them, and they are obliged to keep up their wretched lives by either begging or theft. We point you to this army of destitution and vice and ask what shall we do with it? Barred out from the public schools; barred from the trades by the stringent laws of the trades-unions; in lack of food and clothing, what is left to them but crime? Paris, in the hands of her neglected, ignorant poor, gives us a suggestive warning.

Ignore their condition but a few years longer, and with the ballot-box in their control, the problem of the hour may be, what will they do with us?

We propose as a remedy for this evil, first, the continued aid of the State to reformatory schools, and the alteration of these schools into institutions bearing less of a penal and more of a domestic and educational character. In connection with this point we highly commend the contemplated change of place and character in the Pennsylvania Reform School, which is to be removed from Allegheny City to a large farm,—the family system in lieu of the congregate having been adopted, and the inmates instructed in agricultural work. The tilling of the soil offers in this country the surest chance of employment and the certain removal to a distance from the temptations of city life. The percentage of children trained into good citizens by these schools is set down at sixty at the lowest. These reformatory schools are intended, however, only for the treatment of the real or *quasi* criminal. There is a large number of children in them whose sole fault is a refractory temper or vagrancy, and whose association with the openly vicious can only result in their corruption.

This class and the swarms of youthful beggars outside of the schools have offered a sad and terrible problem for the consideration of thoughtful men in every country. The problem has been solved in Scotland, England, and in some parts of our own country, by what means and with what success a few brief statements will effectually demonstrate.

The first industrial school was opened in the loft of a

blacksmith's forge, in Aberdeen, under the direction of Sheriff Watson, who originated the plan in 1841, "with half a dozen boys dragged in by the police." The results of the industrial school system thus established were:—

	1840.	1870.
Children supported by theft or beggary, . . .	280	None.
Adult vagrants in rural districts for five years,	2,230	349
Children, ...	370	79

Thefts reported from 1845 to 1850, one thousand one hundred and forty-two; 1865 to 1870, three hundred and sixty-one.

These schools in Aberdeen were the prototypes of all industrial schools in Great Britain. In order to insure the attendance of the street Arabs, dependent for food on their own thefts or begging, a soup kitchen was attached to the schools and the police were authorized to arrest all children begging and bring them in.

Reformatory schools received the sanction of Parliament, in Great Britain, in 1853, and industrial schools in 1854. By subsequent acts they were placed under the control of the home office, and an allowance granted, *per capita*, for the education and maintenance of the inmates. There were one hundred of the certified industrial schools in 1872 in successful operation in England and Scotland, under control of different religious or charitable associations, and they are supported in part by voluntary contributions, by government grant, by payment from parents, who send their children voluntarily, and by profits in the industrial department.

In some of these schools the children are fed during the day and return to their homes at night; in others they are fed, clothed, and lodged. The children are governed by the family system, educated as their future position requires, and trained to be practical farmers, sailors, shoemakers, carpenters, bakers, weavers, &c.

The girls are educated in the use of the needle and sewing-machine, in laundry work, cooking, housewifery, &c.

The total number admitted into these schools amounted at the last official returns to 25,376. Of those discharged, the percentage was—

	Boys.	Girls.
Doing well,	75.2	73.7
Doubtful,	6.18	8.8
Convicted,	3.13	2.2
Unknown,	13.3	13.6
Died,	2.2	2.5

In 1856, before the reformatory and industrial system was put into operation, the number of commitments to prison of children under sixteen was 13,981.

In 1870, with a fourteen years increase of population, the commitments were 9998.

Mr. Barwick Baker, who founded the first reformatory school in England, on his own estate, thus testifies to the success of the system:—

"In Gloucester, in 1844, we had seven jails and eight hundred and seventy persons. In 1872, we have pulled down six out of the seven, and have but one hundred and seventy inmates in that."

An example of the benefit derived from a system of industrial schools, differing in detail from those in England, is found near at hand.

In 1852 and 1853, special attention was directed in the city of New York to the subject of juvenile vagrancy and crime, and associations were formed for the prevention of crime. The machinery put in motion by these societies were industrial schools and the removal of children to homes in the West. Of these schools thirty-six are maintained by one society alone. The aggregate attendance at the whole of them reaches 13,606.

The action of these associations is unaided by the State, and unenforced by law. There is, therefore, a lack of thoroughness and force in the system which that of Great Britain possesses, yet the result in ten years of their vigorous and humane efforts, which we append below, is startling in its success.

	1860. Girls.	1871. Girls.
Arrests for vagrancy, ...	2,161	495
Arrests for pocket-picking, ...	59	3
Arrests for petty larceny, ...	959	823
	3,179	1,321
Decrease, ...	1,858	

	1860. Girls.	1870. Girls.
Commitments for vagrancy, ...	5,880	671
Commitments for petty larceny, ...	890	746
	6,770	1,417
	1,417	
Decrease, ...	5,353	

	1860. Boys.	1870. Boys.
Arrests for vagrancy, ...	1,800	1,331
Arrests for pocket-picking, ...	407	46–1871
Arrests for petty larceny, ...	2,987	3,171
	5,194	4,548

	1860. Boys.	1870. Boys.
Commitments for vagrancy, ...	2,708	1,378
Commitments for petty larceny, ...	2,575	2,241
	5,283	3,619

According to the increase of population, the increase of crime should have been twenty per cent., instead of which the commitments of girls for vagrancy, as we see, diminished in ten years five thousand. "Nothing," says Mr. Brace, who presents this record, "can account for this diminution of crime but moral and preventive measures; for during that time a terrible war has occurred with all its necessary evils, and several panics and prostrations of business."

We need adduce no further proof of the efficiency of the plan which we propose, viz., that industrial schools shall be introduced and assisted by the State. The support of a child in one of these, as we stated in our last report, will cost the State twenty dollars per annum. The support of the same child matured into a criminal will cost her $200 per annum. "Our system of industrial schools," says a Swede, "is costly, but not dear. We cannot afford to let a child grow up in ignorance and vice."

Still less can we afford it when the ignorant and

vicious adult will shortly help to make the laws which are to govern us.

The plan we offer is neither costly nor difficult. Considered from the lowest point of view, that of economy, by the statistics given above, it will save the Commonwealth in ten years the expense of at least one-third of her present number of criminals; considered in regard to its humane aspects, we believe it to offer the only means, at once rational and Christian, by which the seething mass of ignorance and crime which underlies society, here as elsewhere, may be reached, and greatly reduced or wholly eradicated.

Profoundly impressed by the truth of the suggestions which we have made to your honorable bodies on this highly important subject, this board has ventured to prepare a bill for your consideration, which will not only effect the purpose of the suggestions, but which will also establish an impartial and uniform system respecting all those classes of institutions which provide for the maintenance and education of destitute and neglected children.

We append to our report on this subject a statement of the numbers, ages, &c., of the inmates of the two houses of refuge or reform schools in the State.

STATE REFORMATORIES.

Of this class of institutions there are two in Pennsylvania, viz., the Philadelphia House of Refuge, and the Pennsylvania Reform School in Allegheny county. The number of juvenile delinquents confined in them on September 30th, 1874, was respectively as follows:—

SEX AND COLOR.	House of Refuge.		Reform School.		Recapitulation.	
White boys,	371		200		571	
White girls,	87		66		153	
Total white,		458		266		724
Colored boys,	99		25		124	
Colored girls,	40		10		50	
Total colored,		139		35		174
Aggregate of white and colored,		597		301		898

The number in both institutions on September 30th, 1874, was eight hundred and ninety-eight, the white being in proportion to the colored as eighty-one to nineteen. It will be observed that but few colored delinquents are confined in the "Reform School," their proportion to the white being but twelve to eighty-eight. In the "House of Refuge," which has a special department for the colored inmates, we find that their ratio to the white is as twenty-three to seventy-seven. The average age of those committed during the year was 13.9 years, or white delinquent 14.5 years; colored, 13.4 years.

PRISON ECONOMY.

PRISON DISCIPLINE.

Prison discipline is one branch of the science of government, and, like every other department of that science, it is progressive. New ideas respecting its purposes and new methods of reducing them to practice will, of course, be developed by patient observation of facts and careful deduction of the principles which they teach.

The moral and physical evils of incarceration have been much abated as Christianity and civilization have advanced. Prisons are spoken of as existing at the times of the patriarchs, seventeen hundred years before the Christian era; but it is believed that they did not become an established part of the organism of the state until the rise of the baronial or feudal system, in the tenth and eleventh centuries. A writer says:—"The prison, as we know it, is as entirely an institution of modern Europe as the church, the school, and the poor-house. Words occur connected with events and customs in the eastern world which we can only translate into modern language or thought by the use of the word 'prison;' but the thing, as we now know it, in the shape of the county jail or the convict prison, was, then, neither known nor anticipated. A systematic committal to prison, as a specific punishment, is a thing of which it may be safely said that no trace can be found in the practices of ancient nations that have come down to us." In early times "prisons" were often excavations in the earth, encased with solid masonry, or dug out in the living rock, and men were dropped into them as into huge bottles, or placed in recesses in the sides and built in with stone and mortar, to drag out a miserable and, sometimes, protracted existence; death offering the only hope of relief.

In despotic countries, the policy of the government has often been to cut off all facilities for the identification of prisoners. When they fell into the hands of power they lost all connection with the living world, and their actual death was known only to the subalterns to whose keeping they were committed.

In the reign of Louis XIV. (one of a race of kings who assumed that states existed for the support of royalty in luxury and self-indulgence) the French Parliament was aroused to do something for the protection from the law's delay of persons seized and incarcerated on charges (sometimes altogether futile and malicious) for which they had not been tried, and to secure for their cases an early investigation; and at length extorted a promise that the case of every imprisoned person should have judical cognizance within twenty-four hours after his arrest. But the fact of imprisonment without trial, and often without guilt, was scarcely a greater cruelty there and elsewhere than the treatment of those adjudged guilty and sentenced to incarceration.

In the reign of George II., through lack of governmental control, and the irresponsibility of the wardens of prisons, greater cruelties were practiced than were common under the most absolute despots. Hogarth's picture of the grated window in one of the dungeons of Fleet street, records better than words of description the miseries of imprisonment in his time.

When these outrages were exposed, Parliament committed itself so far to their correction, that the prison-keepers became more cautious, and abstained from the infliction of unlawful cruelties. But the very prisons themselves were so constructed as to be instruments of mental and physical torture to their inmates, and so continued until the time of Howard. At that very period the prisons of the Dutch (shame to our English ancestors!) far excelled theirs in order, cleanliness, and industry, and were nearly assimilated in these respects to the best establishments of modern times. But the pre-eminent evil of the English provision for the care of prisoners, even to so late a period as the year 1859, was the promiscuous mingling of culprits, great and small. The corrupting influence of such a system can hardly be overstated. The most atrocious and hardened criminals, with such facilities, impart their own measure and type of iniquity to novices in vice, so that the higher measure of wickedness is often reached by these latter almost at a bound.

Even now, in most countries, while the supreme authority has some oversight, and, at will, exercises some restraining power upon the inferior officers of justice, so that they are liable to be checked in the pursuit of any arbitrary or vindictive courses, yet there is no hand to lay restraint upon the chief executive himself, and to protect the prisoner against his caprices or mistakes. England and the United States possess the *habeas corpus* act. These are the ónly countries in which is any power, adequate to the object, that can interpose between the ruler and the alleged culprit and open the prison doors.

These are steps in the way of righteous dealing towards those who have fallen under the condemnation of the law, which do not arrest the course of justice, but only secure its equal administration. They are tokens of a higher civilization, and of a Christianity which has leavened even the civil economy of the state.

The reformation of the prisoner is now, in enlightened communities, no less an object of incarceration than is punishment: so that, in great measure, reformatories and prisons are kindred institutions. The difficult problem which we are now most concerned to solve is, how to maintain the condign severity of the law, and yet to encourage the culprit to attempt, with a hopeful spirit, a new and more honorable mode of life. He must never be suffered to forget that he is under the rebuke of society for his crime. To his proclivities for self-indulgence and evil company, the prison should in no wise give indulgence. *Restraint must be a present consciousness all the time.* Constraint to meet reasonable exactions of work, and of punctuality and obedience to rule, must be as certainly a part of his daily regimen as the supply of his frugal and homely meals. And yet, in the exercise of this quiet strictness and severity, there should be always in the administration the spontaneous *evidences* of humanity, and, in the apprehension of the culprit, the sense that simple justice is dealt out to him. Facilities for improvement must be given; commendation on duties well performed kindly bestowed; and the possibilities of a better life, in after years, suggested and put within the reach of hope. No merely hireling functionary is fit to have the charge of imprisoned culprits. The work of a warden in a penitentiary can be well done only by one who believes in the susceptibilities of manhood, even when brought to the deepest abasement, and who aspires to make an effort to lift it up and help its restoration. He must not be of hasty temper or easily discouraged, but must pursue his undertaking with a quenchless zeal and perform his work in the same spirit of sacrifice with which a missionary of religion leaves his country and gives his life to the reclaiming of men groping in the darkness and degradation of heathenism.

To secure this manner and spirit of administration the most vigilant oversight is required. Very much of what transpires in the various public institutions of our country is secure enough from actual abuse by the publicity of their proceedings. Times of free visitation are appointed, at which whosoever will may pass through them and inspect their arrangements. And this public supervision, supplemented by the official inspection of their board of managers, affords an ordinarily effective mode of bringing to light any grievous wrongs that are practiced upon their inmates. But the walls of prisons are as effectual in keeping critics out as in keeping culprits in. It is especially desirable that impartial men, holding office not for fee or reward, but from motives of philanthropy alone, appointed by an authority which shall possess the highest confidence for its wisdom and its independence, should be invested with powers of oversight and direction, enabling them to look into the inner prisons and the whole economy of treatment and the animus with which it is conducted.

In his first report, after the adoption of our Pennsylvania system of separate imprisonment, the chief officer having oversight of such matters in England wrote:—"I find the result at present to be not only the entire suppression of the corrupt and demoralizing effects of indiscriminate association, but a peculiar seriousness of demeanor is produced by separate confinement, which, except in a few instances, I never witnessed before."

Isolated and temporary experiments of the solitary system had been attempted in Great Britain before; as in the Gloucester Penitentiary, near the close of the eighteenth century, and afterwards, in a modified shape, in the Bridewell of Glasgow.

In 1786, through the influence of the Society of Friends, the solitary system was distinctly developed in the management of the prison in Philadelphia. All punishments of a corporal nature, such as branding and the lash, were at the same time abolished. Alterations were made in the Walnut Street Prison with reference to this new regime. Thirty cells were set apart for separate confinement. Continuous solitude, without labor, books, or manual occupation of any sort, was at first enforced. And the same system was adopted, in some degree, by Maryland, Massachusetts,

Maine, New Jersey, and Virginia. But perpetual solitude was found to be unendurable, unless some employment might be given. A culprit, having small resources of knowledge, and, therefore, meagre material for thought, shut up to brood only upon his folly and crime and punishment, will, if of passionate temperament, be driven to insanity, and, if of sluggish mould, will sink into idiocy. Labor interrupts and mitigates the anguish of remembered guilt and its tribulation. The hands can do nothing unless the mind be more or less engaged in directing their movements, and any diversion of the thoughts from one perpetual, painful subject of reflection, is an unspeakable relief. It is the law of our intellectual, as it is of our physical, nature, that if some faculties be withheld from exercise, others are intensified into abnormal power and activity. As, if the eyes be blinded, the hearing becomes more acute; so, if the operative functions of the mind be repressed, the reflective action is excessively and morbidly increased. He who cannot apply his thoughts to any matter of present interest, recoils upon the past with a fearful energy of memory, of which men in their natural freedom of observation and action are incapable. The American experiment, which, separating prisoners from one another, modified the severity of such solitude by requiring them to labor, gave the first demonstration of the value of those two elements in prison discipline.

But labor is advantageous not only in that it makes solitary confinement endurable, but that it teaches, what most criminals have never learned, the duty of service. "Idleness is the parent of vice." A little investigation would convince any one that in nearly every instance the crimes which consign men to prison have been committed by those who have never acquired habits of industry,—who have either obtained a precarious livelihood by leaning on others for support or by occasional spasms of effort to work, or have lazily, with perpetual reluctance, and with evasion of duty whenever possible, maintained a sham occupation. For such men, especially if they reach prison (the goal of crime) early in life, steady, compulsory labor is a most wholesome discipline. Industry becomes thus a necessity of their situation, both because irresistible authority exacts it of them, and because, in solitude, their own comfort of mind requires it. It is the nearest approach they have to positive pleasure, and so it grows to be agreeable, until a diligence which began under constraint at length ripens into a habit. The criminal who, paying the penalty of a past offense, gains meanwhile this item of personal training, for the lack of which he became a criminal, returns to the world, when his sentence of incarceration is fulfilled, a wiser and a better man, imbued with such new ideas of life that, through industry, he will escape relapse into crimes. But prison labor, to be beneficial in its effect upon the prisoner, must be productive. The crank and the tread-mill only weary the body and vex the spirit. Where a particle of manhood remains, the soul revolts at a mere muscular occupation, which gives no exercise to the understanding, and might as well be done by an ox or an ass. These inflictions are merely penal. Dr. Wines reports of a recent visit to the city prison of London, where as many as seven or eight hundred of the inmates were found "exercising" on the tread-wheel, which is the largest in the world:—"The governor of the prison testifies to the bad effects of this kind of prison labor." They humble the transgressor, indeed, but they destroy his self-respect. They may serve to make the prison odious, and thus operate to make the viciously-inclined more careful to avoid it, but they do him no good—rather positive harm, when once he is lodged in prison as a culprit.

The system of separate imprisonment, with useful labor, avoids alike the danger of contamination by the intercourse of the bad with the worse, and the danger of insanity or imbecility when the guilty are kept idle and alone. Under the old common-jail arrangement the novice in crime was almost sure to go forth, when discharged, an adept. The leisure allowed in the prison-yards, and in the rooms where culprits were herded together, was employed in recounting past exploits in crime and hair-breadth escapes, and in planning future acts of villainy; so that, not infrequently, men were graduated from these schools of vice with a programme of further depredations upon society carefully prepared and determined on.

To preclude communication between prisoners is the paramount idea of the separate system. It does not contemplate the exclusion of ministers of religion according to the denominational preferences of those in confinement; they may come to the wretched exile as often as his spiritual wants require. It does not hinder the access of other conscientious persons whom it may be agreeable and edifying for them to see. In some places it is not thought to impair the efficacy of

this system to allow the prisoners to meet for worship and instruction. In the Western Penitentiary of this State, under a recent law, prisoners come together for labor, restricted, however, from all conversation with one another.

This absolute prevention of all intercourse between the vicious, and exclusion of all outside visitors except those who come to lead them to repentance and a better life, must add great moral force to the influences of religious truth with which they are approached. The privacy of these errands of mercy gives the consciously guilty encouragement to unburden his heart, and to indulge and express feelings of contrition, without the danger of being scoffed at for his weakness. If there be any tender memories, they are likely to be awakened and made impressive and profitable under such circumstances. And besides, undistracted by other objects of interest and topics of conversation, the mind of a prisoner, judiciously guided by conscientious advisers and concentrated upon the recovery of a lost relation of amity with God and man, will most surely reach wise and abiding conclusions.

The dietary arrangements of a prison may be made to promote its reformatory influences. A large proportion of those who are incarcerated as criminals have before imprisonment led dissolute lives. Addicted to intoxicating drinks, their food has been, for the most part, poor and innutritious and taken at irregular times. Surfeited occasionally with inordinate quantities of hearty food, and then almost starved by its meagreness and infrequency, they become worn and sickly, and ordinarily improve in bodily condition after they are

put in durance. This improvement results partially from the uniformity of material of their food, and of the times at which they receive it. It is attributable, also, in some degree, to the constrained inactivity of their lives. And so it often happens that improved in health prisoners come out at the expiration of their sentence presenting an appearance not only in ludicrous contrast with that which they wore when taken into custody, but more indicative of good living than the aspect of honest laborers, who have earned, at liberty, the means of their daily subsistence. A difference so marked ought not to appear, lest poverty be tempted to crime by the seemingly better fare of those who have been convicted of it. Culprits should not be too well fed. They are usually persons in whom the animal nature is predominant, and out of that fact their vices have grown. Repletion of food is often attended with a mental indifference to other things, and a pride and haughtiness of spirit unfavorable to moral improvement. Nor, on the other hand, should the prison be used as a place of physical torture by the withholding of necessary food. It is a nice point to be fixed upon, and it should be determined after the most careful observation, and the exercise of the highest professional skill. What is the lowest quantity of plain food which will preserve a human being, in his normal condition, is the law of subsistence which should find place in prison economy. A certain measure of abstinence is not unfavorable to the best dicipline of the spirit.

Truth is better apprehended when the body has not been satiated with overmuch food; the carnal passions

are less likely to predominate. Such experience is a hint for the management of those who, by the indulgence of wicked propensities, have become dangerous to the community, and are in its hands for chastisement and reform. The regimen of their subsistence should be such, that without detriment to the physical constitution, their whole nature should be kept in the best condition for receiving and appropriating whatever good and reformatory influences may be brought to bear upon them. Especially should there be avoidance of such dietary profusion as could by any possibility make the prison a place of chosen refuge for the idle and thriftless drones of society.

BENEVOLENCE IN PUNISHMENT AND IN PROVISION FOR THE POOR.

Society needs to realize more sensibly than it now does that benevolence, not only towards the stricken and unfortunate, but towards the vicious who fall into its custody, is both its duty and its interest. And they who serve society as custodians of these classes need still more to feel it and to practice it in the administration of their trusts. The perfunctory and heartless care of human beings, whether in asylums or prisons, is a deprivation of that ameliorating influence of sympathy which is at once the right of the persons in ward, and the interest of the community which has them to provide for.

In suggesting a benevolent administration of justice even to convicted criminals, we would not be understood as favoring that weak lenity which would deprive discipline of all its punitive power. The hope of evading arrest, and, if arrested, of escaping conviction; the relief from wearisome labor, and the certainty of good fare in prison, the chances of having the term of incarceration shortened by executive clemency, strip our penal code of almost all its terrors. Through one or more of these loopholes the minions of vice take assurance that they shall escape from the full measure of punishment which the law decrees, and so they venture on crime with the chances, as they think, in their favor. Certainly if condign punishment would be a proximate preventive of crime, uninviting but wholesome food, labor enough to produce daily fatigue, strict but perfectly humane treatment, should be the experience of every convict. In dealing with crime, the public should aim, not only at its own protection by placing the guilty under restraint, but also at the moral reformation of the offender, if for no other reason, for this, that when released he may be of some service to society by his influence and his industry, rather than infect it with the pestilence of his vices and weaken it by his depredations, intensified by hatred and vindictiveness engendered through what he conceives to be the despotism of his restraining imprisonment.

The family relation is the natural one, and should be the type of those larger communities which result from the commercial habits of mankind. The state is a great family, and the animus of its administration should accord with that idea. The father, in no stage of his child's waywardness and alienation, may forget his parental bonds. He deals most wisely with a recreant child who, not sparing the rod of chastisement, makes his offspring to feel, at every stroke, that he is smarting, not under the malignant vengeance of outraged power, but under the effort of aggrieved love to enforce the conviction that the way of the transgressor is hard, and to bring back the offender to duty and reconciliation.

No one, put in durance by the strong hand of society, unless, perhaps, he has committed that extreme offense by which the sentence of death is incurred, should be made to esteem himself an utter and hopeless outcast, whom all men are conspiring to hunt down. When it appears that nobody else has a vestige of hope that a man may be reclaimed, he, himself, loses all hope and abandons all effort of amendment. What is wanted in prison discipline is, not a mawkish tenderness, not a weak consideration for prisoners, as if they were mere unfortunates; but a gracious humanity which recognizes manhood as still existent in the vilest culprit, and would fain do something to bring it out of degrading bondage, and restore it to supremacy. The manual of our religious faith teaches, that while the Supreme permits a transgressor to live, He continues to him the power and the opportunity to return and forsake his evil ways.

But if it be both just and politic to deal even with criminals in a humane and merciful spirit, how much rather should they be stimulated with manifestations of sympathy and encouragement to effort, who have been disabled, by the visitation of God, from earning their own living, and are *unwillingly* forced upon the community for maintenance. We now speak of the worthy paupers, not the professional who oscillate between the county jail and the county almshouse, infected with a double degradation. We may concede that the careless lenity which so generally indulges these consuming lazzaroni, with abundant provision and light labor, is to be deprecated, offering, as it does, a premium for idleness and vice. If such be proper subjects for public maintenance, they should be sternly taught, that "if they will not work, neither shall they eat."

The unfortunate and the guilty are all alike integral parts of the community. Whatever dejects them, enfeebles it. The effective force of society is made up of the power of its individual members, and the confidence of each in all, is one of the elements of that power. The deterioration of any member of the community, even though he be a pauper or criminal, to a certain extent lowers the moral standard of the whole. A modern English writer says:—"It is not to be supposed that the criminal population is a creation apart. No, it springs from, it is a part of, the community; it is composed of the weaker and more excitable part of *every class*.

"The weak, the careless, the vicious of every class find themselves gradually and steadily crushed out of the conflict for that wealth, which every effort made around them by men of higher capacities than their own, tends to exalt their imagination, while it removes them from its legitimate acquisition. The appetite for wealth, which is a disease even among the educated and high-toned of a nation, becomes a foul leprosy in that portion of it, in whom weakness of intellect and strength of passions have not found a compensating control in sound education and early training."

Pauperism, especially, requires to be lifted out of the downward steeps of hopelessness. Our self-respect is largely dependent on our consciousness that others respect us, and loss of self-respect almost certainly leads its desolate victim to the commission of crime. In all almshouses, every inmate should be required to exert his or her ability to labor, however feeble it be, and to that end, diversities of work should be furnished adapted to their individual strength and skill. And this should be exacted, not as a burden or penalty, whose tendency would be still further to crush out the manliness of its victim, but as a stimulus to self-reliance and a proof that the power of self-maintenance may be regained.

This we submit as one method by which the state, the embodiment and executive power of society, may characterize its administration of those departments in the great household, where the transgressing, the inefficient, and the unfortunate members are provided for, under rules of the firmest discipline, but by a generous and wholesome benevolence. And through an agency of its own charged with this mission, and imbued with a right spirit, it is believed that much may be done to repress evil, alleviate misery, and promote future improvement in those restraining methods and influences which are now in practice.

CRIME AND PRISON ECONOMY.

It is a trite maxim, that the prevention of evil is better than its cure; and nowhere is the maxim more true than in relation to crime. To destroy its seeds or hinder their germination—to dry up its sources or turn their flow into some harmless or useful direction—to eradicate or neutralize its causes—is better than all efforts at its repression or even its reform. It is easier, as well as better, to throw off the incipient fever than to stay its full-grown progress. It is easier and wiser to guard against or extinguish the first kindling of the fire than to stem the sweeping conflagration. Both processes, the preventive and the remedial, will always be needed; for neither disease nor conflagration nor crime will ever be utterly abolished among men; but each process should be applied in its proper place and in its due proportion. In the former reports of this board, therefore, attention has already been most earnestly called to the unspeakable importance of adopting effectual measures for securing the universal education of the young in learning, industry, and good morals; for hindering truancy and vagrancy, idleness and intemperance, and for furnishing the destitute poor with such shelter and support as may preserve them from either miserably perishing or preying upon the peace and property of society, as well as giving occasion to still greater multitudes of idle vagabonds to impose upon its charity. Such preventive measures cannot be too urgently pressed and pushed forward. They are the most humane, the most beneficent, the most effective, and, in the end, they will prove the cheapest. Still, measures of repression and reform, to which it is now proposed to invite attention, will always be necessary; and they will continue to tax the highest wisdom of the legislature. Indeed, no subject connected with the science of legislation or of public economy possesses a deeper interest than this. After due preventive enactments, no other has a more momentous bearing upon the welfare and progress of society. No other demands profounder consideration or more patient inquiry, as a condition of wise and beneficent legislation. *Beneficent* legislation, we say advisedly and purposely; for humanity and charity are concerned in it as well as policy and wisdom; or, rather, in this case, they *are* both policy and wisdom.

Not that the inspection and examination, which this board has made, of the penal and reformatory institutions of the Commonwealth, even from the special point of view suggested by its very title, have tainted the minds of its members with any mawkish sentimentalism over "the poor, suffering" criminal, or inspired them with any frenzy of philanthropy, or with any sympathy for the imprisoned convict as a mere "victim of misfortune." Far from it. We look upon crime with horror and detestation, and we regard the criminal as richly deserving punishment;—often severe, grievous punishment,—punishment sometimes greater than man can inflict. But all this does not hinder that he should be an object of humane, kindly, and beneficent regard. In wrath, mercy may be remembered by man as well as by his Maker; by the state as well as by the individual. The criminal is still a man. He is a criminal and must be punished, ought to be punished; he is a man and must be treated, must be punished, *as a man.*

This board does not forget that it is the creature, the agent, the representative of the legislature; and that it has no proper functions or aims which lie beyond and outside of the functions and aims of the legislature. Its business is to represent the true character and spirit of the legislature, and no more. But it rejoices to remember that it has been constituted and designated to represent that character and spirit in their most generous, their humane, and benevolent aspect. Such an aspect it is firmly believed they have and, of right, ought to have. That such an aspect of character and spirit is not alien to its functions the legislature has formally acknowledged and declared in the very act of creating the board itself. Let it not be supposed that it is intended to push the inference too far. This board fully recognizes the fact that the state is not a mere benevolent association, or the legislature a philanthropic club; that the state looks with a calm, large view at general results and the common weal, rather than with a sentimental absorption at the relief of particular cases of hardship and suffering; looks at political interests rather than at moral and religious ends; that the public good is the fundamental condition and aim of all legislation; and, particularly, that punishments are inflicted upon criminals in order to prevent the further commission of crime by others as well as by themselves. But these general doctrines are sometimes misunderstood and misapplied; are overstretched on their exclusive or negative side, and in their antithesis to views supposed to be conflicting; or are urged in a manner quite too bold and peremptory. It may not be irrelevant, therefore, in introducing the general subject which has been proposed, to premise a brief preliminary consideration of what is meant by the general good as a principle of legislation.

What does this principle involve, and what does it exclude, as considerations proper or improper to be taken account of in making laws?

Here the broad statement may be ventured, that a regard for popular intelligence and virtue, that sentiments of justice and honor, of humanity and charity, are proper motives for legislators, and their promotion and prevalence in the community proper objects of legislation, as well as the protection or advancement of the common physical well-being, or the increase of the pecuniary wealth or resources of the state; they are *included* under the idea of promoting the general welfare.

In regard to intelligence and virtue, most Christian states have, in their legislation, practically acknowledged the truth of the statement. Our own State in particular has emphatically acknowledged it in providing the elements of instruction for all, and in encouraging and fostering the higher institutions of science and learning, as well as those for the moral and religious training of the community.

The claims of justice, too, are generally admitted in practice. It is admitted that the state may not commit injustice herself,—however much it might seem to promote the public good,—and that it is a principal part of her office to administer justice between man and man, to redress wrongs and to prevent injuries. This is admitted to be involved in the idea of promoting the general welfare; and, if so, surely a nice *sense* of honor and keen *sentiments* of justice cannot be unfitting motives to sway the mind of a legislator; or, to secure their prevalence in the community, an improper object of legislation.

Thus far there is no considerable dispute. The great conflict occurs at another point. It seems to be very generally thought and assumed that at all events the sentiments of humanity and charity have nothing to do with statesmanship and legislation; that *here* the legislator is bound to look directly, strictly, and exclusively at the public *interest.* But if the helpless poor, the deaf, the blind, the idiotic, the decrepit, were left to perish, and if the insane were forthwith put to death, society might be relieved of a great burden, and its physical well-being greatly improved. Only humanity and charity forbid. And all civilized and Christian states have in their legislation recognized the authority of these sentiments; have recognized their exercise and prevalence in these relations as being of more importance to the general welfare than mere dollars and cents. How is it possible, then, that those who act for the state in making its laws should find it unfitting to be themselves influenced by the same sentiments and motives in framing their enactments?

In like manner, in the treatment of criminals, it is believed and maintained that regard should be had to the claims of humanity, to the good and reformation of the offender, as well as to the claims of justice or to the security of the state, in the removal of burdens or the deterring of men from the commission of crime.

Otherwise, all criminals of whatever age, under whatever circumstances, guilty of crimes of whatever degree, might upon conviction be straightway put to death. If the legislator is to look simply with a cold-blooded regard to the public interest, why should they not be? If it should be thought that public justice, or the public good, in any point of view, forbid it, because they require a gradation of punishments according to the enormity of offenses, that requisition might be met by marking the greater crime with the more excruciating mode of execution, or by the infliction of various degrees of preliminary torture. Thus society would be summarily relieved of an oppressive burden of expense, and men would most effectually be deterred from the commission of crime, so far as severity of punishment could deter them. But not the spirit of Christianity alone, the voice of humanity and the genius of civilization, cry out against the Draconian code. Such a society, a society with such a code, a society thus discarding all the sentiments of humanity, would be a society of savages. And shall the customs of savages furnish the purest illustration of the highest ideal of human legislation, of a wise and single-minded aim at the *public good?*

It may perhaps be suggested that in a civilized community such a code would, in fact, encourage instead of preventing crime, and thus defeat its own object and operate against the general good; because, with such a code, judges and juries would not convict or sentence men guilty of crimes, especially in the case of minor offenses, and thus the great mass of evil-doers would actually escape punishment altogether. If this suggestion is made, it is cheerfully and frankly admitted; but, in the same breath, the whole point here contended for is admitted also; for it is thus admitted that legislators, in their penal enactments, cannot safely ignore the sentiments of humanity and charity; they cannot safely so look at the public good as to leave these sentiments altogether out of account as motives in shaping their action.

Nor can the force of this argument be parried by saying that these sentiments must, indeed, be recognized by legislators as existing facts in the community, but not as proper motives in their own minds; that, rather, they are to be regarded as unfortunate external impediments which they are compelled to take account of, while they seek, as directly as possible, and in spite of these hindrances, to reach their proper end—the general interest of the state. This implies that, from a legislative point of view, it would be desirable that all such sentiments should be abolished in the community, and thus a great impediment removed from the direct path to the accomplishment of the proper purpose of legislation,—in short, that the savage is superior to the civilized state. But this is too absurd to be openly maintained for a moment. No Rousseau can longer be found ingenious and hardy enough to defend the thesis. Rather, it is unquestionably in the highest degree desirable, that sentiments of humanity and charity should pervade the community; their prevalence is a most important condition and element of the general welfare. If it is the duty of legislators not to be influenced by these sentiments, it is equally the duty of judges and juries not to be influenced by them; and still more emphatically is it their duty, if it is made and declared such by positive law. Are the oaths of judges and jurymen less binding than those of legislators? And if not, why is it to be assumed that the former are more likely to disregard the solemnity of their oaths than the latter? Are legislators the only honest and trustworthy part of the community? But why are legislators called upon to abdicate their humanity, while judges and jurymen are allowed to retain it? If this "humanity" is a weakness and a vice, both in the makers and the administrators of public law, would not consistency require that, while seeking to abolish it in one department, we should aim at its abolition in all other departments, instead of yielding to it in any? The fact is, this ignoring of humanity by statesmen is, after all, a lesson not so easily learned or practiced. Men cannot easily make themselves mere abstractions or mere legislative machines: they will still be men. And if men are to govern men, the governors must not only retain their own humanity, but must also recognize the manhood of those whom they govern.

Nor does the principle here contended for rest on merely theoretic grounds; it is no matter of mere speculative sentimentalism; it has been practically confirmed by actual legislation. The claims not only of justice, but of civilization and humanity have been distinctly recognized by the modern state—in the abolition of all forms of torture and of ignominious inflictions for crimes; in arranging a due gradation of punishment; in consulting for the comfort and health of prisoners, by providing for them warmth, ventilation, and wholesome diet, and in establishing reformatory institutions for juvenile offenders, as well as in providing or aiding from the common treasury hospitals and asylums for the poor, for the blind, for deaf mutes, for the aged, the feeble-minded, the insane, and the inebriate. As a matter of fact, and to a large extent, the Christian state has adopted, in her legislation, the principle of humanity and charity, instead of unadulterated social selfishness.

The simple question now is, will the state repudiate her own practical principles out of deference to an extreme, purely speculative, and savage doctrine of the "public good;" or, retaining them, will she *carry them out in a thorough and consistent manner?*

In the progress of Roman civilization, it came to be felt that a Roman citizen, however criminal, was a person too sacred for scourging or crucifixion ; these were punishments reserved for slaves. In modern civilization, till quite too late, have lingered the pillory and the rack and bloody whipping-posts, the mutilations of noses and eyes and ears and hands, the slow pressing to death of recusants and the cutting out of the hearts of traitors, while the ingenuities of inquisitorial torture and burning at the stake have been reserved for the holiday amusement of religious bigotry. That bigotry, alas, is not quite extinct, but in general it has learned to be content with less horrible modes of gratification. Some remnants and relics of those other cruel and ignominious inflictions still disgrace the statute-books and judicial usages of some Christian states; but even when they were in full operation, under the brutal codes of feudal institutions, they were usually accompanied with what was at once an insult to humanity and an acknowledgment of its claims, in the shape of an exemption from them in favor of the members of the governing aristocracy. Modern civilization has, for the most part, entirely outlived them. With *us*, especially, they are quite obsolete. We have no slaves, on the one hand, and no aristocratic exemptions on the other. Every American citizen is, as such, a person as sacred and respectable as the Roman citizen of ante-Christian, or the feudal baron of mediæval, times; and American laws will not discriminate against the persons of those who come to us as guests or as prospective citizens. In short, it has been found that contempt and contumelious treatment of our fellow-men is not good, either for them or for us; that the spirit of wanton and vindictive cruelty cannot promote the general good and happiness of society, and, least of all, when organized, sanctioned, and executed by the authority of the state, as an act of the whole body politic; that the state cannot afford, by the ignominious degradation of humanity, even in the person of the grossest criminal, or by the infliction of any punishment whatever for the mere purpose of inflicting pain or suffering on the offender, to encourage or sanction the spirit of inhumanity or cruelty in the community. A sacred regard for human kind, or respect for the dignity of man as man, a prevalent spirit of forbearance and kindness, and a prevailing horror of cruelty, are better safeguards of personal rights and the public good than all the tortures and scourgings and pillories and bloody mutilations that ever were invented.

Men will often, if not always, best promote their private interest, not by a course of pure selfishness, not by making that interest the direct and exclusive end of all their plans and conduct, but by cherishing and acting upon the sentiments of justice, humanity, and charity. If a farmer, a merchant, or a manufacturer, having a number of men in his employ, would have them serve him most heartily, faithfully, and efficiently, he must show that he takes a cordial interest in them and in their welfare; they must be made to believe that he has such an interest; and the best, the only honest, if not the only possible way to make them believe it, is, actually to have it and cultivate it. In like manner individuals, if not legislators, will often best promote the public good, not by seeking it as the direct and absolute end, but by consciously aiming at the ends of justice and charity, of humanity and civilization, of morality and religion. *And even legislators will wisely aim at these ends so far as the public good requires, and seek the public good only in such ways as these higher ends permit.* The public good is too closely interwoven with those ends to be separated from them, either in fact or in purpose, even by the most abstract and imperturbable legislative coolness.

For example, whatever a crude idea of the public good might seem to require or sanction to the contrary, the sentiments and the ends of humanity and equity evidently require a *gradation of penalties* according to the enormity of offenses. In the end, the public good requires it too, and so, as already said, all civilized legislation has practically recognized the principle. For if the theft of a dime were visited with the same punishment as the commission of murder—even though that punishment were death—the petty theft might indeed come to be regarded with greater horror, but the crime of murder would certainly be most perilously cheapened. For this the highest punishment should be reserved ; on this the extreme penalty should be inflicted, and the infliction of the extreme penalty in this case is demanded quite as much by the *natural sentiments of humanity* as by any regard to the public welfare. Yet even this extreme penalty should be executed, not with any adjuncts of needless ignominy or cruelty, not in malignity or vindictiveness, but in as mild a form as possible, and with every token of reluctance, of sympathy and humane regard. If the pricipal end of all punishment should be the prevention of crime and the restraint of criminals, capital punishment should remain to deter men by the highest penalty from the greatest of crimes, and to restrain the criminal absolutely, *i. e.*, to remove him, once for all, beyond the possibility of repeating his offense. While, then, the sentiments of humanity and charity undoubtedly require that the infliction of *capital punishment* should be reduced to a *minimum*, the same sentiments of humanity and charity, with a due regard to the demands of justice and the welfare of society, require that it should be retained at the *apex* of any system of penal jurisprudence. But it is no part of our present purpose to discuss the right or the expediency of capital punishment. We only desire to disavow any advocacy of its abolition, and to protest that a consistent regard to the claims of humanity and charity, which we *do* advocate, does not require its abolition, but just the contrary. The fact that the reformation of the offender ceases to be an object of this extreme punishment, does not at all hinder that it should be a proper and most important end to be sought in all those cases and modes of punishment in which there are room and opportunity for seeking it. A due regard for the public good will itself make the distinction in these cases. The public good may not require the reformation of the criminal who is once for all put out of the world, and yet it may imperatively require that reformation in the case of those who, after their term of punishment is fulfilled, are to be restored to the bosom of society.

Take another example on the other side. Laws enforcing by penalties the duties of inward and private morality, or the profession and practice of true religion, are not to be enacted by the state, because, on the whole, they would subvert instead of promoting the highest good; and that, although the prevalence of the strictest personal morality and conscientiousness, and the profession and practice of the true religion, must be in the highest degree beneficial to the whole community, and the prevalence of their opposites the greatest of public calamities. So, too, with *sumptuary laws;* although the prevalence of temperance, frugality, and economy cannot fail to be most desirable and salutary, yet the state cannot undertake to enforce them by legal penalties without occasioning more harm than good. Thus the ends of the public good on one hand, and the ends of humanity, charity, morality, and justice on the other, are co-ordinate motives for the statesman, and neither can be safely followed to the entire disregard of the others. Such a following of the public good would often fail to reach it; and in legislation such a pursuit of the ends of humanity or morality would often be the surest way of missing them. By the wise statesman the two must be combined in one view.

As the board are about to suggest certain changes and reforms in the prison economy of the Commonwealth, they have ventured upon these preliminary statements in order to "define their position," to place in front the principles upon which they proceed, and to forestall the too-prevalent objection that all such schemes of prison reform are the mere dreams of a very respectable but unstatesmanlike philanthropy, of an amiable but ignorant and unpractical sentimentalism; having no basis in the public weal, and undeserving the attention of enlightened legislators. These preliminary statements have been entered upon, *not to instruct the legislature, but to explain ourselves.* We shall ask for no reform which cannot be shown to be demanded by the public good, taken in any large and statesmanlike sense; but we shall not hesitate to urge in support of reforms so demanded all the motives of justice and morality, of humanity and civilization.

We may as well make up our minds that great reforms will be made in this department of our legislation and public policy. The movements in this direction, which have been going on in the civilized world during the last twenty years or more, and which have been annually increasing in vigor and volume, show beyond mistake that such must eventually be the result. In former times Pennsylvania took the lead in prison reforms and improvements; and much real progress was made. Since then she has been too much disposed to rest upon her early laurels, while vastly more yet remains to be done. The question is, will she, in the further progress of this great work, follow up in the rear or take the lead? Will she allow Russia and Turkey to get the start of her, or will she again give her lessons of example to all western as well as eastern Europe?

1. THE REFORMATORY USE OF IMPRISONMENT.

That the protection of society or the prevention of crime, in a large sense, is the whole object of imprisonment, is freely admitted. That it should aim at the exemplary punishment of crime, and the restraint of the criminal as well as his reformation, though by some extreme philanthropists it may be denied, yet is here assumed to be so generally admitted that it is not felt necessary to attempt any formal argument in its proof. It is deemed more to the purpose, in the present state of jurisprudence and of prison economy, as well as of public opinion, to emphasize the other side of the positive statement, and to claim for the *reformation of the criminal* its rightful, but much forgotten and neglected, and often contested, place among the proper purposes of penal restraint. It is claimed on four distinct grounds:—First,

Of Humanity.—Even the criminal, as already said, has not ceased to be a man; and those must be extreme cases in which we have a right to assume that any man is so degenerate and utterly corrupt that no efforts for his amendment can be of any avail. Even in the worst and most abandoned of men, there almost always remain some relics, some feeble echoes, at least, of right feeling; some susceptibility to good on one side or another; some avenue to some buried and dormant sparks of ingenuous and manly emotion; of right and virtuous affection. Shall all these be neglected? and shall the poor wretch, by the solemn legal action and systematic arrangements of a civilized and Christian community, be heartlessly cast out, consigned, unaided and unfriended, like a wild beast, to the unalleviated and unsoftened influence of mere penal infliction—infliction which, as he is not a beast but a man, with human sensibilities and resentments, must ordinarily tend to harden him more and more in the recklessness and desperation of inveterate crime? Every generous and honorable and kindly feeling of human nature cries out against it; against mere vindictive punishment; against cool and unmitigated cruelty; against the infliction of one particle of pain beyond what is necessary for the protection and well-being of society; and demands, that if the reformation and restoration of the offender be by any reasonable methods possible, such methods should be sought out and applied.

It is claimed, secondly, on the ground of

Simple Right and Justice.—Society, in electing the penalty of a term of imprisonment instead of capital punishment, has acknowledged that, in her judgment, the offender is not a person of such a desperate character that her safety requires him to be summarily and once for all put out of the way; she has acknowledged that he may not be incorrigible. As imprisonment, personal restraint, and detention are a necessary practical condition of any reformatory measures or discipline, so such measures are a necessary logical result or concomitant of imprisonment. In depriving the man of his own free choice and self-guidance, and taking his control into her own hands, society has assumed an unavoidable responsibility for his future moral course and character. He has become her ward, and she owes him a *duty* analagous to that which the parent owes to the children whom he retains under his government. While she chooses to maintain this relation to him, she has no right to neglect any means in her power for his reformation and moral improvement, and, in general, for his preparation to discharge his duties as an industrious and virtuous member of society, when he shall be restored to its bosom and placed again under his own control. This simple justice requires, and whatever it may cost to meet it, the state cannot rid itself of this responsibility. But, in fact, to meet it manfully will be found to save the public more than it costs.

It is claimed, then, in the third place, as demanded by *the public good,* and this in a threefold way:—

1. As a most effective example deterrent to vice and encouraging to virtue. The spectacle of penal inflictions, severe and persistent, yet adapted to and resulting in the reformation of the criminal, must have an unspeakably greater power to deter men from crime than the mere infliction of mere punishment, though tenfold more rigorous, and however sanguinary and cruel. It shows, clear as the sun, the unutterable

folly of crime; it cows down all its defiant bravado, and quells all its bitter hatred against society; it turns, by a flank movement, the last intrenchments of its dogged spirit of martyrdom and its pride of heroic endurance. Every reformed criminal, returned to the bosom of society, while he is thus a living and constant lesson of rebuke, of repression, and of humiliation to the criminally disposed, must be also a monument of encouragement and strength to the feeble endeavors of those who, in the midst of temptation, and after many failures, would gladly persevere in the effort to raise themselves from the moral degradation into which they have fallen.

2. Every criminal reformed is a positive diminution of the number of criminals to infest society; and this, though such cases should be but few, is no insignificant gain, when compared with the process of returning the criminal, who has served out his imprisonment, hardened in crime, hardened by the very punishment he has sullenly endured, and rankling with revengeful malignity against that society which inflicted the punishment; returning him to reinforce and marshal the ever-swelling army of malefactors who are pressing on in his footsteps.

3. Such reformations, to the full extent to which they take place, tend powerfully to prevent the education of others in crime. That education comes very largely from the old adepts, both in prison,—where they are promiscuously mixed up with the other prisoners, from the youthful novice to the hoary offender, as they natur-

ally will be when no account is made of the reformation of convicts,—and out of prison, after they have been discharged unreformed from their term of punishment. Prisoners discharged without reformation have taken their doctor's degree as teachers of crime.

It is claimed, in the fourth place, as necessary to *consistency in our legislation*.

The principle of making the reformation of the convict one of the chief objects of his imprisonment, has been distinctly engrafted upon the legislation of this Commonwealth. In connection with county jails it is provided by the act of 14th April, 1835, that the matron should give the (female) convicts under her charge "such instructions as may tend to their reformation, and to render them useful members of society." And, in connection with the State penitentiaries, it is provided, by the act of 23d April, 1829, that "it shall be the duty of the instructor to attend to the moral and religious instruction of the convicts in such manner as to make their confinement as far as possible the means of their reformation, so that when restored to their liberty they may prove honest, industrious, and useful members of society." In establishing her reformatories for juvenile offenders, the State has also most clearly recognized reformation from crime as a proper object of public legislation. In thus selecting juvenile offenders she has undoubtedly selected both the easiest and the most important portion of the work. But reformation, if possible, is also desirable in the case of adults; and, if not possible, at what precise age did the possibility cease? In the very name of "penitentiary," which the State has given to some of her prisons, she presupposes that it does not cease with adult years.

The reformation of the criminal, therefore, is solemnly acknowledged by the State to be an important end of his penal restraint, and at the same time it is acknowledged that restraint will not of itself effect the purpose, but that some other special provision is required for its accomplishment. Now, these points being conceded, consistency plainly demands that the law should not stop until it has found some effectual provision for so important an end, if any such provision is possible consistently with the other ends of imprisonment and the requirements of the public good.

At all events, when the reformation of the criminal is urged as one of the ends of penal legislation, let it be remembered that the existing statute endorses the demand; and when such arrangements of prison discipline and management are proposed as shall most effectually accomplish this end, the proposer is not to be bluffed off with any polite allusions to sentimental philanthropy, or the easy utterance of any mere phrases of disparagement. It is to be seriously and candidly inquired and earnestly considered whether such proposed plans are feasible, and are consistent with the other ends of public justice and with the public good. If so, they should be forthwith adopted.

II. LABOR OF CONVICTS.

We here take for granted that the reformation of the convict is one of the objects of his incarceration; while fully admitting that punishment is another—for incarceration *is* punishment. It is accordingly assumed that, so far as possible, such means are to be joined with the punishment as will render that punishment itself reformatory, which alone would not be so. Labor is believed to be such a means; and it is now proposed to set forth, in some degree at least, *how* this means may be made most effectual to that end.

1. There are, first, certain important questions as to the proper character and conditions of convict labor; among them are the following:—

(*a.*) The labor itself may be considered a part of the punishment; but should it be purely punitive, or also productive?

It is believed that labor of a merely punitive character can have no reformatory and little deterring effect. It sours, irritates, hardens. It seems to be now generally conceded that the tread-mill, as a form of labor or a substitute for it, is productive of little if any good, but rather of much harm; and it is to the credit of French prison discipline that, though French history has had its Bastile, the French language has no term whereby to translate the name of this engine of punishment. In its expensive uselessness, it is a merely vindictive and degrading infliction. It is, moreover, unjust and unequal, imposing what may be an easy exertion for one and a most exhausting, if not dangerous, exertion for another. And finally, the tread-mill system taken instead of productive employment is a manifest and wanton waste of what might just as well be utilized as thrown away. If employed at all in prisons, it should not be as a constant thing, or as a general substitute for proper work, but it should be reserved for some special and extraordinary occasions, as a punishment for gross violations of order, or for the health of the prisoner who positively declines to work. If labor is to be made even a wholesome punishment, still more if it is to be made a means of reformation, *it must be productive.* However grievous, it must be attended with the apprehension that it has some other object than merely to punish, and with the encouragement that it accomplishes something. It must have so much the character of ordinary labor as to tend to form habits of mind and body which will be of service to the prisoner after his release.

(*b.*) Shall the labor be performed in cells or in common workshops, in individual separation or in groups?

This might bring up the whole vexed question between the solitary and the congregate systems of penitentiary discipline, which it is not proposed now to discuss; nor is it necessary, for reformatory labor can be appropriately combined with both. But, as will be seen in the sequel, there are weighty reasons for the conclusion that it cannot *completely* answer its best purposes if confined exclusively and throughout the whole period of discipline to either.

To this subject we have already referred in our former reports. In that of 1870 we alluded to "a change in the Pennsylvania system which has recently taken place in one of the penitentiaries of the State, under the sanction of law. By recent legislation, namely, under date 8th April, 1869, the congregate system is allowed in the Western Penitentiary for the several purposes of labor, learning, and religious instruction. The government and officers are unanimous in the approval of the system thus introduced." In regard to this partial introduction of the congregate system, we added:—"There are embarrassments which oppress every unprejudiced mind in its reflections upon this grave subject. It cannot fail to discover, with other advantages, vigorous and remunerative labor, which is always morally healthful, accomplished on the one side, and a discipline exerted under circumstances accordant with man's nature and condition; and on the other side, it sees as plainly, baleful exposures of convicts to mutual acquaintanceship and probably contamination—the possibly innocent, the certainly unhardened, with the obdurate and insensate criminal; and the want, also, of that opportunity of intro-reflection which, if not enforced, may never come, and which is a necessary foundation for a trustworthy reform."

In the report of last year, having pointed out the extreme peril of "relieving a man from solitude after a few months of effort for his reformation, by transferring him from an apartment in which he had no society, except when visited by the benevolent for his good, to the common receptacles for men convicted of crime," we added:—"Prevention of intercourse between convicted criminals, from first to last, we esteem indispensable to successful effort for their reform. Let them have stated and, so far as may be, diversified occupation; let them have carefully selected books for entertainment; let them receive visits from judicious friends and counselors seeking their good; but keep them away, while in the custody of the State, from intercourse with each other."

We beg now to observe that, in that connection, we could not be supposed to mean that no intercourse whatever between any two convicts, however carefully selected at any period in their course of reformation or for any purpose or under any circumstances whatever, would be safe or should be allowed; but that they should be kept away from that sort of general or indiscriminate intercourse which prevails ordinarily under the congregate system; to which system, conducted in any such way as we have had the opportunity of observing, we remain, as in the past, thoroughly opposed. Besides which, as we have said in another place, we must "take things as they are," and as they have been qualified and determined by public sentiment and legislation founded thereon, if our views are to be made practically suggestive.

Thus, after the earnest advocacy of the strictly "separate" system of imprisonment by some of the best and most philanthropic minds of the State, often against strenuous opposition; and after an example of its practical application for nearly half a century in what may be called model establishments, designed in all their appliances for the perfect carrying out of the system, what do we find? Not one prison or penitentiary in the State in which it is conducted in its entirety. We find the authorities of one penitentiary repudiating it and demanding its overthrow there, and the legislature acquiescing in their demand; while, at the same time, it denies to the other the full realization of the opposite views—held with equal tenacity by high, even exceptional ability, influence, and experience—by keeping the penitentiary accommodations so restricted as effectually to prevent, in many cases, the separate confinement of its prisoners.

And the "separate system" is equally neglected in the county establishments. In these, with the exception of an inconsiderable number, where it partially obtains, there is no attempt to follow the system in any one respect. Premising this we proceed:—

Strictly solitary confinement for a long period, *without labor*, is a punishment altogether too cruel to be imposed; it is more than human nature can bear; it must undermine and break down the health both of body and mind; it is killing by inches, inflicting capital punishment by slow degrees; or if the convict survives, and is at length released, he is let out upon society vastly more unfit and more unlikely to discharge his duties then, and earn an honest livelihood, than he was before his incarceration. And even if solitary labor be added to such confinement, continued through the entire period of penitentiary discipline, while all must admit that much of the cruelty, and many of the physical and moral evils may be avoided, it may be seriously questioned whether the prospect, upon the convict's release, will be most favorable to the discharge of these duties. It is at least fair to inquire:—Is he likely to continue such labor when restored to liberty and to the influence of free society? What training has it furnished him for meeting the accumulated trials and difficulties and temptations that surround and oppress him the moment he is thrown again upon society and his own resources? His labor has not been pursued under the ordinary circumstances, motives, and influences. His discipline may have made him an excellently well-behaved convict, but has it prepared him to meet the perils, and perform the duties, of a free and industrious member of society?

On the other hand, if the congregate system of labor is applied indiscriminately, and throughout the whole period of imprisonment, to all grades and classes of convicts alike, mixing all up together in working gangs,—young and old, novices and adepts in crime; those committed for greater and those for lesser offenses, for longer and for shorter periods; those convicted for the second or the third time, and those under punishment for their first offense; the old long-wonted inmates of the prison and the new-comers,—it will scarcely be possible, by any methods or contrivances for enforcing silence and shutting off communication, to prevent such companies from becoming schools of increasing corruption and wickedness, instead of amendment and reformation. The only preventive must be a free and familiar use of the *lash;* a mode of punishment so inhuman and degrading that it is scarcely allowed by enlightened and civilized jurisprudence to be inflicted for any crime, even upon the sentence of any magistrate or judge, high or low; a punishment, therefore, one would suppose still less to be left to the daily discretion of mere prison-keepers or underling overseers. And if all objections were removed, labor under such circumstances is, as we shall endeavor further on to show more fully, little fitted to train men to earn their subsequent livelihood in habits of free and virtuous industry.

In order to approximate the desired reformatory result, would it not be better that the two systems—the separate and the congregate—should be combined, each at its proper season, in its proper degree, and with a due regard to the natural disposition and habits, the temper and character, of the different prisoners? It is believed they may be so combined most effectually and advantageously. Indeed, the latter system, under any tolerable existing arrangement, is so far combined with the former as to provide for the distribution of the prisoners into separate cells by night. How the two systems may be best combined in connection with the different periods of the term of imprisonment and the different classes and characters of the prisoners, it is proposed to develop under another head.

The importance of labor as an element of corrective discipline, as well as the importance of combining the two systems of labor, is thus set forth by one of the earliest and most earnest advocates of the separate system, Mr. Edward Livingston:—

"Of all the crimes in the catalogue of human depravity, four-fifths are, in different forms, invasions of private property; and the motive for committing them is the desire of obtaining, without labor, the enjoyments which property brings. The natural corrective is to deprive the offender of the gratifications he expects, and to convince him that they can be acquired by the exertion of industry. The remaining proportion of offenses are such as arise from the indulgence of the bad passions, and for those also solitude and employment are the best correctives. But whatever corrects the desire or the passion that prompts the offense, acts in the double capacity, first of punishment, and, afterwards, when it is effected, of reformation. * * * The prisoner who labors lessens the expense of his support; he who works skillfully and diligently may more than repay it. The advantage of this beneficial result must be felt by the prisoner as well as by the state; if the proceeds of his work should not be sufficient to cover his expenses, it yet produces for him a better diet; and if preserved in and accompanied with good conduct, for certain probationary periods of six and twelve months, during which he is permitted, in the day, to leave his cell and pursue his solitary employment in the court, he is indulged with the *privilege of working and receiving instruction in a small class*, not exceeding ten."*

(*c*.) Another question is, should convict labor be purposely made servile and degrading, or as cheerful and elevating as possible?

To answer this question, we have only to propose and answer to ourselves another question: is it our purpose, by the temporary incarceration of criminals to make them worse, and then turn them out upon society again; or to make them better fitted and better disposed, upon their return, to discharge the duties of virtuous and industrious citizens? Our means must be adapted to the end we have in view; and we are *responsible* for the end to which our means *are* adapted. But what right have we forcibly to seize upon a bad man and make him worse? What right have we to

* Livingston's Criminal Code, pages 309 and 337.

deprive an erring fellow-mortal of his own free choice, unless we, at the same time, use all the means in our power so to control and guide him as to reform his errors and turn him into the paths of virtue and rectitude? The man is dejected, desponding, distrustful of his power of self-control or of virtuous living; shall we discourage him still more? Shall we drive him to desperation? He is degraded, degraded in fact, degraded in his own eyes; shall we degrade him still more? He is reckless and malicious; shall we sink him to lower depths of recklessness, and add a new fund of venom to his malice? If not, if we propose to raise and reform him, shall we make the very labor on which we rely for that end a badge of degradation? Let it be understood, once for all, that no degrading inflictions whatever can restore a spirit of manliness to the corrupt and depraved. Labor, imposed under such a category, is not likely to be continued after release, nor can it be regarded by the released convict with complacency or respect. And yet that complacency in labor, that respect for labor, are precisely what it was above all things necessary to associate with it in the convict's mind; so that, after release, he might be weaned from his evil courses and disposed to resort to the proper methods of obtaining an honest livelihood. To this end his labor, while in detention, should be made, as far as possible, cheerful and attractive, a constant means of encouragement and elevation. That this need not be inconsistent with his severe and terrible punishment, will, in the sequel, be made sufficiently clear.

(*d.*) Should convict labor be enforced or voluntary? This question covers the principle which controls the case; it embraces and sums up most of the other inquiries.

The effort to get the benefits without bearing the burdens of labor is the occasion of most of the offenses committed against society. To correct this disposition is the grand business of penitentiary discipline. Enforced labor may do something towards this end by forming certain physical habits, and imparting or rather impressing a certain degree of training to orderly routine and manual dexterity; but the motives and associations under which this is done are such that there must be the greatest danger that the best-behaved and most industrious and skillful convict will lose his good habits, and disuse or misuse his skill, as soon as he is committed again to his own control.

We venture to retrace here somewhat at large Mr. Livingston's plan of voluntary convict labor.

"No succession of involuntary acts to which adults may be coerced is likely to produce permanent habits of reformation; they must be the effect of the will, operated upon by the judgment, producing a conviction that such acts are beneficial; and experience must enforce this conviction by giving the actual enjoyment of some, and the certain hope of other, benefits that are the result of these acts. With evil habits it is different; for the most part they are acquired by the repetition of acts procuring sensual enjoyment; and the judgment has so little agency in procuring them, that it must be silenced or perverted before the acts of indulgence are done or repeated. It is for this reason that the work of reformation is more difficult than that of perversion; the one requires intellectual power sufficient to prefer a distant and moral good to a present and physical enjoyment; the other coincides with the natural propensity for present enjoyment, reckless of what an uncertain futurity may produce. And for this reason, also, it is that the work of reformation is slower in its operation than that of corruption. * * * The spring which sets in motion my whole machinery for producing reform is this:—That all the acts which, by their succession, are to produce habits of good, are to be performed voluntarily, and are offered as alleviations of the severity of the sentence; the will must act, or the repetition will produce no effect. But, to operate on the inclination, sufficient inducements must be held out to overcome the natural repugnance to labor. * * * Privation of employment is denounced as a part of the punishment; and this circumstance alone would, with most men, cause it to be considered as an evil, and the experience of its effects will soon cause it to be felt as such; of course it will be connected with the idea of suffering; and occupation being denied, will, from the propensity to wish for that from which we are expressly debarred, be estimated as a good, and desired with an intensity proportioned to the strictures and length of the privation. To strengthen this natural desire other inducements are offered. * * * If the prisoner acquires such proficiency in the business as to make the proceeds of his industry exceed the expense of his support, he is allowed the immediate enjoyment of a part, to be laid out in books or such other articles as he may desire. Those of food or drink are excepted, in order to avoid irregularities that otherwise would be unavoidable; and the residue of the surplus is an accumulating fund to be paid to him on his discharge. To give the greater effect to these inducements, they are not offered to the convict on his commitment to the prison; first, he must know and feel the unmitigated punishment; his own reflections must be his only companions for a preliminary period, during which he is closely confined to his cell; he must live on the coarse diet allowed to the unemployed prisoner; he must suffer the tedium arising from want of society and occupation, and when he begins to feel that labor would be an indulgence, it is offered to him as such; it is not threatened to him as an evil, nor urged upon his acceptance as an advantage to any but to himself; and when he is employed, no stripes, no punishment whatever are inflicted for want of diligence; if not properly used the indulgence is withdrawn, and he returns to his solitude and other privations, not to punish him for not laboring, but merely because his comduct shows that he prefers that state to the enjoyment with which employment must always be associated in his mind, in order to produce reformation. If it has been shown that involuntary acts will not produce a lasting habit, then, if there be any such as will not accept these alleviations of their imprisonment upon them the imprisonment must operate solely as a punishment. But experience shows that these exceptions will, if any, be very few, for employment, even under the lash, is in most cases preferred to solitude." (Pages 336, 337.)

To this we might propose to add, as will be seen, a further but cautious introduction of social labor (still voluntary), with increasing degrees of liberty, as the process of reformation goes on, until the reformed convict passes into society in full freedom, by an easy step, with habits ready formed for his new condition, prepared to act upon the same motives after his release as before, and without any great shock either to society or to himself.

It may be objected that, in the plan above described, the labor is, after all, enforced; that the remanding to the solitary cell, without occupation, is coercion as much as the lash. We answer, first, that it involves no degradation; secondly, it is self-inflicted—a deliberately chosen alternative; thirdly, in its nature it leads not to passion but to consideration; fourthly, when the labor comes it comes not as a punishment, but as an alleviation of punishment; and, fifthly, the labor, if enforced, is enforced by the same sort of motives by which it is enforced in ordinary life, *i. e.*, as a means of obtaining certain objects of desire, of comfort, and gratification.

It may be objected that, in its ultimate working, this plan leaves punishment out of account altogether, and aims exclusively at reformation. We answer, no; the proper punishment yet remains in full force—imprisonment, solitude, want of occupation either for the mind or body, coarse aliments, hard lodging, clothing of the roughest kind. These are the evils of which punishments are composed; their duration, their intensity, their cumulation, are the means of adapting them to different offenses, and are to be duly prescribed in each sentence; their alleviation in different degrees and after the prescribed interval, by permitted and encouraged labor, is the means of producing reform.

It may be objected that thus the deterring power of punishment is destroyed. Again we answer, no; the punishment, with all its terror, still remains, in such degree and for such period as the law judges necessary; but the remedial system is added,—a system which, itself also, teaches all criminals and criminally-disposed persons that the only way to escape the punishment is to resort to that very labor, the hope of avoiding which is their most ordinary temptation to crime.

(*e.*) Is the reformatory labor to be performed under the immediate oversight and direction of the prison authorities, or by the intervention and under the control of contractors?

The answer is, emphatically, the former and not the latter. Nothing has led to greater deterioration of prison discipline, corruption of the prison-keepers, and demoralization of the prisoners than this system of contract labor, wherever it has been adopted. It completely annuls the idea of reformation as an object of prison labor, and makes it merely a means of petty profit or pecuniary relief to the state (in which it sometimes signally fails), and of untold and irresponsible oppressions and cruelties on the part of the interested and unfeeling overseers and drivers. The labor should be performed under the eye and control of responsible parties, who have no selfish ends to accomplish by it, and who will take a humane and personal interest in the welfare and amendment of the convicts. Not the present profit of the labor, but its bearing upon the future good of the laborer is the absorbing concern. The health, strength, and previous habits of prisoners are to be considered; not the amount of product, but faithfulness and diligence are to be rewarded.

(*f.*) And here the general question may be raised, whether the products of convict labor should inure exclusively to the benefit of the state, or also to the present and future benefit of the convicts.

In answer, we have no hesitation in saying that if it is to accomplish its reformatory function to any considerable degree, its profits must be permitted to inure in part and sensibly to the benefit of the convict. This is an essential point. The state should undoubtedly have the first and largest portion of the proceeds, not from any petty economical motive, but because it is highly important for the convict to learn and feel that he owes a debt for his past iniquity and for his present support, which he is bound in reason and honesty to pay. The next largest portion should be appropriated, if needed, towards the relief or support of his dependent family during his detention, that he may learn the blessing which labor confers of making others happy whom we desire to benefit. The next part, to be determined according to fixed rules, in a certain proportion to industry and good conduct, should be set aside to accumulate, if not forfeited in whole or in part by misconduct, as a fund to be used and enjoyed after his liberation; that he may learn the next lesson of honest and thrifty labor—to deny himself for the present in order to provide for the future. And, finally, a certain small surplus, to be determined in like manner, should be placed at his immediate control, as a means of purchasing such present alleviations and comforts as are consistent with his state of detention and punishment; that he may learn the final lesson of labor that all the alleviations and comforts of a hard life are the proper rewards of a patient and persistent toil. Thus his convict labor will powerfully tend to his practical and permanent reformation.

2. It may be proper, in the second place, to present in one view the benefits of such reformatory convict labor.

(*a.*) It will promote the health and well-being of the prisoners, both in mind and body. Without some labor bodily health—and without such labor, mental health—must terribly suffer; a kind and degree of suffering which we have no right to inflict.

(*b.*) It will promote their moral improvement, gradually developing the power of self-control, and forming habits of provident and voluntary effort in industry and toil. It will prepare them to become virtuous and useful members of society.

(*c.*) It will facilitate the preservation of good order and discipline in the prison. The wise management of the reserve fund and of the present reward for diligence and good conduct will enable the prison-keepers to dispense, in almost all cases, with all other means of enforcing in the prison the rules of good government.

Thus prison life will be divested of most of those horrible abominations which so often render it a means of much greater evil than good.

(*d.*) It will give the convicts the essential preparation for gaining a livelihood after their release; first, by forming habits of voluntary industry; secondly, by securing a little fund to aid them during the critical period of transition from prison to social life; and, thirdly, by instilling a moral character which will enable them to resist the temptations of their old associates and commend themselves to the confidence of the community.

(*e.*) It will promote the good of the state; first, in presenting the most efficacious example to deter or wean others from crime; secondly, in diminishing the expense of maintaining prisons; thirdly, in preventing the relapse of the criminal; and, fourthly, in adding to the resources of the state the industry, and to its well-being the virtue, of another citizen.

3. It is sometimes objected to productive convict labor that it *interferes* with the rights and interests of labor in general.

One hardly knows where to begin or end in showing the absurdity of such an objection. It belongs to the category of the exploded outcries against the introduction of labor-saving machinery, or of any improvements in the processes of production, whereby it was said the demand for laborers would be diminished and their wages reduced; whereas it has turned out that just the contrary has been, in the long run, the uniform and natural result.

We have seen that, whatever may be the effect upon the wages of labor, or upon the price of its products, we have *no right*, instead of hanging or shooting our fellow-men, to inflict upon them the outrageous punishment of incarcerating them for years in solitary cells without any occupation, or, still worse, of shutting them up in mixed congregate masses of all sorts of criminals and leaving them in sheer idleness to make one another as thoroughly corrupt and diabolical as human nature is capable of becoming; and, if we have the right, it would be the most egregious political folly to do it. Moreover, we have seen that labor, to serve any good purpose, must be productive. We meet the objector, then, at this point; and we say that, according to him, when this labor has resulted in creating a certain amount of valuable products, it would be more for the interest of society—if the interests of labor and society are identical—that all those products should forthwith be committed to the flames or cast into the sea, than that they should be preserved and applied to their appropriate uses! If it is rejoined that the competition of such labor is unfair because, unlike the ordinary laborer, the convict is supported independently of his work; we have only to say, let the products of prison labor be disposed of at public auction or at market rates, and no one has a right to complain of the competition for its tendency to reduce prices. Every addition to the supply might be complained of for the same reason. The state, not the convict, is the owner of the articles; and the state is as directly interested in getting the highest price for these articles, that thus she may meet the expense of maintaining the convict, as any laborer is in getting the highest price for his products to meet his own expenses.

The plain state of the case is this: all in the community must be supported; the fewer idlers, therefore, to be supported by the rest, the better for the rest; and if this alleged reduction of price in consequence of this competition of convict labor exists, and *is* a tax, it is the *smallest tax possible*, if convicts are to be supported at all, upon the labor of the community—and upon that labor all taxes must ultimately fall.

4. The laws of Pennsylvania actually require provision to be made for the labor of all convicts, whether in the State penitentiaries or in the county prisons.

For the penitentiaries, it is required, by the act of 31st March, 1860, that "whenever any person shall be sentenced to imprisonment at labor, by separate or solitary confinement, for any period not less than one year, the imprisonment and labor shall be had and performed in the State penitentiary for the proper district: *Provided*, That nothing in this section contained shall prevent such person from being sentenced to imprisonment and labor, by separate or solitary confinement, in the county prisons now or hereafter authorized by law to receive convicts of a like description." And, by the act of 23d April, 1829, it is required of the inspectors that "they shall direct the manner in which raw materials, to be manufactured by the convicts in said prisons, and the provisions and other supplies for the prisons shall be purchased, and also the sale of all articles manufactured in said prisons."

For the county jails, it is declared, by the act of 5th April, 1790, that "the malefactors sentenced to hard labor as aforesaid, in the several counties of the State, other than the county of Philadelphia, shall be employed in the several jails and workhouses in the respective counties, in such hard and servile labor, and fed and clothed in such manner as is hereinbefore directed; * * * and the duty of the said keepers shall be to superintecd and direct their labors; * * * and they shall have authority to confine, in close durance, apart from all society, all those who shall refuse to labor, or be idle," &c.

"The keepers of the jails and workhouses or houses of correction, shall, once in every three months, or oftener, if required, furnish the commissioners of their respective counties with a complete calendar or list of all persons committed to their respective custody, under sentence of such servitude, &c.; * * * and the said commissioners shall, at the charge of the proper county, provide * * * such articles and materials of labor and manufacture as shall be most suitable for the employment of all those who are capable of labor or manufacture, and deliver the same to the said jailor or workhouse-keeper, taking a receipt therefor; and the jailor or workhouse-keeper shall render an account quarterly, or oftener, if required, to the commissioners, of the work done by the said malefactors, and dispose of the same in such manner as the commissioners shall direct."

"If any jailor shall neglect or refuse to give notice

or furnish a complete calendar, &c., * * * he shall forfeit and pay, for every such neglect or refusal, the sum of one hundred dollars; and if the said commissioners of any county, after the receipt of such notice or calendar, shall neglect or refuse to procure sufficient articles and materials of labor and manufacture, * * * such commissioners, or any of them, so neglecting or refusing, shall forfeit and pay the sum of one hundred dollars for every such neglect or refusal."

In relation to the Philadelphia County Prison, similar provisions are made by special statutes.

Now we must confess that the language of the statutes seems rather harsh; yet we have a right to presume that the terms "hard" and "servile" labor mean no more than *manual* labor carried to the extent of bodily *fatigue*. We admit, also, that it is *enforced* labor for which provision is made by the law; but even enforced labor, whether with solitary or social confinement, is unspeakably better than sheer idleness, both for body and mind, for the morals and the future prospects of the convicts. But when the prisons are so wretchedly constructed or mismanaged or overcrowded, that the system of separate confinement is practically abandoned, and the convicts are mixed promiscuously together, or thrown into cells by pairs or in companies of three, four, or half a dozen, and these *left without employment*, we have as bad a system as could well be conceived. If the worst enemy of mankind were to invent a school for the propagation of vice and crime, he could invent no better. And, alas, notwithstanding the stringent provisions of the statute, this is, to an alarming extent, the condition of the county jails of this Commonwealth. The labor designed by the statute is not provided for, is not required, is not performed. *The convicts are defrauded of the employment to which they have a statutory right.* They suffer the consequences, and the State must suffer them too.

The State provides for labor—enforced labor, as we have said; but this is not all. The State provides also for *reformatory, voluntary labor,* both in the jails and in the penitentiaries. The State declares that "it shall be the duty of the inspectors, sheriffs, or other persons having charge of any penitentiary or jail within this Commonwealth, to transmit to the secretary thereof, on or before the first day of February, in each and every year, a full statement in detail of the condition of such penitentiary or jail, * * * and whether an opportunity is afforded to the prisoners *for doing overwork,* or *for receiving in any other manner the profits of their labor.*" Now this implies that the "hard and servile labor" enforced is not intended to be of so extremely exacting a kind as might be imagined; for it is not to be supposed that the State would mock her convicts. The enforced labor leaves time and strength for more work. Certain reasonable tasks being presumed, provision is made for "overwork," for voluntary work; and even for the convict receiving in other ways, as an encouragement, a portion of the profits of his labor. The statute recognizes the principle for which we contend, the beneficent end we would accomplish.

What is needed is: First, that *the statute should*

be enforced, so that its beneficent purpose may not be frustrated by neglect and abuse; and secondly, that further provision should be made for carrying out the principle recognized, by improving the structure and enlarging the capacity of the county prisons, and by *expanding the sphere of voluntary labor*, and systematizing its operation, so as to render it a means of general and permanent reformation. Such a means we firmly believe it might be made, and the State might rather gain than lose by the arrangement, even in the lowest pecuniary point of view. If voluntary were substituted systematically for enforced labor, fixed rations might be abolished altogether, and the prisoner required to earn his food, as well as his other privileges and comforts.

III. INSTRUCTION TO CONVICTS.

For the general protection of the community against crime, the importance of instruction in the case of the young and of juvenile offenders, is, at least in theory, commonly admitted. One after another, civilized states are waking up to the necessity of a more thorough application of the theory in practical legislation. Our own State has done much in this direction, although it must be admitted much more remains to be done.

The case of adults, and of adults already criminal, is more difficult and less hopeful. They have habits—it may be inveterate habits—of evil to be eradicated; they need habits of good to be initiated and confirmed; they are slow to apprehend and receive the lessons of instruction, and quick to lose what they have learned;

in them the valvular system has been inverted so that the avenues for the entrance of knowledge and of good influences are almost closed, while the passage for egress and leakage are open and free; they resist good impressions like a surface of flint, and discharge them like gum-elastic. All this is extremely discouraging; and when the mass of criminals is looked upon as they pass through the hands of the police and the dock of the criminal court into the prison cells, no wonder that most men shake their heads incredulously at the idea of their possible restoration to the paths of manly virtue and the companionship of good society.

There is much truth, though quite too little of hopefulness, in the nervous utterance of an Edinburgh police detective:—

"The simple truth is, that punishment hardens. It is forgotten by the hopeful people that it is clay they have to work upon, not gold; and, therefore, while they are passing the material through the fire, they are making bricks, not golden crowns of righteousness. Enough, too, has been made of the evident-enough fact, that they must continue their *old* courses, because there is no asylum for them. You may build as many asylums as you please, but the law of these strange nurslings of society's own maternity cannot be changed in this way. I say nothing of God's grace—that is above my comprehension; but, *except for that*, we need entertain no hope of the repentance and amendment of regular thieves and robbers. They have, perhaps, their use. They can be made examples of to others, but seldom or never good examples to themselves. That they will always exist is, I fear, fated;

but modern experience tells us that they may be diminished by simply drawing them, when very young, within the circle of civilization, in place of the old way of keeping them out of it."

We would not say a word to diminish the motives for carrying out this last suggestion, or to detract from its force. It presents the true, radical remedy for the appalling evil. But the exception which the policeman has made may have a wider and deeper significance than he seems to suppose. That "grace," however incomprehensible to him or to us, furnishes the true *point d'appui* for all our efforts—it is neither to be despised nor ignored. We have no right to despair of the salvability of the most depraved and degraded men. We must try all possible means—more than one plan, and that a hackneyed and fruitless plan—before we give up all hope. We must remember that, if these "strange nurselings of society's own maternity" are what and where they are, not so much by their own fault as because we have failed to draw them or to attempt "to draw them, when young, within the circle of civilization," the blame for their condition is after all more our own than theirs. They are to blame, no doubt; they have sinned; they must be punished; society must be protected. But, if society punishes them, she must punish them, not with pharisaic insolence, disgust, and contempt, but in a spirit of regretful kindness, and with an earnest and honest endeavor to make amends to them for her past neglect. She will best protect herself by reforming them. Hitherto punishment alone, or almost alone, has been tried—and "punishment hardens." Now let patient instruction and a scheme of reformatory influences be tried—systematically, consistently, and perseveringly tried—before we hopelessly abandon them to their "fate." The appeal to "fate" is quite out of place. Because disease and death are "fated" always to remain in the world, we do not abandon the use of remedies. Some sick men may be cured, though many die. Which may be saved we know not; but our general principle is, that while there is life there is hope. Hitherto prisoners, upon their discharge, have been compelled to "continue their *old* courses, because there was no asylum for them." Let us then provide an asylum for them, and try it. Hitherto, if we have had no experience of drawing back to the circle of civilization adult men who had wandered from it, it is because the effort has not been seriously and patiently made upon any principles or methods affording a reasonable promise of success. But we have *some* "experience" of men being thus drawn back; and it remains for us to study and apply the principles and the method on which it has been done.

The shrewd and striking statement above cited has been thus enlarged upon, because it has been felt that it contains, in a condensed and pointed form, an expression of the desponding judgment, which is quite too prevalent in the mass of the distant and unobserving community, sustained by the dicta of some of the keenest and coolest proximate observers. It certainly needs to be carefully reconsidered.

As ignorance and the want of a right education are the concomitant causes of most offenses against society, so instruction is a necessary condition of the efficiency of any scheme of reformation. Any scheme having reformation for its principal or even incidental object is imperfect, if not utterly useless, if it do not contain a regular and permanent provision for education in knowledge and virtue. The old rubbish must be removed and a new foundation of principles must be laid; a new set of motives must be brought into play; the intellect must be aroused, and such knowledge imparted as will qualify the recipient for intelligent and manly occupation. One great point to be reached in the process of reformation is to counteract in the will the natural preference of present enjoyment to future good. To produce this effect the mind must be improved by intellectual instruction; it must be taught that there are other pleasures besides those of sense. The conscience must be awakened and quickened, and religion must be brought to bear its part in the work of amelioration. Her lessons must furnish the basis for all the rest; but her lessons will be offered to the greatest advantage, when, combined with instruction in useful knowledge, they are offered as they should be; not as a part of the sentence of punishment, but as an alleviation of its rigor. Bodily exercise will profit little. It is the mind, the soul, of the convict that is to be gained.

"Let it not be said that the idea of moral reclamation is too refined to be adapted to depraved and degraded convicts. Convicts are men. The most depraved and degraded are men; their minds are moved by the same springs that give activity to those of others; they avoid pain with the same care and pursue pleasure with the same avidity that actuate their fellow-mortals. It is the false direction only of these great motives that produces the criminal actions which they prompt. To turn them into a course that will promote the true happiness of the individual, by making him cease to injure that of society, should be the great object of penal jurisprudence. The error, it appears, lies in considering them as beings of a nature so inferior as to be incapable of elevation, and so bad as to make any amelioration impossible; but crime is the effect principally of intemperance, idleness, ignorance, vicious associations, irreligion, and poverty,—not of any defective natural organization; and the laws which permit the unrestrained and continual exercise of these causes are themselves the sources of those excesses which legislators, to cover their own inattention or ignorance or indolence, impiously and falsely ascribe to the Supreme Being, as if he had created man incapable of receiving the impressions of good. Let us try the experiment before we pronounce that even the degraded convict cannot be reclaimed. It has never yet been tried."

When, in spite of ample knowledge and instruction before received, men have committed crimes and become hardened in wickedness,—and we must admit that this is sometimes the sad and chilling fact,—their case is indeed almost, but *not quite*, desperate. All possible remedies must be tried before we give them up for lost; and can we tell when the bounds of possibility have been reached? Line upon line, line upon line, precept upon precept, precept upon precept; the same old means must be renewed and repeated under a change of circumstances, which we may hope to be more favorable. And if, after years of earnest, kindly, faithful, and patient trial, all means fail to accomplish the hoped-for and hopeful amendment of the hardened convict, what then? Having served out a certain term of imprisonment in sullen obstinacy or with increasing irritation of malice against society—for if he has not been made better by his incarceration, he has probably been made worse,—shall he be forthwith discharged upon the community to renew his career of crime and iniquity? What folly or inconsistency could be greater? Let those, therefore, who so readily set convicts down as irreclaimable, remember that if such be the fact, then the only reasonable course to pursue with them is, either to put them to death and be rid of them, or to keep them under restraint as long as they live, and that without wasting the slightest thought or effort for their reformation. If we shrink from thus summarily deciding their destiny for time and eternity, either by taking their lives or by shutting them up in the dungeon of despair, what remains but that—leaving a ray of hope to penetrate to the mind of the convict, which we ourselves may fail to perceive—we should keep him in restraint, not until he shall die, but until he shall be reformed; and then faithfully use all possible means for his reformation as long as his incarceration lasts? At all events, such a convict should not be released until he is reformed. To suppose that his imprisonment, without such a result, is going to deter him or others from the commission of crime in the future, is one of the greatest and strangest of mistakes. For himself, such a released convict may have become more cunning, but will not be less persistent in his career of crime; and by his busy and crafty efforts, and bravado of heroism, he will do incomparably more to incite and encourage and train others in similar courses, than all that his temporary incarceration will do to deter them. Let us not be too ready to pronounce any criminals absolutely incorrigible, until we have made a fair trial for their reformation; or, if we really have such incorrigibles on hand, let us by no means turn them loose again to prey upon society.

The proper view of the case is that all convicts are the *wards of the state*, and when they are discharged are to be discharged better than they came, prepared to be good citizens. To this end they must be instructed, and the state having deprived them of their liberty, and assumed the control of them to herself, is morally bound to give them such instruction as is fitted and needed to attain that end. Such instruction

1. Will instil and enforce good principles, the greatest need of all.

2. Will awaken the hope of something better to be attained in the future.

3. Will give birth to a sentiment of self-respect,—a feeling in the convict's mind that, after all, there is something in him too precious to degrade and lose,—a feeling which is one of the mightiest levers of moral and social elevation.

4. Will furnish or increase the power of honest self-support after his release.

The subjects of such instruction will be found—

1. In some trade or handicraft, if needed.

2. In the elements of learning; in reading, writing, &c., if needed.

3. In further intellectual training and employment, as there may be a capacity and a readiness for it.

4. In habits of economy and of good morals.

5. In religion; which alone must furnish the fundamental and crowning motives for a reformed and useful life.

The method of instruction must be adapted to the peculiar case we have to deal with. It is not children but adults that are to be taught; it is with the perverted minds of criminals and not with the ingenuous minds of virtuous men that we have to do; our lessons are addressed to persons under restraint and not to free men. Under such circumstances the ordinary methods of school instruction must be expected to prove failures; prisoners will not perform literary tasks like children. Teaching by lectures, too, cannot be successfully used without many special cautions and modifications. We must be prepared in any event for unusual and extreme trials of patience. Our methods must be largely informal and different for different cases; there must be a vast deal of labor in detail, of individual, personal effort. And especially must the method of instruction vary according to the progressive stages of general improvement, and to the degree of confidence which may already be reposed in the different classes of prisoners. No particular rules of method, therefore, can be laid down. We can only say that, while ordinary scholastic methods are mostly out of place, a person of good sense and discretion, of kind feelings and patient temper, penetrated with a deep interest in the personal welfare of the convicts, and possessed with an earnest faith in his work, an assurance and a determination that it shall succeed, such a person will not be long in finding the true method, and cannot fail in the use of it. The *spirit* is everything, here, as an element of success.

We must again repeat that such kindly reformatory instruction is not at all incompatible with the idea of restraint or punishment. It leaves that punishment and restraint just as they were; it is itself based upon them as its own necessary condition; and one of its greatest lessons is to impress upon the mind and conscience of the convict the justice of his penalty. Nor is such instruction incompatible with the fullest deterring power of punishment; for, if unsuccessful, that punishment should still be continued; it is only when the instruction is successful and ends in the convict's reformation, that he is released. And surely nothing could more effectually deter the criminally disposed from the commission of crime than the practical assurance that in case of its commission, he will be placed under penal restraint from which there is no release until, by a course of instruction and discipline accompanying it, he is transformed into a virtuous man and fitted for the duties of free society.

The particular principle of instruction, as well as the

general principle of reformation—and the two run into each other as elements of prison discipline—has been already recognized by the statutes of this Commonwealth.

The statute in regard both to jails and penitentiaries requires an annual report to be rendered as to "what provision is made for the instruction of prisoners in such penitentiary or jail." The statute already cited, relating to the duties of the matron in the Philadelphia County Prison, recognizes and enjoins the duty of giving to prisoners "such instruction as may tend to their reformation, and to render them useful members of society." In the penitentiaries the statute establishes the distinct office of "religious instructor;" and we repeat its declaration, that "it shall be his duty to attend to the moral and religious instruction of the convicts, in such a manner as to make their confinement, as far as possible, a means of their reformation, so that when restored to their liberty, they may prove honest, industrious, and useful members of society."

With such principles avowed, what is needed is a faithful and thorough enforcement of the existing law, with such an enlargement of the statutory provisions, such an increase of appliances, such improvements of method, and such a consistent, systematic, and persevering working out of the whole scheme, as shall not leave it a mere barren excrescence, but shall secure to it that degree of success which we have reason to expect, and which the public good imperatively requires.

IV. KIND TREATMENT OF CONVICTS.

This is due from officials, and is commonly accorded, even to prisoners guilty of the most shocking crimes and condemned to suffer the severest punishment, and even in the very act of inflicting upon such persons the extreme penalty of the law. There are none of us who would not be scandalized at the conduct of any warden or jailor or sheriff or other officer, were he wantonly to indulge in any violent or taunting acts or words towards such a convict under such circumstances, or in any harsh or opprobrious treatment, one hair's breadth beyond the strict requirements of the law and the sentence of the court. This is sufficient to show that kind and humane treatment on the part of officials is perfectly compatible with the infliction of condign punishment.

It is a great mistake to suppose that when a man has been condemned to imprisonment for his crimes, his jailor is required to carry out the *analogy of the law*, by the most unfeeling, rigorous, and contumelious treatment; that he is conscientiously bound to shut up his bowels of compassion, if he has any; to abstain from any kindly personal interest in the convict, from all the amenities, courtesies, and charities of human intercourse, and, instead of recognizing in his ward a fellow-man, to hold him at a distance as a detestable outcast, a venomous viper, or a malignant fiend. The truth is, the law neither requires nor sanctions any such duties by way of analogy, any such discretionary and arbitrary inflictions, or methods of re-enforcing its own inflictions. It prescribes the precise punishment it would impose, and does not authorize any man to aggravate it by "one jot or tittle." The wardens and keepers of prisons are no more to add, directly or indirectly, properly or constructively, in kind or degree, to the punishment denounced by the law, than to release from it or relax its severity; and any unnecessary exercise of acerbity or rigor in the mode of administration, any unfeeling exhibition of scorn or contempt, is as much an addition to the punishment as an increase of its term would be.

Nor, on the other hand, are prison-keepers mere heartless or soulless machines, to execute with mechanical precision the punishment imposed; but they are moral agents, human beings, of like passions with those placed under their charge, and it is intended by law that they should, by all means, retain and not put off this character, for they are to represent, not so much the majesty or the severity, as the *spirit* of the state in punishing, and this is a spirit of kindness and good-will, not of vindictiveness or contempt or unfeeling cruelty. The punishment is necessary and must be inflicted—inflicted in its full measure and rigor, yet more in sorrow than in anger, and with a manifest desire, not to degrade and crush, but to encourage, elevate, and save.

The evil consequences of the harsh and unfeeling treatment of prisoners can scarcely be exaggerated. By it every movement towards good in them is repressed, and everything that is bad in them is excited and provoked to its fullest intensity. At best they are cowed down and lose the last remnants of manly aspiration which crime had left in their bosoms. Their worst passions are kept in exercise or only under sullen constraint, and it will be well if through constant irritation, and the pent-up accumulation of revengeful feelings, the discontent with society and with themselves, with which they entered the prison, is not changed to a fixed and inveterate malignity or desperation before their release; so that they will be discharged upon the community hardened, infuriated, and intensified in wicked purposes, to pursue with tenfold earnestness their career of vice and crime. Thus our prisons become gymnasia and seminaries for the most thorough discipline and development of criminal character. Thus "punishment hardens."

It may be said that the crushing and unmitigated punishment thus inflicted, with all these circumstances of contumely, opprobrium, of repellent scorn and unfeeling rigor, of cruel and insolent asperity, will be the more fearful example to deter others from the commission of crime. But is that punishment likely to deter others from crime, which does not deter him who suffers it? that punishment which rather confirms and hardens him in wickedness? If so, it must be because those others are more afraid of becoming confirmed and thorough-bred criminals than they are of the punishment; and thus our simplest plan would be to make every criminal that should fall into our hands as bad as possible in the shortest way, and then hold up the result as an example to frighten others from entering upon a course which should lead to such an end; somewhat as the ancient Spartans are said to have made their slaves drunk that the degrading spectacle might deter their children from intoxication. But then

who would be responsible for the education of those adepts and inveterates in crime? The state cannot afford to incur such a responsibility, especially since incurring it would, according to the known principles of human nature, infallibly fail of the ulterior end referred to. Such a punishment, with such a result, would deter nobody from crime. Both duty and interest equally and imperatively require that the state should, if possible, secure the reformation of the criminals whom it punishes.

But if reformation is to be made at all an end of prison discipline, *humane treatment*, a spirit of kindness and sympathy towards the convicts, the practical manifestation of a real personal interest in them and their improvement, is the essential condition, the very key to any effectual scheme for that purpose. Without it, all other appliances and contrivances will be in vain; success is impossible. Whatever other qualifications a prison-keeper may have, he is unfit for his place unless he possesses a genuine kindliness of nature, a spirit of compassionate sympathy, faith in humanity, a profound respect and regard for man as man, however fallen and degraded, an earnest, patient, indomitable purpose to reclaim and raise the wretched and guilty outcasts committed to his care. The precise point is to rekindle the dormant spark of humanity in the breast of the criminal, to develop a spirit of manliness and of human kindness; and to this end he must be treated with human kindness, and his manhood must be recognized.

The want of proper interest in the prisoners committed to their charge, if not so great a fault as positively cruel treatment, is a much more general defect, and one, therefore, which may practically result in a much greater amount of evil. Prisoners probably suffer more from mere neglect than from harshness or personal abuse. The sheriff or the jailor puts the convict into the cell or the common prison, locks the door, sees that he is kept safely and is properly fed; and, for the rest, leaves him "to make the best of it."

Prisoners need positive and kindly attention; and that positive efforts be made for their present well-being and their eventual reform. The consciousness of this on their part will furnish the strongest support in the struggle for their reformation. They are not likely to work it out by their own suggestions, or from the mere influence of detention.

Criminals are not ordinarily beyond the reach of good influences, yet criminals in crowds are annually discharged through mere flux of time, who are proclaimed altogether *incorrigible*. But it has been denied, on the ground of actual experiment, that there are any such whatever. The preliminary report of the United States Commissioner to the late International Prison Congress contains the following just and weighty suggestions:—

"There are many prisoners weak, and some deplorably wicked; but so long as Divine Providence is pleased to retain men in this world of probation at all, our right may well be disputed to regard or pronounce any to be irreclaimable. Our duty is first to try some new method; to try indeed any and all hopeful methods to reclaim them. But under present notions we reject all rational means of promoting their recovery; and, then failing (rather the means we *do* use failing), we quietly pronounce them irreclaimable; just as an engineer might do, who, when charged to reduce a strong fort, should fling away his trenching tools and pronounce it impregnable. In such a case, with whom really lies the blame, the prison officers or the prison inmates? And which are the irreclaimable, while such a system is persisted in? It was the opinion of an able writer, and equally able as well as successful prison manager, that prisoners could be saved to a man by the application of right principles and methods in prison administration. He feared neither bad habits nor any other difficulties. He believed that while life and sanity are spared, recovery is always possible, if properly sought. There is infinite elasticity in the human mind if its faculties are placed in healthful action, and neither diseased by maltreatment nor locked up in the torpor of a living grave."

We have the assurance of this same prison manager that his remarkable success was not the mere result of peculiar personal qualities:—"My task," says he, "was not really as difficult as it appeared. I was working with nature and not *against* her, as all other prison systems do. I was endeavoring to cherish, and yet direct and regulate, those cravings for amelioration of position, which almost all possess in some degree, and which are often strongest in those otherwise most abused. Under the guidance of right principles, they rose easily to order and exertion. I did not neglect the object of punishment in my various arrangements, but I sought it in the limits assigned alike by the letter and spirit of the law, not by excesses of authority beyond them. The law imposes imprisonment and hard labor, and these, in the fullest sense of the words, my men endured. Every one of them performed his government task," and, besides, his other voluntary labor as he could catch opportunity. "But he was saved, as far as I could save him, from unnecessary humiliation, and encouraged to look to his own steady efforts for ultimate liberation and improved position. And this—not the efforts of an individual, zealous as they certainly were—was the real secret of success."

Such are the views of the most intelligent, experienced, and close observers of prison discipline, in reference to its existing deficiencies, and the proper principles and methods of reform. Such are the prevailing tendencies of opinion among the most thoughtful men. Such are the results at which our advancing civilization evidently aims, and which it will eventually—and that at no distant period—accomplish. That is to say, the attempt will be made, and, if made, there can be no doubt of a reasonable degree of success. Absolute success may not be attainable, and should neither be promised nor expected.

The best and wisest of prison-keepers will still be imperfect intellectually and morally; and the best and wisest are but few. Even if they were many and, besides, were perfect, some criminals might not be saved by their treatment, however kind and judicious. We need not hold that there are absolutely no "incorrigibles." But more will be reformed in this way than in any other.

The experiment has been repeatedly tried by Maconochie, by Crofton, and many others; and always with the most encouraging degree of success. That perfect success is unlikely is no objection to any plan for the government or improvement of mankind. If it were, then one thing is plain: our whole cumbrous system and expensive machinery of penal jurisprudence should be instantly and utterly abolished; for it is patent and notorious that it has ever fallen far short of perfect success. Legal penalties have never swept away crime from human society; but we do not, therefore, propose their abolition. They may have done something towards the desired end. We propose an improvement of their mode of administration, whereby they would accomplish vastly more. But, after all, much will undoubtedly remain unaccomplished; much that will lie quite beyond the power and ingenuity of man to effect. Let us do what we can.

V. CLASSIFICATION OF PRISONERS.

Classification is not needed so long and so far as the separate system of confinement is absolutely adhered to. Each prisoner is then dealt with by himself, and on his own separate merits. But separate or solitary confinement has never been practically introduced, nor, so far as we know, has it ever been, even in theory, seriously proposed, for all persons under penal restraint, whatever their sex, age, or degree of criminality. Houses of correction for adults, and houses of refuge for juvenile offenders, have always been arranged on a different principle. Usually, convicts confined for minor offenses and for shorter periods are allowed more or less of companionship; and if so, the sexes are separated, or ought to be. Some degree of classification, therefore, seems to have been generally admitted to be proper and necessary. In the Western Penitentiary of this State, the separate system is by law allowed to be modified. The inspectors of the Philadelphia County Prison, in their last report, tell us that "the separate system, once the pride of Pennsylvania, has been long abandoned in every department of the prison, and even in the convict corridors two, three, and even four prisoners are placed together in a single cell." The history of the past and the present state of facts compel us to assume that the separate system will not, in the future, be thoroughly and universally carried out in this State. And if not, the classification of prisoners becomes a matter of most serious moment. *Taking things as they are*, its wider application would, in our judgment, be productive of the most important and beneficial consequences. From this point of view we propose to pursue the discussion of the subject—that is to say, *taking things as they are, and supposing that the separate system will not be universally and thoroughly carried out.*

Not a word need be said to show the unutterable absurdity and the terrible consequences of the free mingling together of all sorts of prisoners, or of thrusting them, indiscriminately, by the couple or the half dozen, into the same cell. Nothing could be more utterly subversive of all the purposes of punishment, whether exemplary or reformatory. No better contrivance could be invented for giving vice the fullest opportunity for fermenting and festering and propagating its contagion. Prisons thus become training-schools for crime. As far as reformation is concerned, such prisons are like hospitals in which all sorts of patients, with all sorts of diseases, from the plague, the small-pox, the cholera, the typhus and yellow fever, down to the rheumatism, asthma, catarrh, gout, or dyspepsia, should be indiscriminately huddled together in the same wards, and even in the same cots.

Leaving aside, therefore, this extreme case of the neglect of classification, which finds no defenders, we proceed to say that this same neglect is the occasion of many and capital defects in the "congregate system" of prison discipline, as it ordinarily exists, even under its best methods of management, and under the most favorable circumstances. To remedy these defects, not only must the labor of the convicts be made voluntary, instead of being enforced by the lash, but their classification must be carried out so far that the members of the several parties or companies or squads shall be left, and safely left, to very great, if not perfect, freedom of intercourse, as in ordinary social occupation.

Such a classification has sometimes been alleged to be impossible consistently with the purpose of reformation. By no one has the objection been placed in a stronger light than by Mr. Livingston. His views are thus expressed:—

"To remedy this evil (*i. e.*, the corrupting consequences of indiscriminate intercourse), what is called classification was first resorted to; first, the young were separated from the old; then the analogous division was made between the novice and the practiced offender. Further sub-divisions were found indispensable, in proportion as it was discovered that in each of these classes would be found individuals of different degrees of depravity, and, of course, corruptors, and those ready to receive their lessons. Accordingly, classes were multiplied, until, in some prisons in England, we find them amounting to fifteen or more. But all this while the evident truths seemed not to have had proper force: First, that moral guilt cannot always be discovered, and, if discovered, so nicely appreciated as to assign to each one infected with it its comparative place in the scale; and that, if it could be so discovered [appreciated], it would be found that no two would be found contaminated in the same degree. Secondly, that if these difficulties could be surmounted, and a class could be formed of individuals who had advanced exactly to the same point, not only of offense but of moral depravity, still their association would produce a further progress in both, just as sparks produce a flame when brought together, which, separated, would be extinguished and die. It is not in human nature for the mind to be stationary. It must progress in virtue or in vice. Nothing promotes this progress so much as the emulation created by society; and from the nature of the society will it receive its direction. Every association of convicts, then, that can be formed, will, in a greater or less degree, pervert, but will never reform, those of which it is composed; and we are brought to the irresistible conclusion that classification once admitted to be useful, it is so in an inverse proportion to the numbers of which each class is composed, and is not perfect until we come to the point at which it loses its name and nature in the complete separation of individuals. We come, then, to the conclusion that each convict is to be separated from his fellows." (Page 309.)

But even Mr. Livingston seems elsewhere to modify this absolute rejection of the principle of classification, and to admit the association of prisoners with very cautious provisions. We have already seen that he proposes classes of not more than ten for working and receiving instruction together. Again he says:—"I discard the use of the lash, therefore, being firmly convinced that, as an instrument of punishment, it is not only defective and dangerous, but that it cannot be brought to produce that reformation which is one of the essential parts of my plan. But social labor, whether general or in classes,—*if these classes are at all numerous* [*i. e.*, if each is numerous in individuals],—cannot be carried on without it, unless the security and order of the prison be put to hazard. Social labor, therefore, must be abandoned, *or so modified and admitted with such precautions* as to render this anomaly [the use of the lash] unnecessary." (Page 334.)

That these modifications and precautions can be introduced has been demonstrated by successfel experiment. The importance of the end to be attained by adopting them, and of adopting them in order to attain that end, can scarcely be over-estimated. The difficulties and the cost may be great, but success will abundantly repay the expenditure. Those who have tried the experiment also triumphantly defend their plan, even on general and theoretic grounds.

It must be plain, on a little reflection, that the opposite plan necessarily leads to absolutely "separate" or solitary confinement or segregation, *through the whole term of imprisonment;* for the other alternative—the *indiscriminate* association of the prisoners for all or any of the time, is out of the question. Such a plan, therefore, is inconsistent with the non-application of such confinement to less gross offenders, or to those sentenced to shorter periods of incarceration, as in houses of correction or workhouses, or even to juvenile convicts, provided the idea of reformation in those cases of greater criminality is admitted at all, for, if these last are ever reformed, they must reach reformation *gradually*, and must, therefore, before it is complete, reach stages of advancement in which they can be trusted with mutual companionship, *as well as those whose original criminality was less.*

But if criminals—even the grossest offenders, the most corrupt and desperate—are to be reformed and discharged at all, they must be so reformed as to be prepared to live, and to live safely, in society. They must be fitted for society, its motives, its processes, its trials, and its temptations. Can they be so fitted wholly outside of these tentative and experimental influences? Certainly solitary or separate confinement should have its place at the beginning, *and as much of it as is thought necessary in each case.* It is invaluable to secure a period for serious reflection and quiet instruction, and for preparing the prisoner to accept, with further instruction, society and even labor and all reformatory agencies, as great benefits and privileges. It may also have an appropriate use for temporary punishment afterwards, instead of resorting to the lash, or other degrading or violent remedies. If, by itself, it really succeeds in reforming the criminal, so as to be prepared for his full discharge at once into society at large, he will certainly be prepared, with entire safety to himself and others, to be transferred to the system of social discipline here suggested. If he leaves the solitary cell with good resolutions, indeed, but with resolutions not sufficiently strengthened by practical trial, that system will need to be added to to confirm and complete the work already begun. In any event, the social system is important to be applied as a test, before the hopefully-reformed convict receives his full discharge.

It will be understood, as a matter of course, that the classification here recommended must not be made on an arbitrary basis, as of age, length of the term of imprisonment or portion of that term elapsed, supposed criminality, identity, or similarity of temperament, or the like.

"Like all other exercises of mere authority, authoritative classification will prove a pure delusion; and in fact very few practical men, even now, are not ready to pronounce it such. There is no rule by which to regulate it. If by offense, this is the mere accident of conviction; if by age, the youngest criminals, born and cradled in sin, are very often the most corrupt; if by supposed similarity of temper or antecedent character, no one can certainly pronounce on this, and men are as often and oftener improved by associating with their opposites as with those who resemble them. It is impossible to attain real benefit by such means. One general difference between prisoners at the same time does exist, which it will be important, on many occasions, to keep in view, but not with the aim of separating them; it is this:—The difference between men who have erred from having more than an average amount of physical energy, and men who have sinned from having less than an average of moral principle. The treatment of the two should very considerably differ, and it might not be impossible or unwise to subject this to regulation." The classification, which alone this writer approves, is based on character, conduct, and merit, as shown in the daily routine of prison life.

Such a classification undoubtedly requires, on the part of the prison managers and keepers, a great share of knowledge of human nature, of good judgment and sound discretion, a habit of close observation and constant watchfulness, patient and indefatigable effort, and a deep, whole-souled, devoted interest in the work in hand.

The hypocrisy of criminals is proverbial, and must be carefully guarded against. Meanwhile this social system is one of the best tests that can be applied to the evil, and, if the evil exists, will infallibly lead to its seasonable exposure.

To render this scheme of classification systematic, self-working, and not merely discretionary or perhaps capricious, the "mark system," as it has been called, may be made an important accessory. The working and character of this system will be more fully considered further on.

But, with the exercise of all possible discretion and devotion, and with the use of all possible helps, it must be expected that mistakes will sometimes be made; it will sometimes be necessary to retrace steps that have been taken, and even ultimate failure will sometimes ensue. But these means will accomplish what can be accomplished; they will accomplish much; and we have no right to rest satisfied until these have been tried to the fullest possible extent. The experiment has been made by Captain Maconochie, to whose suggestions we have already referred, and by others; and wherever it has been fairly and faithfully tried, it has proved eminently successful.

VI. SELECTION AND TRAINING OF PRISON-KEEPERS.

Nothing is so important in prison economy as the right spirit and style of administration; to it everything else is subordinate; without it everything else is unavailing,—whether structure of prisons, structure or arrangement of cells, ventilation, diet, labor, instruction, separate system, or whatever else,—all may be spoiled by a wrong method of treatment. Everything, therefore, hinges upon the character of the wardens or keepers.

It may be thought an insuperable objection to the plan thus far developed, that the qualifications indicated as requisite in these functionaries are quite extraordinary and exceptional; in short, that enough of such men cannot be had. It may be said that a Maconochie, a Montesinos, a Crofton, or a Pilsbury may indeed accomplish wonderful effects in the way of reforming criminals, or rendering them orderly or industrious, by personal and moral influences, but that it is a mere Utopia to think that such a plan can be carried out as a general system. The genius, the magnetic power, the extraordinary personal qualities cannot be made to order, or collected in sufficient quantities to meet the demand. This may be said, plausibly said, and so men may turn away quite self-satisfied, as if the whole question had thus been settled and foreclosed, and prison discipline must be left to go on in the future substantially as it has gone on in the past. "The whole plan is a mere theory—a philanthropic dream," was the first cry. It was thereupon put to the test of experiment, and succeeded, and then we are told—"ah, but the men who tried it were extraordinary men, and one swallow does not make a summer." Let the experiment, we reply, be faithfully and earnestly continued; let the attempt be made to find more such men; let this too be tested by trial, and they will be found. What man has done, man can do; and where there's a will there's a way. These are the true mottoes for all good undertakings.

What we have to do is, first, to make up our minds what are the proper qualifications for the keepers and managers of prisons, what are the qualifications which the public service and the highest ends of prison economy require, and then with that degree of earnestness and diligence which the case demands to proceed to find and judiciously select those who approach nearest to the standard. Perfection, of course, is not to be attained, and, therefore, should neither be demanded nor expected. But surely it does not follow from this that it is reasonable to proceed without any standard or system, at pure hap-hazard, and with no effort at discrimination, flattering ourselves, and endeavoring to persuade the community, that such are the difficulties of the case we and they must be content with whatever material may chance to fall in our way.

In making the selection there is one point which must be laid down as absolutely essential; no political influence must be allowed to sway or interfere in the slightest degree to impede or determine the choice. It should be a matter of religion with all parties to exclude such influence altogether from the case. Political considerations have no more proper bearing upon this function than they have upon that of a professor of mathematics. Moreover, no men who have been elected or appointed for quite different functions should be suffered *ex officio* to be employed in this. County sheriffs, for example, are no more likely to be fitted for this office, or for determining who possess the proper qualifications for it, and, perhaps, on the whole, are less likely to be so fitted, than the general average of intelligent men. And yet the sheriffs of the several counties have, by law, the exclusive control of almost all the county jails or prisons, holding in their hands the appointment of all the keepers and under officers, which appointments they have the opportunity, and are under the temptation, to distribute to themselves or their friends, as petty political prizes, or as a matter of private and family patronage. While such a system is allowed to continue, what right have we to expect that the keepers of such prisons should have the spirit of a Howard, or emulate the example or exhibit the tact and talent of a Pilsbury or a Crofton? If we cannot expect this, is it because of the inherent difficulty of the case, or because of the egregious and stupendous folly of the method we persist in applying to it?

This is a special function and requires special aptitudes of mind and qualities of character; and if enough men fitted for it by nature, or by their own efforts and experience, cannot be found, provision should be made for the *special training* of others.

Considering the direct and important bearing of this business upon the public weal, what good reason can be given why men should not be especially trained for *this* function, in a sort of *normal institute*, as well as for the function of school teachers? Indeed, as there is a best way of managing prisons and prisoners, and as it is not only a peculiar, but a very complex and intricate business, involving most important principles of mental and moral philosophy, as well as infinite practical details, it is a serious question whether any one should undertake so delicate and responsible a task without a special training for it. The distinguished warden of the Albany Penitentiary, to whom allusion has several times been already made, undoubtedly owes much of his remarkable power of efficiently working a prison—and that in spite of grave defects of general principles in his system—to the training he received from his father and to his own life-long experience. Mr. Pilsbury and other men of similar ability and knowledge of their profession could in no way turn their powers and acquirements to better account or make them in a higher degree subservient to the public good than by training and instructing others who may succeed them in the exercise of their art, and thus bequeathing to posterity the secret they have mastered. And by concentrating upon such an institution the reflection, experience, and wisdom of the country in this department, further secrets would be discovered and the art would be developed as well as propagated. We venture to recommend the establishment of such a school by State authority, with such a system of regulations in regard to examinations, to the choice of prison wardens and keepers and to their systematic promotion, upon experience, from lower to higher grades and from less to more responsible positions, as will speedily secure the enjoyment of its benefits to all the jails and penitentiaries in the Commonwealth.

The dismissal of prison-keepers should not be left to be determined solely upon specific charges of misconduct or ill-treatment, good reasons though these are; but the proportion of the convicts discharged from the care of each, who should prove to be reformed or otherwise, or who should be re-convicted for crime, should be ascertained by careful statistics; and, the cases having been carefully considered, in connection with all the circumstances, incompetent or unsuccessful keepers should be forthwith dismissed.

There is one object of the highest moment, to facilitate the accomplishment of which the training-school would most powerfully contribute, and that is the elevation of the position of prison-keepers in the social scale and in the public regard. This profession should be as honorable, and should be made to be held as respectable, in general esteem, as that of school teachers or college professors, or superintendents of asylums for the insane or the blind. In the nature of the case, there is no reason why it should not be so. The reason why it *is not* so regarded is twofold: first, the want of training and culture and high character in so many who exercise the profession, the prevalent notion that men of mere ordinary or inferior abilities and qualities are quite equal to this work; but secondly and chiefly, it is because the business of a prison-keeper is supposed to be, and, hitherto, to a large extent, has been, merely to secure and superintend the infliction of punishment—an office of unfeeling coldness and sternness, of heartlessness and cruelty; an office calling for no exercise of the higher and kindlier human affections, but rather requiring their repression. Such an office cannot command the sympathy or respect of mankind. It is not in human nature to look upon it otherwise than with repugnance and a recoil of disgust,—the human heart can apprehend no elements of honor in it. Let us recognize and weigh well this verdict of humanity. Let us be thankful that, though led astray by the principles of a mistaken policy, our prison economy is sunk so low, yet our common human nature is not sunk so low with it as to regard it with complacency or reverence it with honor, but instinctively repudiates it with a sense of loathing.

But let our prisons be made and looked upon as schools for reformation rather than dungeons of punishment, as institutions for raising the fallen victims of vice, instead of crushing and trampling them deeper into the earth; and let the managers and governors of such penitentiaries receive a thorough culture and training for such an office, and they will soon come to be regarded as one of the most unselfish, high-minded, honorable, and elevated classes of human society. So ought they to be regarded.

VII. COMMUTATION, OR THE SUBSTITUTION OF REFORMATION FOR LAPSE OF TIME, AS THE CONDITION OF DISCHARGE.

All the punishments of criminal jurisprudence being imposed for the good of society, within the limits of justice and under the guidance of humanity,—as we trust has already been shown,—reformation must be included among the ends of punishment, and, moreover, its inclusion must be an important condition of the right and complete accomplishment of any other proper ends. It must, therefore, be the highest end of all. It is not denied that punishment should have reference to the past; but we have no right to punish our fellow-men for the past in utter and heartless neglect of their future. It is not denied that punishment should be inflicted as a vindication of justice and a deterring example to others; but it will accomplish these purposes only—or, at least, thoroughly accomplish them only—on condition of its having a reformatory character.

If, then, punishment looks to the future *rather than* the past; if the imprisonment of criminals is for the protection of society *rather than* for vengeance upon *them*, it follows that the mere lapse of time is no proper measure for prospectively determining the length of its continuance. Until the reformation aimed at is accomplished, the same reason exists for the continuance of the detention which existed for its beginning. If society is to be protected from the further crimes of the particular offender, and his imprisonment was mainly intended to secure that protection, what is it short of folly to dismiss him from that imprisonment while he is as ready and able to assume and pursue his career of violence or depredation as when he was first incarcerated? If, by the example of his punishment, others are to be deterred from similar, or from any, crimes, how else could this purpose be more effectually accomplished than by their seeing that, if convicted of such crimes, there is no way of their escape from perpetual imprisonment, but by giving satisfactory evidence, through a severe process of long and searching test and trial, of sincere and thorough reformation? Surely nothing could be *more* effectual than this; but it may be suggested that something short of this may accomplish something, or even much, in the same direction. But it is doubtful whether any punishment of offenders can have much effect in deterring others from crime, when those offenders are released more hardened and defiant than they were before; and still more doubtful whether any punishment can, on the whole, diminish the general amount, or check in the community the growth, of crime, unless, by that punishment, the offenders are absolutely prevented from returning to their old courses and their old associates.

The true plan, therefore, would seem to be, either the imposition of much longer time-sentences than the statutes now impose, *with greatly increased* opportunities to secure a commutation; or, what is more consistent *in principle*, the conditioning of every discharge from prison—at least in cases of felony or gross offenses—simply and absolutely upon *good conduct and evidence of repentance and reformation.*

In determining the weight of this evidence, the character and history of the parties previous to their incarceration should be taken into the account; and the estimation of good conduct should not depend simply upon orderly behavior, obedience to prison regulations, and the punctual performance of imposed tasks, but much more upon such habits of voluntary and provident industry, and such constant faithfulness, under circumstances of increasing exposure and temptation, as may guarantee a preparation of character for the labors, burdens, and trials of free life in actual society.

The idea of reformatory punishment is apt to be thought quite too mild and gentle for dealing with the rough and reckless characters of the mass of depraved and hardened criminals; it is apt to be dismissed with a quiet sneer as an unstatesmanlike and unpractial Utopia of men, very kind and humane, but very ignorant of human nature. It would not be surprising, however, if now, upon a full development of the idea, its opponents should entirely change their tune, and charge it with an excessive and intolerable severity—a severity quite inconsistent with the rights and privileges of the free citizens of a free state.

We must defend it, therefore, against this other charge; and we say that such severity is just that which offends against no principle of justice, humanity, charity, or religion; and which, at the same time, is needed for the full protection of society against the encroachments of the dangerous classes.

As the population multiplies and cities are thronged, as civilization advances and wealth increases,—and poverty, too,—crime, unless checked by special means, will also increase in a still greater ratio; roughs and rowdies and desperadoes, gamblers, swindlers, and knaves, thieves and pickpockets, garroters and robbers, murderers and assassins, will multiply apace, until the courts are overwhelmed and the prisons crowded; and yet the vast army is recruited and filled up faster than it is depleted by all the efforts of sheriffs, judges, and juries. The continual passing of a few through the pains-taking process of arrest, trial, and brief imprisonment, only to return with increased skill and malignity as heroic leaders to their old associates, as instructors to the host of novices gathered in their absence, will never remedy or remove the evil. It is but the labor of Sisyphus. When one looks at this immense and swelling host of the "dangerous classes," and considers how capable they are, in these days of guilds, brotherhoods, and associations, of a much more thoroughly organized combination than they have yet betrayed, one trembles for the future of modern civilization. There are only two remedies for the appalling evil, and the second is only supplementary to the first. These are, first, the universal training of the children in knowledge, morals, and religion, including, especially, the outcast, vagrant, and neglected classes of children; and, second, insisting upon the reformation of all those who are duly convicted of crime before they are again let loose upon the community. Both these remedies are, in our judgment, imperatively required for the public welfare and safety. And if what the public safety and welfare require is ever to be enacted into a law, it would seem to be when the voice, both of justice and humanity, both of rigorous right and of gentle charity, joins in the requisition.

Besides the common demand of reformation *in all cases*, the different degrees of criminality may need to be distinguished by a *graduation of punishment*.

For this purpose there might be imposed, in the original sentence, longer or shorter terms of strict solitary confinement, or of rigorous hard labor; and it might be provided that, in any event, the discharge of the prisoner should not take place *before* the lapse of a certain prescribed period of time, and this, especially, in the case of re-convictions.

Short terms of simple imprisonment might still be imposed, as the whole punishment, for misdemeanors and lesser offenses, without any violation of the principle contended for, which applies only to crimes in the stricter sense. But persons so imprisoned should either have a house of detention entirely separate from that of convict felons, or should be retained in solitary or separate confinement during the whole period of their punishment.

There is a class of crimes which some may think it incongruous to treat under this idea of reformation as an absolute condition of discharge: it is the case of those persons who are guilty of acts of personal violence in sudden brawls or intemperate excitements, but who do not belong habitually to what are called the "dangerous classes." But we think their cases sufficiently provided for by the foregoing remark, that, in estimating the character and standing of convicts, their habits and history previous to conviction must be duly taken into account; and, indeed, the scheme of prison discipline which is here in view seems to us, in this connection, to have a special advantage, to which we cannot refrain from directing particular attention.

Most of the felonious acts just referred to are occasioned by habits of ungovernable passion, or of intemperance in the use of stimulants. The temptations of this class of persons are chiefly *social*, hence they cannot be presumed fit to be intrusted again with the control of themselves in free society until they have stood the test of some degree of freedom of choice in the companionship of their fellows. *The remedy must be social.* Enforced abstinence, quiet reflection in solitude, theoretic instruction, and good resolutions, with the removal and absence of all temptation, can hardly give sufficient reason to trust in the permanence of the promised amendment, when the prisoner is suddenly liberated from his solitary cell, and returns to the actual temptations and trials of social life.

The scheme suggested would require the progressive classification of convicts according to their progressive and various developments of conduct and character—greater privileges and greater degrees of freedom being accorded in proportion to their grade of advancement, and all to be earned and purchased by their own efforts. Such a scheme, of course, requires, in its managers, close observation and a nice, discriminative judgment. To secure the fair and proper working of the scheme, leaving as little as possible to arbitrary determination and loose general judgments, a complete, detailed, and constant record of each prisoner's conduct and character from day to day should be made and preserved, to be to the prison manager what his "log" is to the mariner. This is, substantially, what is called the "*mark system,*" a full description of which is not here required.

Nor is it essential that any particular, precisely prescribed "system" should be adopted. What is essential, or, at least, extremely important, is, that some detailed daily record should be regularly kept, of every prisoner's character and conduct, merits and demerits, and of all rewards and punishments. There should be *some system and some definite record*, for the inspection of official visitors, for the information and encouragement of the prisoner, and as a guide and check for the prison managers.

But, after all, a great responsibility must rest upon these managers and the inspectors, and what some may think an excessive power must be committed to their hands—a power no less than that of practically determining, by the recorded estimates and judgments, the term of imprisonment for every convict. Passionate severities, favoritism, and other abuses of power, must be, by law, guarded against in every possible way. The detailed record above mentioned would do much as a guide and as a check—a guide to correct loose and general impressions; a check against sudden and passionate judgments. The *results* in the case of discharged prisoners would serve to expose and correct over-laxity; and the frequent visits of official inspectors would, with the aid of the record of marks and the personal examination of the prisoners, be the means of detecting any undue severities.

We have only to add, under this head, that the *principle* of modifying time-sentences, by allowing the commutation here advocated, has been *already adopted in the legislation of this Commonwealth.*

The statute of 1st May, 1861, enacted that "every prisoner or convict, sentenced as aforesaid, who shall have no such infraction or violation of the said rules recorded against him or her during any month of the first year of his or her imprisonment, shall be entitled to a deduction from the term of his or her sentence, &c. * * * *Provided*, That it shall be lawful for the inspectors of said penitentiaries or prisons, if any such convicts or persons shall willfully infringe or violate any of said rules or regulations, or offend in any other way, to strike off the whole or any part of the deduction which may have been obtained previous to the date of such offense.

"The said inspectors shall have full power and authority to discharge the said criminals, whenever they have served out their term of sentence, less the number of days to which they are entitled under the provisions of this act."

And then it is further provided that a certificate shall be given to such discharged prisoner. This act applies alike to county jails and State penitentiaries.

What we ask is, that the *principle* here involved should have a much wider, higher, and more consistent application; that instead of being the exception it should become the rule; and, instead of the commutation being based merely upon obedient submission to prison regulations, it should be based upon industry, diligence, moral conduct, and progress in practical reformation. The greater benefits which would then ensue may be judged of by the benefits which have followed upon the partial application of the principle. In their last report, the inspectors of the Philadelphia County Prison testify that "the commutation act, by which prisoners, who conduct themselves without charge of misconduct, are entitled to a deduction in the terms of their sentences, has been in operation in the prison since May, 1870. Its effect upon the discipline of the prison has been apparent, and we see no reason to doubt that its general reformatory influence has been good."

VIII. INTERMEDIATE PRISONS OR DISCHARGING-HOUSES.

The reformation of criminals is the object in view; and this object is presumed to be eventually attained. The process is in its nature gradual; and the course of progressive classification adapts itself to the advancement from stage to stage, both recognizing and promoting it. But something more distinct and decisive seems necessary to mark the highest and final stage. Those who have reached this point are supposed to be already substantially reformed. Like the piece of ordnance before its transfer to actual service, they need only a final testing to ascertain whether they will bear the strain of free society. They are really in a transition state, not quite ready to be trusted with entire freedom, and yet not to be treated simply as convicts. It seems eminently proper, therefore, that, at this stage, they should find themselves in a new atmosphere, surrounded by new associations, under new circumstances of recognized respectability as well as of responsibility, where the character of the man should begin quite to overshadow and efface that of the convict. For this purpose new quarters, quite separate and distinct, both in character and in name, from those of the less advanced prisoners, would be required. Such quarters we venture to call "intermediate prisons," or, better, perhaps, "discharging-houses." They should be regarded not so much in the light of prisons as of simple reformatories. In them the idea of punishment should give place entirely to that hopeful, voluntary amendment, or confirmation of amendment. Only in case of misconduct the right would remain to the superintendents or controlling managers of a summary remanding of the offender to the prison proper.

As the reformation, so the transfer to entire freedom would thus be made by degrees. And this last degree is a most important preparation for the full discharge. We do not propose to suggest the details of arrangement for these houses or prisons; they may be greatly varied, according to circumstances, and according to the personal judgment and peculiar aptitudes of the superintendents. The general principles to be carried out should be to give much greater freedom of action than in former stages,—perhaps entire freedom within certain limits of time,—to manifest much greater personal confidence in the men, retaining the feature of mutual watch and responsibility, and the absolute requirement upon all to be at their quarters before a certain hour in the evening.

Some may think it a crushing and final objection to any such scheme that, in their opinion, many, if not all, the prisoners under such treatment would make their *escape* and disappear. But such an objection is the child of despair. It proceeds from an entire want of hope that criminals can ever be reformed. For only those who are presumed to be substantially reformed—whether under the separate or the social system—are to be placed in these circumstances and allowed these liberties; and, when placed here, should they *all* make their escape, it would be no worse than if, instead of being placed here, they had all been forthwith discharged. But they will not all escape; some may; it is to be presumed that some will. Still, we shall retain this advantage, that they will be *escaped prisoners*, and, upon arrest, can be restored to their incarceration without being arraigned, tried, and convicted for some new crime against society. Most of such runaways would be arrested.

If it be thought that, while the fear of such arrest and its consequences might be a restraint, yet such restraint would, after all, be a sort of compulsion, and would not prepare for a state of entire freedom; we answer that such an objection proceeds upon the idea that nothing but entire freedom can prepare for entire freedom; it rejects all approximation, and annuls the idea of preparation altogether. Whereas, we believe that self-control, exercised under such a motive, would not only test its own power, but would confirm a habit of self-control, with a view to the future, which would be one of the most powerful preservatives from a resumption of criminal courses, after the full discharge and restoration to entire freedom.

It may be thought that this plan would require a multiplication of prison establishments, and thus entail upon the State a great additional expenditure. But, even though this were the case, still, provided the plan were liable to no other valid objection, and provided it would be productive of the benefits proposed, no such petty objection of expense should weigh for a moment against them. Such an outlay would be a good investment. It would go to prevent the waste of much of the other expenditure which crime entails upon the State. Penuriousness is often the greatest extravagance. But no multiplication of prisons need result, even temporarily, from the plan proposed, but only a special distribution of them; for, while we should confidently believe and maintain that, in the long run, it would tend to diminish the number of prisoners, it would not, even at the first, necessarily increase their number; for prisoners might naturally be transferred to these intermediate houses of detention somewhat sooner than, without them, it would be thought proper to risk their complete discharge.

As for the current expenses of these establishments, our idea is that—with the exception, of course, of the sick and the infirm—all prisoners, both here and in the former stages of their confinement, but especially here, should by their own industry pay for their maintenance.

Under a judicious management they would not only do this, but would rapidly accumulate their reserve fund, to be received by them upon their release. As a general rule, none would be transferred to this intermediate position who should not already have earned and accumulated such a fund; and this fund being still at risk, and liable to be forfeited for misconduct, would be a further pledge for good behavior, as well as a guarantee for their current expenses. Here is another motive of restraint which some may stigmatize as of the nature of compulsion; but it is the same sort of compulsion as that under which all men are called upon to act in ordinary life. It is, therefore, most appropriate as a final preparation to return to that life, with its temptations and its responsibilities.

IX. REFUGES AND OTHER PROVISION FOR DISCHARGED PRISONERS.

This is an indispensable part of every effectual scheme of prison economy. It is the clincher of the whole. Without it the rest of the scheme, however perfect in itself, will largely fail to accomplish its end. The State, therefore, cannot afford to leave this portion of the process entirely, as is commonly proposed and has hitherto been done, to the kindly but uncertain and inadequate efforts of private charity.

To cause the stream of criminal life to circulate through the penitentiary, without change or improvement in its character, must be to small purpose. It is only a brief arrest of the current's rapidity. It is as a dam thrown across a river; the waters are checked and accumulated for a time, but in the end just as much is discharged below as is received from above.

And scarcely to any more purpose will it be to reform the prisoners before returning them to society, if upon being so returned they are to be treated as outcasts.

Yet hitherto they have been so treated, whether reformed or unreformed. There has prevailed in the community an almost unconquerable, and, as things have been managed, a not unnatural or unreasonable, feeling of distrust and aversion, of shrinking repugnance and even of fear and horror, towards discharged convicts. They have found no sympathy, no encouragement, no helping hand, no shelter, no employment, no means of honest subsistence. Every man's hand has been against them, every back turned upon them, every door shut in their faces and barred against their intrusion. They have been turned out of prison into a dark passage, walled up to heaven on either side, their only alternative either to lie down in it and perish, or to follow it out to its only exit among their old associates and in their old trade.

Shall this continue? And what is to be the end of these things? Surely these questions address themselves, not merely to philanthropic sentiment, but to the coolest and most calculating regard for the public interest. No wonder that under the present system the proportion of re-convictions should be very large. We know it to be large; but it is unquestionably much larger than can ever be ascertained, owing to the great extent of our territory and the distribution of our penal administration among so many independent States.

With our present prison management and with the circumstances of discharged prisoners left as they are, it may be seriously questioned whether it is reasonable or just to condemn re-convicted criminals, as is so often strenuously urged, to an aggravated severity of punishment. The first step in remedying the evil must be the full and frank adoption in prison discipline of the principle of reformation, carried out through the intermediate trial above recommended and supplemented by the *refuges* here suggested. Let this course be adopted, and while, in accordance with the very nature of the reformatory plan, the re-convicted criminal would be placed under a severer and more cautious course of discipline and trial, it would also be both manifestly reasonable and highly important that the absolute or *minimum* length of his time-sentence or task-sentence should likewise be increased.

While the present plan and working of prison discipline continues, it will also continue impossible to revolutionize or greatly to modify the public sentiment in regard to discharged convicts, to remove or sensibly to mitigate the feeling of distrust and repugnance towards them. Nor if it were possible would it be reasonable to attempt it, for to a very great extent the feeling is well founded.

The revolution must begin in the policy of the state. Her treatment of imprisoned convicts must be changed before the reception of discharged convicts on the part of the community can be changed. Let it not be suggested that this state of degradation, in which released convicts find themselves and this repulsion which they meet with on all sides, is their own fault, is a natural and proper part of their punishment. If so, the state ought to take their lives or shut them up in perpetual incarceration. She has no right to turn them out and spurn them from her and say, "Steal or die; and it is your own fault." Here again the first step for the state is the adoption of the principle that reformation is the great end of the detention of criminals in prison. If this principle is once adopted and successfully carried out, it will tend most powerfully toward removing the popular prejudice against discharged convicts.

Still, in order to facilitate the healthy re-absorption of such convicts into the mass of society, there would remain for a long time, and perhaps always, a necessity, or at least important office, for such establishments or refuges as we here propose. It has sometimes been suggested and attempted to secure their re-admission to the bosom of society by carefully concealing their character as discharged convicts. What we propose is, an open admission of that character, by an acknowledged connection with a public establishment expressly kept up for their resort. This is the open and honest course of dealing with the community, without subterfuge or deception. Discharged convicts are thus not smuggled into society under a mask, or thrust in an underhand way on those who employ them. They are not called upon to hide or deny the fact that they *are* discharged convicts, while all the time fully aware that if this fact were known they would be rejected and refused employment, thus beginning their new lives with the practice of a lesson in swindling and falsehood.

These refuges or establishments for the resort of discharged prisoners should contain:—

1. The means of lodging and maintenance for such numbers as would be likely to resort to them, with considerable elasticity as to enlargement or contraction.

2. They should be supplied with workshops, implements, and materials for the employment of such as should not find opportunity for employment elsewhere.

3. They should be supplied with means of good advice and instruction, of mental and moral improvement, as reading-rooms, &c.

4. It should be understood that those who can find employment elsewhere should have their lodging here as long as they desire it.

5. All should be required to pay for their board, lodging, and other expenses by their own earnings or out of their reserve fund.

6. The reserve fund, accumulated by each prisoner before his release, should be held on deposit at the refuge, to be set against his current expenses if necessary; and the whole to be paid up to him, not at once, but in installments within such time (whether he remains in the refuge or not) as may be judged expedient and established by a fixed rule. Such arrangements could easily be made in respect to the *plan* of his receiving the several installments as he should desire; and such precautions could be taken as should be necessary to secure against their undue or their premature transfer to other parties, to the prejudice of the original claimant.

7. Should the reserve fund, in any case, be exhausted, and the man seek to remain an *idle hanger-on* at the refuge, it would simply be proved that the reformatory discipline had, in his case, failed of the hoped-for effect. Such instances might of course occur. It would not be very difficult to devise the proper means of dealing with them; and we are quite confident that they would be but few. But we shall pursue them no further.

We have merely to add that the suggestions here made have in some form or other received the support of almost every writer on prison economy in the present century, their voices only increasing in earnestness as the years roll on. Indeed, it may justly be claimed that the general consent of all experienced and thoughtful men for the last ten or fifteen years has been pitched in one key—"longer sentences, steadier discipline, rewards for good conduct, and assistance to discharged prisoners."

X. THE PARDONING POWER.

There can be no doubt that this power has sometimes been grossly *abused*. And this abuse has been fruitful of some of the greatest evils that beset the economy of penal jurisprudence. Men have been pardoned, because they had influential friends, or from mere caprice. Men have been pardoned in view of private and personal, and not of general and public, considerations. Men have been pardoned, and that by no means unfrequently, who have soon found their way back to prison again; and sometimes these same men have been pardoned out a second time. Men have been pardoned without any proper evidence either of innocence, or of any mitigation of criminality, or of reformation. Men have been pardoned, if not from corrupt, yet from altogether improper and insufficient motives. In short, men have been pardoned in such numbers, and with such entire disregard of fixed principles, as to encourage the commission of crime, breaking down the certainty of punishment even after conviction, and opening to the most abandoned criminals, when receiving their sentence, a door of hope, that very likely, after all, they will not be obliged to serve it out.

Still, the pardoning power must be retained; it must be lodged somewhere; it cannot be dispensed with. There may be cases of persons who, after having been sentenced and committed to prison, are found to have been convicted on false testimony or by some mistake; others in whose cases circumstances greatly mitigating their offense are subsequently discovered; others whose enlargement may be required for the ends of public justice, as that they may be qualified to testify as witnesses; and others, whose offenses having been committed in some scene or occasion of great public or political excitement, their release is afterwards demanded, before the expiration of their sentence, by considerations of state policy and expediency; and so on.

What is needed, therefore, is not that the pardoning power should be abolished, but that, in the first place, it should be hedged about as far as possible by constitutional limitations; and, for the rest, it should be held in constant check by an awakened and watchful public sentiment. This is needed as a safeguard against the abuse of all discretionary and irresponsible power; and too much cannot be said and done to keep such a sentiment always alive and in vigorous exercise.

But we dismiss this point with these brief remarks, not because it is unimportant or irrelevant to our general subject, but because, not being a matter of legislation, it is, strictly speaking, aside from our proper office.

XI. IMPRISONMENT FOR LIFE.

It is difficult to conceive of a case of crime in which imprisonment for life would be an expedient or appropriate punishment. This judgment may seem strange or paradoxical; but we believe that the grounds upon which it is founded are entirely tenable.

Imprisonment for life as a constant substitute for capital punishment is scarcely defensible, for if *rigorously carried out* it involves unnecessary lingering cruelty, and at the same time has not the deterring power which belongs to the dread penalty of death. It is really killing by degrees, while it seems not to kill at all, and so far as the punishment is to operate upon others, the seeming is of more consequence than the reality. It is a protracted execution, yet so protracted that the terrible impression, for want of concentration, is dissipated. On the other hand, *if not rigorously carried out—always* rigorously carried out, it is plainly, as regards its exemplary influence, a still more perfect failure; and it will not be rigorously carried out unless death, before the lapse of many years, should intervene to cut short its duration.* One generation will not consent to be the executioners or jailors for another. The convict whose crimes have faded from recollection will be pardoned and released.

Such imprisonment, as an occasional substitute for capital punishment, is still more awkward; for if capital punishment should ever be inflicted, its infliction is apparently required in those cases of crime in which it

* We believe that the average term of imprisonment for "life sentences" is about ten years.

is judged absolutely unsafe for the guilty man ever again to live at large in human society.

Looking at the subject, in the next place, in relation, not to the direct external effect, but to its bearing upon the convict himself, and upon the good of society as indirectly involved in his good, imprisonment for life must be condemned on other grounds.

It is utterly and manifestly inconsistent with the idea of reformation as the object of penal detention. It cuts off at once all hope, all stimulus to effort, all motive for self-denial or self-control.

If the hopes of a future life are suggested, how weak must be their influence; how dim and distant their view, unsupported by nearer and lower motives, under circumstances of aggravated temptation, and especially with a sense that *there is time enough yet*, and more than enough; that time, indeed, is the greatest burden, and that the principal object is to find out how to kill it as fast and effectually as possible; and how inconsistent to urge a man, in the name of the state, to be good, and at the same time to tell him that, even if he should become a saint, you will still treat him as a scoundrel as long as he lives.

If the hope of a discharge at last, through executive clemency, is suggested, this removes the idea of reformation still farther from the prisoner's mind, and, besides, annuls the very fact of imprisonment for life, and, of course, all the influence that the anticipation of such a fact could have upon the prisoner's mind, or upon the minds of others.

If, finally, the hope is suggested of a discharge in case of manifest reformation, this, to have its full effect, or to be at all reasonable, must not be uncertain or capricious—a mere *may be*—but must be on system and by fixed rules; and if so, then it is manifest that the imprisonment has ceased, even in theory, to be for life; it is placed upon a new principle; it is simply imprisonment terminable upon reformation, and upon reformation only. As such, we have not a word to say against it. It is precisely the kind of imprisonment whose systematic adoption we have ventured to suggest as the best of all remedies for crime.

XII. COUNTY JAILS AND MUNICIPAL PRISONS AND STATION-HOUSES.

We here touch upon one of the most important, because among us the most neglected, departments of prison economy. Our State prisons or penitentiaries, and a few of the principal county prisons, which, from their connection with large cities, belong, in a manner, to the same class, have attracted and absorbed almost the whole attention of those who have interested themselves in the improvement of prison discipline. Upon what has been done in these have been exclusively based our too-confident boasts and over-weening self-satisfaction in view of the supposed vast progress by which we have flattered ourselves with having outstripped the rest of the world. In them some progress has unquestionably been made. They have been better constructed. Their management has been raised to a much higher standard. Their wardens and keepers are generally most respectable, zealous, and intelligent men. They are visited, watched over, and managed by faithful and judicious inspectors. They are kept before the eye of the public, which takes in them a lively interest. Much earnest effort is made—though not always successfully—to preserve them from confusion, over-crowding, negligence, and abuse. In short, the system which they have adopted, such as it is, is worked with most commendable fidelity and large efficiency.

When we turn from these and look at the average of county jails and city lock-ups, the scene changes. Here the grossest abuses keep uninterrupted carnival. Bad construction, bad ventilation, bad management, reckless treatment, indiscriminate mingling of prisoners,—with no separation at all, except that of the sexes, and not always even that,—intolerable crowding of cells, no kindly sympathy, no moral or religious instruction or influence, disregard of health and cleanliness, no provision or opportunity for labor,—in plain violation of the statute,—the practice of all sorts of petty tyranny, these are their characteristics; and the people love to have them so, or pass by them on the other side, or look upon them as places too low, rough, and foul to be approached or meddled with. Few besides the sheriff, the policeman, or the alderman—and the inmates—know anything about their interior condition or history; and the officers, even though endowed with much natural goodness of heart, grow so thoroughly accustomed to the abuses and abominations that reign around them, that they become hardened to the scene, and lose all idea of the possibility or desirableness of reform. And as for the keepers, they must often be not much superior, either in intellectual or moral character or culture to those who are placed under their care. Many of these city establishments, if inspected at an early morning hour, would suffer in comparison with the prisons of Turkey or Persia or Hindostan. Yet through them, as a kind of heart, the criminal, the vagrant, the drunken and quarrelsome part of the population, is continually circulating—festering and fermenting together. In comparison with the number of persons who are annually locked up in these establishments, and detained for a longer or shorter period, the number of those sentenced to the State penitentiaries is as nothing. It is true some of the county jails are not so crowded as the city prisons and lock-ups; and in general, the same abuses and evils do not exist to the same extent in all these institutions alike; but they exist to an alarming extent, and more or less, almost everywhere.

What is absolutely required in all these places of detention is:—

1. Such an enlargement of the accommodations—at whatever cost—as may furnish for every inmate a separate, well-aired, cleanly, and healthy lodging for the night, and proper distribution for companionship by day (if companionship is allowed), with wholesome and well-served food; and,

2. Such a provision of keepers, of high, respectable, and responsible character, as will insure the humane and judicious treatment of the prisoners.

But, in connection with these jails and ward-houses, the greatest evil and most crying injustice of all remains to be considered. It relates to the detention of witnesses, of vagrants, and of persons charged with crime.

Not only are persons charged with crimes of all kinds and degrees, in company with idlers, drunkards, vagabonds, and rioters, all crowded and mingled together, for a night, and sometimes longer, in these municipal Bridewells; but, in the jails, all these are thus huddled in, sometimes for many months, with persons detained as witnesses added to the company; and all, in many cases, left in perfect idleness, or busy only in deepening their own depravity or imbibing that of others; the old adepts maturing their plans of crime, and inoculating all around them with their pestilent corruption. If all these were convicted felons together, it would not only be most unwise and impolitic, but most inhuman and abominable, to subject them to such a regimen; but who can express the enormity of its injustice, as well as its folly, when it is added that to it are subjected persons acknowledged to be perfectly innocent, who are detained by the highest stretch of the civil authority, merely in order to secure their testimony, which is presumed important to the ends of public justice; and persons charged with crime, indeed, but either charged upon suspicion, which may prove most foul and unfounded, or committed upon *ex parte* testimony, which may prove prejudiced or malicious! The witnesses, we say, are confessedly innocent, it may be virtuous men, whose only fault is that they are poor and friendless, and therefore cannot furnish a satisfactory guarantee for their appearance at the required time. The state may have a right to detain them—

she may have a right temporarily to deprive them of their liberty, as she has a right to take private property for the public good; but what right has she to thrust them in to herd with vagrants, thieves, pickpockets, and murderers, as their associates day and night? If it be thought that as virtuous men they will be in no great danger of being harmed, but may do some good in such society, it must be remembered that some of them may be young and inexperienced, or intellectually or morally weak; in any event, that an honest man or woman must look upon the imposition of such society as a gross and horrible infliction; and that to *compel* men to be missionaries has never been recognized as one of the rights of the state.

As to persons committed or detained under a charge of crime, the phrase of the law is that all such persons are "presumed innocent until they are proved guilty." Is this phrase a mere magniloquent sham, mere sound, meaning nothing, keeping the promise to the ear but false to the hope? When persons are thus incarcerated, which are they treated most like, the innocent or the guilty? It is true this maxim of the law could never be reasonably supposed to be taken in that absolute and sweeping sense in which it is perhaps popularly understood, and is often urged by over-zealous attorneys and advocates. It cannot be meant that, in the case of a person charged with crime, it is to be presumed, until his guilt is proved, that his innocence is proved and established; for, if that were so, he ought at once to be acquitted and discharged. His case is a case of doubt. Strictly speaking he is to be treated neither as innocent nor as guilty, but, according to the true state of the case, and just as what he is—a person charged with crime. And the legal maxim referred to, if it means anything, must mean as much as this, that a man charged with crime presumably may be innocent, that such a man is not to be treated as guilty until he is proved so, and that the burden of proof is on the side of the prosecution. Such a man the state has a clear right temporarily to restrain of his liberty, to detain before trial, as long as necessary, and no longer. But the state can have no right to add to that detention one particle of hardship or discomfort, of exposure or privation, of contempt or ignominy, beyond what is reasonably required to secure his person and prevent his escape. In all other respects he has a right to be treated with all possible consideration, respect, and kindness.

It must be observed, and the state must be presumed to know it, from past experience, that a certain percentage of persons thus detained are bad and corrupt men, guilty of crimes of greater or less enormity, and most dangerous, as well as most repulsive, companions for the far greater percentage, who, it is equally known, will prove to have been innocent, or nearly so. A proper concern for her own protection and welfare, as well as a just regard for the feelings, the rights, and the moral safety of the latter parties, should forbid the state to thrust all these into one indiscriminate company, before ascertaining which are the bad and which the good. She knows that both bad and good are there, and that, by companionship, the bad will make themselves and others worse; yet she leaves the business to take its course. And what, in connection with the city of Philadelphia, adds unspeakable outrage to unspeakable folly, is the temptation which, by law, is thrown in the way of police magistrates, and to which they are notoriously and constantly yielding, to commit large numbers of persons to prison on the most trivial charges, for the mere purpose of blackmailing them—unless the explanation is that they make a wholesale business of compounding felonies—and thus swelling the fees, and perhaps other perquisites, of the committing and discharging magistrate;—yes, "the magistrate," we are obliged to say; but, in such a case, which is the magistrate and which the thief?

The inspectors of the Philadelphia County Prison, in their last annual report, have again urged this subject most earnestly upon the attention of the legislature. This is their statement:—"Of the prisoners committed for trial during the past year (nine thousand eight hundred and twenty-three), six thousand six hundred and ninety-seven were discharged by the committing magistrates, and in the cases of four hundred and fifteen the bills of indictment were ignored by the grand jury. These figures show a larger than usual proportion of persons discharged without being brought to trial (nearly three-fourths of the whole number committed), who, as a general rule, *settled* their cases, as it is termed, with the committing magistrates. It is obvious that so long as the income of these officers depends directly upon the fees accruing from cases brought before them, commitments for trivial or unnecessary cases will be multiplied."

The board again desires to express its opinion of the

necessity of a reform in the police magistracy of Philadelphia, and in view of the proposed convention to reform the State Constitution, it would invoke the aid of all good citizens to secure the necessary change in our organic law for this purpose. As has been often urged in these annual reports, we would here again submit, that the great and foremost evil in the criminal department of Philadelphia is the system of police magistracy; and no reform is so much needed as a change at least in the mode of compensation of our committing magistrates. So long as their receipts are directly dependent upon and swollen by what must be stated to be simply a traffic in the manipulation of petty crime, it is idle to anticipate radical improvement in the treatment of this class of prisoners. It is difficult to believe that such a system of magistracy can be tolerated in a city like Philadelphia, and that her citizens can sit quietly under so great a reproach. If our police magistrates were removed from the sphere of politics, by a change in the mode of selection; if they held their offices by a good-behavior tenure; were required to be learned in the law, and were compensated by adequate fixed salaries, in place of fees, a reform would be accomplished the effects of which upon social improvement can scarcely be estimated.*

Here, then, is one per cent. of all the population of Philadelphia subjected annually to this scandalous process, this organized system of arbitrary oppression and plunder. How we should pity the darkness and degradation of Turkish or Egyptian society, if such a

* See report for 1871, pages 17 and 18. The Constitutional Convention made the change suggested. (1877.)

shameful system of abomination, under color of the administration of justice, were allowed to be practiced among them from year to year. Yet such is the system of police magistracy in the city of Philadelphia.

There is a very common feeling, it is true, that these persons, though not actually convicted of crime, are yet in all probability guilty of it; or, if not guilty of the precise crime alleged, are guilty of some other—at all events, are bad men, keeping bad company, suspicious and dangerous characters—that, therefore, they deserve little consideration in their treatment, and that no great mistake can be committed in consigning them at once and together to a common prison. This feeling ignores the fact, just brought to view, that by far the larger part—nearly three-fourths—of those who are committed to prison charged with some violation of law, are actually released without trial; while of those who are brought to trial more than three-fifths are acquitted. Now, whatever deductions may be reasonably made from the magnificent largeness of the legal maxim above referred to, that "a man is to be presumed innocent until he is proved guilty;" and whatever may be the loose estimates in the private judgment of individuals, or in the popular mind, in regard to probable moral turpitude in any cases, the state is bound,—and it is the state that is here the responsible agent, for it is she that arranges prisons and detains prisoners,—the state is bound, to presume those to have been innocent whose guilt she has failed or not even attempted to prove, or who, upon solemn trial, have been acquitted. Indeed it would seem not unreasonable for the state, which holds herself bound to pay for the private property which she takes for the public good, to make to such parties some amends, if possible—and still more in the case of detained witnesses—for the mere detention which they have suffered, even though that detention had been attended with no unnecessary aggravations. If such aggravations, and that to a most outrageous extent, have been needlessly added, how ought the state to be visited with compunctions, as well as with a desire to make all possible reparation,—yet no reparation is ever made.

It is true that the large and increasing class of suspicious characters, of idle, desperate, and dangerous men that congregate especially in large cities, and prowl about the streets by day as well as by night, may need to be dealt with in some special and more effective way than has yet been invented. It is indeed very difficult to contrive any such way of dealing with them consistently with the principles of our common law and our free institutions. But, whatever method is adopted, it should not be by indirection or caprice,—it should be straightforward, square, open, regulated. If these men are to be punished, they should be punished *as being* just what they are, and should not be mixed up indiscriminately with men fully indicted for definite crime, on the one hand, and, on the other, with men charged with no crime or suspicion.

We venture the following general suggestions:—

1. All persons sentenced to jail to be imprisoned at hard labor, should either be kept in strict solitary confinement, or, when they desire it, being properly classified, should have the means of employing themselves

daily in productive labor. Their being allowed to herd together in idleness is one of the gross abuses of some of our county jails.

2. Persons committed as idlers and vagrants should be treated in the same manner,—only in entire separation both from convicts and from all other classes of prisoners.

3. Persons detained as witnesses should also have entirely separate quarters from all others, whether convicts, vagrants, or suspected persons. They should have the means of perfect privacy or of mutual association at pleasure; also, the means of reading and writing and of such employment at labor as they may choose. With these might be joined another class, which fortunately is likely to be but small, viz., persons committed for contempt. Such persons may be highly respectable men, guilty only of some impropriety of conduct or bearing or of declining to perform some legal mandate, and that sometimes from high though mistaken motives of duty; and it is most unreasonable that they should be thrust into prison among felons and vagabonds. The restraint of their liberty and that for an unlimited time,—for, curiously enough, this is the only class of persons whose period of imprisonment is, under present law and usage, terminable only upon reformation,—such restraint is leverage enough wherewith to act upon their wills, without forcing upon them the grievous alternative of submission or of "rotting" in such a jail.

4. Persons committed under charge of crime should also have their separate quarters and should be treated, in general, as the last-mentioned classes of prisoners; but with some important modifications, such as, that those charged with graver crimes should be secured with the greater caution, and that they all should be more or less rigorously confined to their separate cells or classified for mutual association, if they so prefer, according to their conduct, known history, and ascertained characters.

5. We most heartily and earnestly endorse the recommendation of the inspectors of the Philadelphia County Prison, above cited, in reference to the reform of the police magistracy of that city.

Now we are aware that all this may be met and smothered in the cold blanket of a calculating economy. It may be avoided by running away. It may be buried and forgotten under arithmetical estimates. The cost, the huge outlay, the enormous expense of making such immense and sumptuous provision for the entertainment of prisoners! We answer that here we will not enter into any petty calculation of dollars and cents. If this thing ought to be done, if it is due to the classes of men whom the state thus takes into her custody, then is the state bound to do it at whatever cost. The state cannot afford to practice inhumanity. The state cannot afford to commit injustice, still less can she afford to commit it systematically and on an enormous scale, deliberately and from year to year, and talk of saving a few paltry dollars.

The truth is, and we repeat it, this mixing together in the society of one common prison, and often crowding into the same cells, by night as well as by day, all these various classes of persons in custody—thrusting them, like so many swine, into one pen—is nothing less than a burning disgrace to the police and jurisprudence of a civilized state. It is an outrageous injustice, an unspeakable abomination. It is simply astounding that it should have been allowed to continue, without a thorough remedy, to the present day.

But this is not all. Such a state of our prisons is not only an injustice to the individual, it is a great public evil; it is one of the most fruitful sources of crime, furnishing the most admirable contrivances for inviting and facilitating its propagation. Thus the wrong reacts upon the wrong-doer; and the penurious system of injustice costs more than the generous remedy. It turns out here, as it always will, that the course of humanity and right is the cheapest in the end.

So far as the "generous remedy" has been tried, it has proved abundantly successful. Say the inspectors of the Philadelphia prison:—"The decrease in the number of the commitments of females is much greater than in that of males, and is so large during the four years that have elapsed since the *extension* of the female department, that it may be fairly attributed to the increased accommodation for female prisoners, that was secured by the transfer of the old debtors' apartment to the female department. The separation of female prisoners, which was thus accomplished, with the greater facilities for the enforcement of prison discipline, has resulted in a marked diminution of vagrancy and crime in the female population of our city. The expenditure originally involved in the extension of the female department has proved a true economy, and the results attained support the arguments which have been so repeatedly urged in favor of an extension of the more important and over-crowded male department of the prison." They add:—

"The board would here repeat the views expressed in previous reports, upon the subject of an extension of the prison, and again call the attention of the legislature to the incapacity of the prison for the proper confinement and employment of its large male population. In every aspect, sanitary, moral, and economical, the injurious effects of its over-crowded condition are manifest. The results of improved accommodation in the female department, previously cited, have shown that the great growth of crime and vagrancy is directly stimulated by the undue congregation of prisoners. It can scarcely be doubted that the collection of a number of prisoners in a single cell soon reduces all to the moral level of the worst prisoner; and the unceasing intercourse which results from the original construction of the prison, with a view to the separate system, fosters the moral contagion more actively than in prisons not designed for this system. * * * The board feels that this subject can be no longer overlooked, and that either the extension of the convict blocks, or the construction of a new prison, has become a necessity."

Hitherto convicted felons have been the heroes of our prison economy. They have been treated with great respect. They have been a sort of little standing army. Their discipline has absorbed the almost exclusive attention of all parties, while the organizing and training of the militia has been neglected. We need now to turn our attention emphatically to the municipal bridewells and all the over-crowded houses of primary detention; to the *police* arrangements which precede the processes of trial and conviction, or which, perhaps, through gross abuse and mismanagement, not only never lead, but are never even *intended* to lead to such a conclusion.

XIII. SUMMARY.

The board begs now to resume and recapitulate the principal points which they have endeavored to make, in relation to the whole subject of crime and prison economy, including, with those which have passed under discussion, some which have been merely alluded to as preliminary, and presenting all in one connected view.

1. For dealing with crime *preventive* rather than *remedial* measures to be chiefly relied upon—among these:—

(*a.*) A thorough system of universal education.

(*b.*) Special and effective measures for the care of truant, vagrant, neglected, and over-tasked children.

(*c.*) Reformatory schools and houses of correction to be provided to a much larger extent for the various grades of juvenile offenders.

(*d.*) Due provision for the proper care of all the poor and helpless.

(*e.*) Effective laws for the suppression of intemperance, which is one of the most prolific sources of crime.

(*f.*) Due provision for the restraint and employment of all idle vagrants.

(*g.*) Due provision in the county and municipal prisons for the separate and proper treatment of vagrants, detained witnesses, and persons charged with crime, as well as convicts.

2. The *remedial* system, or prison economy proper. This should be based upon the fundamental principle of *reformation through punishment*, and not of punishment only as its proper end. It should contain, among others, the following features:—

(*a.*) Sufficient provision for the separate confinement of each convict.

(*b.*) After a longer or shorter period of separate confinement, and the performance of certain prescribed tasks, provision made for the employment of the convicts in voluntary, productive labor, as a means of moral improvement, as a preparation for their future self-support, and as necessary for their present health of body and mind.

(*c.*) Unless solitary labor should be preferred, this labor to be performed in small companies or families, properly selected, the members having free intercourse together, and ultimately being mutually responsible for one another's conduct.

(*d.*) The proceeds of the labor to be appropriated:—First, to defray the current expenses of the convict and indemnify the state; secondly, to contribute to the support of the convict's family if necessary; thirdly, to the convict himself, to go partly to form a reserve fund against the time of his release, and partly as he may choose, for procuring present alleviations and comforts.

(*e.*) Instruction should be given to all the convicts, as they may need:—First, in some trade or handicraft; secondly, in the elements of learning and knowledge; and, thirdly, in the principles and practice of morality and religion.

(*f.*) Considerate and humane treatment to be emphatically insisted on, using, as far as possible, moral influence instead of physical force, and endeavoring, above all things, to develop the self-respect and manhood of the prisoners, and their better and kindlier natures.

(*g.*) A careful classification of the prisoners to be constantly kept up, and from time to time corrected;—not based upon any external or arbitrary considerations, but upon character and conduct.

(*h.*) Provision to be made for securing a corps of judicious, trained, and, eventually, experienced keepers, for rendering their profession honorable and respectable; and, to this end, a special school for their training to be established.

(*i.*) A commutation of meritorious conduct and probable reformation for mere lapse of time, as the ground of final discharge. That is to say, convicts may earn their release by such evidence of meritorious conduct and habits as will imply their probable permanent reformation.

(*j.*) That there shall be, in the case of each convict, a certain time-sentence, graduated according to his offense, but, in each case, for a much longer period than at present, so as to leave full opportunity for the effect of the commutation and the working out of the reformatory process; premising that the ideal perfection of the plan, which makes the discharge of every prisoner absolutely dependent upon his reformation, would require too great a revolution in legal and popular ideas to be as yet expected or asked for.

(*k.*) Some definite and detailed record or system of marks to be kept, which, under fixed rules, may be a guide for classification and rewards, as well as for the final judgment; having a debit as well as a credit side, and providing for loss of standing and class, or even for a remanding to the cell, in case of misconduct.

(*l.*) Intermediate prisons or houses of discharge to be provided, where the prisoners—still remaining undischarged from their sentence—may be finally tested, by being trusted with a great degree of liberty, and left in large measure to control themselves, under most of the ordinary temptations of social life, yet liable, for unfaithfulness, for misconduct, or attempted escape, to be degraded and sent back to begin their work over again.

(*m.*) Refuges to be provided for released prisoners, to facilitate their re-introduction to the bosom of society, and where they can have, at their own expense, lodging and maintenance and means of employment, until they can procure employment elsewhere.

Such are the outlines of a general plan of criminal police and prison economy. It is by no means presumed that every point is unquestionably established, still less that the plan is complete for working purposes. No name is given to it of any system, whether old or new. It is not denominated the separate or the congregate or the mixed system, the English, the Irish, the Belgian, the Massachusetts, or the Pennsylvania system. It must stand, not upon the prejudices or the associations, whether favorable or unfavorable, connected with a *name*, but upon its own intrinsic merits, in detail as well as in gross. In view of these, then, it is respectfully submitted for dispassionate consideration. If it shall have the effect to awaken such an interest in the subject and its discussion as shall lead to systematic practical action, this board will be more than rewarded, more than satisfied.

What is especially needed in this matter is a well-considered, complete, and consistent system. Our whole scheme must be remodeled to meet the demands of the times, the state of our modern civilization, and the progressive ideas of free, popular government. Partial expedients and reforms lead only to eventual disappointment and discouragement. They are only a piece of new cloth patched upon an old garment, wasting the good and making the whole worse.

Such a complete system would, of course, require *unity of control.*

All the prisons and houses of detention in the Commonwealth, whether State, county, or municipal, should be placed under the supervision and direction of one head, or of one board of management, representing the authority of the State. In respect to all matters of prison construction and prison discipline, the county and municipal authorities should be required to act under the direction of this central and supreme authority.

That something must speedily be done in the path of reform seems to be beyond question. To judge of any mode of prison discipline, four tests have been proposed:—

1. Does it secure the *custody* of the convict?

2. Does it pay its own expenses?

3. Does it check and diminish crime?

4. Does it reform the criminal?

Of these tests the first is of prime importance as a necessary condition of all the others. If prisons are not secure they are useless for any purpose. The second test is of some incidental importance, but of no essential consequence. The third and fourth bring out the great objects of imprisonment. The fourth is of the highest importance, practically as well as morally, for on it the third also is largely dependent. Now our prisons, with a few exceptions, are places of secure custody, and so far our present system succeeds. But in view of the other three tests, and particularly of the last, we fear it must be pronounced a failure; and if so, where is the fault, and how can it be remedied? These are the questions to be earnestly pondered. We have endeavored, though in a very fragmentary and imperfect way, to show how they should be answered; and while our suggestions have been, for the most part, the result of our independent observation and reflection, and must stand upon their own merits, and no man's authority, it may yet be of interest to add that, according to the report of our highly respected fellow-citizen, Joseph R. Chandler, Esq., the International Prison Congress lately assembled in London reached the following propositions or general results, as stated in the concluding report of their executive committee:—

"*First.*—Recognizing, as a fundamental fact, that the protection of society is the object for which penal codes exist, the committee believe that this protection is not only consistent with, but absolutely demands, the enunciation of the principle, that the moral regeneration of the prisoner should be the *primary* aim of prison discipline.

"*Second.*—A progressive classification of prisoners should be adopted in all prisons.

"*Third.*—In the treatment of prisoners all disciplinary punishments that inflict unnecessary pain or humiliation should be abolished.

"*Fourth.*—To impel a prisoner to self-exertion should be the aim of systems of prison discipline, which can never be effective unless they succeed in gaining the will of the convict.

"*Fifth.*—*Work, education,* and *religion* are the three great forces on which prison administrators should rely."

The board conclude this branch of their report with earnestly and formally recommending to the legislature the prompt *appointment of a commission* of prudent and cautious men, learned in the law, fully abreast with the times, and imbued with the spirit of progress, as well as of conservation, who shall not only make thorough inquiry into the principles and practice of penal jurisprudence and prison economy, but shall be empowered and directed to revise all the existing statutes on these subjects, and to mature and present for adoption by the legislature a scheme of legislation based upon the principle of the *prevention* of crime, and the *reformation* of criminals, as its fundamental ends.

The board recommends the appointment of a special commission, not for merely making a report to be read and printed and forgotten; not for mere curious inquiry or idle investigation; but for *immediate practical action.*

Let Pennsylvania once more take the lead of the civilized world in this great and pressing reform.

All which is respectfully submitted.

By order of the board.

GEO. L. HARRISON,
President.

NOTE.

To show how far the views above set forth have approved themselves upon further investigation and experience, and to bring the state of the question down to the present time, the following brief statements are added:—

In Ireland, the progressive system of imprisonment is still prospering. Denmark has adopted it in its entirety. Sweden and Norway are pressing towards the same goal. Switzerland is following fast. In several of the cantons the whole system has been adopted, with the exception of the intermediate prison. Neufchâtel is upon the point of introducing it complete—intermediate prison, provisional or preparatory liberation, and all. In Italy, similar arrangements have been inaugurated. Progress in this direction has been made in England, especially in respect to the patronage of discharged prisoners. In Belgium and Holland, the cellular (separate) system still maintains its ground; though in Holland the progressive principle has found numerous adherents. In Germany and

Austria, the subject of prison economy and reform is undergoing a general investigation and discussion. The result cannot be doubtful. Great reforms have been made and are in progress in France and Russia. Several of the States of our own Union, and particularly New York, have been making great progress in the same direction. Pennsylvania, it must be acknowledged, has done little as yet to maintain or recover her ancient prestige.

At the meeting of the International Penitentiary Commission at Bruchsal (Baden), three questions were distinctly raised: (1) Can criminals be reformed? If so, (2) on what principles should reformatory treatment be based? (3) By what agencies or methods should such a system be worked? And they were distinctly answered in favor of the progressive system, as outlined in the foregoing report of 1872.

M. Guillaume, commissioned to prepare a draft for a penal system in several cantons of Switzerland; M. De Fleury, commissioned for a like purpose in Brazil; Messrs. Michaux and Marsangy, members of the great French parliamentary commission on penitentiary reform,—all, without consultation or concert, have, in elaborate reports, reached substantially the same conclusion.

1. Proper care and training of the young is premised in forefront of all measures for the prevention of crime.

2. Cellular separation is recommended for short terms of imprisonment, as a preliminary detention for long terms, and as an occasional corrective.

3. They all earnestly support, for long-term prisoners, a system of progressive classification, with labor and instruction, in which the fate of the criminal is largely placed in his own hands, and which is gradually relaxed and softened as he earns increased indulgence and privilege; until,

4. Through the intermediate prison, with little more than moral detention, he passes into

5. Conditional liberation, with kindly supervision; and thus, finally, to his complete discharge, a reformed and useful and happy man, "redeemed, regenerated, disenthralled."

The International Prison Congress in New York, in 1876, besides a general approval of these same principles in regard to the management of prisons and treatment of prisoners, very strongly and distinctly endorsed the views of this report, in the matter (1) of the imprisonment of witnesses, (2) of county jails, (3) of the treatment of discharged prisoners, and (4) of reformatory institutions, especially for juveniles.

PRISON REFORM.

In presenting again to your honorable bodies the subject of prison reform, the board ask for your thoughtful consideration of a question the most momentous and grave which can be laid before you.

Temporary matters of law or polity submitted for your decision, are in comparison but of local and superficial importance, but the problem of the lessening of the mass of crime and vice and ignorance in our penitentiaries and prisons and reformatory schools, the alleviation of the cankering sore, never to be cured in the body politic, is one which touches not only the moneyed interest, but the civilization, the vitality, and the religion of the state.

We have grown apathetic to the existence of the criminal classes. Nothing so dulls the moral sense as custom, and we have seen the barred windows of the county jail, or the massive walls of the penitentiary since childhood; have learned to look upon the miserable wretches behind their bolts and gratings as human beings, perhaps, but as alien to ourselves,—as creatures of another race and age.

These strongholds of misery, and the thieves and murderers who tenant them, have come to appear to us as commonplace, though inexorable a fact, as the ground on which the prisons are built. It is difficult for the best man actually to realize that he personally has a duty to fulfill to them. The thief, the murderer, the degraded woman, are here; but why they are here, by what strange mischance they missed their place in nature's wise economy in this life, or where they are to go when this life is over, are questions with which society has hitherto troubled itself too little. The ordinary citizen has no uneasy doubts that part of the guilt of their existence rests on himself, and shows no anxiety for their sake or his own, that they should be brought, if possible, to the same level of decency, honest living, and chance of elevation. If one of these wretches jars against his own orderly life, he promptly locks him in jail or penitentiary, or hangs him, and then washing his hands in self-righteousness, declares himself, like Pilate, "free from the blood of this man."

After a year, or term of years in prison (during which the orderly citizen is taxed for his support), the convict is released, to become, through crime or pauperism, a yet heavier burden upon the tax-payer, and hardened and embittered by punishment, to spread more widely his virulent moral poison.

Here, in plain words, is the ordinary history of the treatment of crime; and there is assuredly no function of government in which society has proved itself so willfully blind to its own interests, putting aside all question of humanity. When a fatal epidemic is abroad, doing its deadly work upon our bodies, all the skill and foresight and care which we can command are brought forward to foil or banish it. Municipalities and individuals alike bestir themselves with eager zeal to purify the air, to remove every trace of stagnant water, carrion, or other foul deposit which may breed disease; the medical science of the growth of centuries is summoned to detect the secret agents of these subtle poisons, and to counteract them. But since society was organized this contagion of crime, fatal alike to soul and body, has been at work, and what has been done to combat it?

The sole remedy suggested by the wisdom of ages was the locking up of the criminal, and at a given period, his release, with whetted appetite for his unwholesome work. It is precisely as though we should cover over a malarious swamp for a certain time until its vapors had gathered fresh malignant venom, and then set them free on their death-dealing errand.

It should be observed here that, in the examination of this question, we are not to consider special cases of wise and beneficent administration of prison or penitentiary; or on the other hand the most besotted and barbarous treatment; but we must look at the *general* character and condition of prison economy and discipline, as we find it in our own State, and as we know from personal observation or other knowledge that it exists anywhere.

We can point to examples of most just and creditable concern for the welfare of the incarcerated human beings under certain management, and again to the grossest neglect and abuse of these unhappy criminals in the other direction. It is the terrible fact that stares us in the face that, at least in every moral point of view, the latter is the general characteristic of the prisons of the whole world.

As a means of improvement in the administration of our own county jails, we strongly recommend now, as in the past, the enactment of a general law, which will take from the sheriffs of the counties the control of the prisons, and provide for boards of inspectors, who will appoint suitable persons as wardens to administer these institutions.

In consideration of the progress made by mankind in science and knowledge of every sort, the cruelty, and in many cases the barbarity, of its modes of dealing with crime appear almost incredible to the student of political economy. Something has been done within a few years to solve the problem with the broad and enlightened truths and sound practical sense which it deserves, but the success has been but meagre, consisting so far more of attempt than execution. That Pennsylvania may at least endeavor to keep pace with that little, is the motive of your board in bringing the subject thus urgently before your honorable bodies at the present time. We will summarize as briefly as possible the present status of the reformatory effort, and its desired promotion at your hands.

The motive idea of the treatment of criminals was, until a comparatively recent date, simply punitive and deterrent, not unmixed, in coarser grades of society, with the sentiment of revenge. The ill-doer was to be driven to repentance, or at least terrified from a repetition of his offense, by actual physical suffering. One hundred years ago this mode of treatment had reached its full development even in Christian Protestant England. Capital punishment was inflicted for two hundred different offenses; men were hanged for stealing a loaf of bread, for breaking a hop-pole, as certainly as for murder; debtors suffered the same treatment in the jails as other prisoners, and this treatment consisted in the herding of men and women promiscuously in cells reeking with filth, and wet with the foul damps oozing from the ground, with only an aperture of four inches by eight to admit the already poisoned air from the dark passage-way. "Debtors in gangs were padlocked by the leg to the different links of a long chain stapled to the wall, and at night the prisoners were laid on their backs and caged by iron bars passing over their bodies, while spiked iron collars about their necks prevented any movement of the head." The sole employment of these prisoners was gambling and drinking; a bar for prisoners being kept by every jailor, whose interest it was to lead them into debauchery and excess.

The labors of John Howard removed many of the abuses of this system. Prisoners no longer rot out half their lives in English and American prisons from inability to pay the extortionate demands of brutal keepers. They are not suffered to die in darkness, filth, and foul air, of jail-fever or starvation; but while the physical discipline is ameliorated by reason and humanity, the moral treatment in our jails is founded on the same principle as in the days of Howard. The prisoner is punished precisely as a dog is made to feel the lash to deter him from ill-doing, while no more attempt is made to convince him of his guilt, or to put in his hands the means, when discharged, of avoiding his evil courses, or gaining an honest livelihood, than if he were in reality a brute.

Even in the penitentiaries where the labor has been made part of the punitive and reformatory discipline, there is still large limit for reform. In many state prisons the contract or leasing system is in use, by which the convict is regarded simply as a money-making machine for the contractor.

In the most humanely governed of these institutions the application of moral influences is but occasional and unsystematic. The exhortations of a chaplain, however zealous and faithful, to several hundred prisoners, must necessarily prove less efficacious in prompting the individual convict to the exertions which will give him his lost place among honest men, than a legalized, unalterable system which will affect all his hourly and daily work and thoughts, and, through them, inspire with hope in the future and that faith in himself and in the humanity of his fellow-men, of which a long course of crime has robbed him.

There is such a system, conceived in the purest spirit of humanity, and based upon a profound knowledge of the needs and requirements of human nature. It has already been tested thoroughly, and we present, or rather re-present, a modification of this system for your consideration. Having submitted it heretofore with much amplification, we shall not dwell upon its details at any length, but touch only upon a few points. readily attainable, and which furnish a sure outlook, as we believe, to salutary results.

The ideal plan in its entirety is probably impracticable in the present condition of public sentiment. Its plain idea was to generate in the convict's mind the incitement of hope rather than the sullenness of despair, which is the slow outgrowth of an inevitable punishment. It was devised and partially carried into execution by Captain Maconochie in a penal colony in Australia, and the jail at Birmingham, England.

This method was briefly as follows:—The convict was not to be sentenced for any given time, but until he should have earned a certain number of marks according to his crime. These marks were given for good conduct, industry, neatness, &c. They were reckoned as money, and with them he was required to pay first for his clothing, food, &c.; out of the surplus only could he buy his release. The prisoner also passed through certain stages or conditions, being subjected at first to solitary confinement, low diet, absolute idleness, with but a small opportunity of gaining the marks of approval by his patience and obedience. The permission to labor was received as a relief. From this period the way lay open to him to earn better food, lodging, and, finally, freedom.

The principle of this method will, we are confident, be recognized by you as that which underlies every wise system of government. It is simply the attachment of inflexibly certain rewards and punishments to good and bad conduct. This is the outline of the great scheme of polity established by the Creator for His rational creatures in this life, and we can not assuredly act unwisely in imitating it, however feebly, in our dealings with those of our unfortunate brethren who, from mischance of birth or education, are thus made dependent upon us to gain their knowledge of Christianity, or faith in its teachings.

A modification of this system has been practiced for nearly twenty years in Ireland by Sir Walter Crofton. Here there are three prisons through which each convict passes. The first penal, with solitary confinement; the second reformatory, where the inmates are divided into classes, earning their advancements by good marks. "The majority of persons," we are told, "earn the maximum of marks and secure their promotion within the shortest period allowed." The third "prison" is in fact no prison, but an open farm, where there is neither bolt nor bar to prevent their escape, the detention being simply that of moral influence. Yet during the twenty years in which this experiment has been tried, not more than a dozen escapes have been made. Lusk, is, in fact, an intermediate halting-place, where the men have an opportunity to test the value of the moral and other teachings which they have received during their confinement. They work together, or singly, and "their constant thought is what they shall do when they are liberated, what wages they will be likely to obtain, how they can win honest bread and an honorable position." Nor in these twenty years has there been cause for a single complaint from any of the farmers living in the vicinage, although there is neither restraint nor discipline at Lusk other than that maintained over ordinary farm laborers.

We cite these facts as proof, if any is needed, of the wisdom and expediency of appealing to the more hopeful and higher elements of manhood in our dealings with even the most degraded of human beings.

Make treaty with the ill-doer as with a fellow-creature, and it is more than probable that he will stand to his agreement; but treat him as a brute and he will promptly fulfill your expectations by acting as a brute.

We have referred thus briefly to these experimental efforts for the reform of the dangerous classes, believing that Pennsylvania is fully aroused to the necessity of such efforts, and, through her legislature, is prepared to take a leading part in them. That the necessity is urgent, the very name given by popular consent to the class which we approach signifies, conveying at once their history and the ominous presage of their future. Nor is it only in this country that the grave attention of governments and of thoughtful men has been anxiously directed to this fatal element in the body politic. The International Prison Reform Congress, although it had its inception in the United States, numbered, also, at its late meeting in London, delegates (scientific and learned men,—experts in dealing with crime, and philanthropists) from every nation in Europe but one, and from Chili, Brazil, Australia, and India.

Nor need we wonder at the startled surprise and alarm with which the world regards the criminal member of, or rather outlaw from, society. At no period in history has his existence been so perilous to the best interests of civilization; never before has so much education been given to him, an education, however, abused for want of moral truth to guide or give it the proper direction. The criminal is no longer the brutalized boor of two centuries ago, whose passions, needs, and ambitions were almost wholly animal; he wears no collar of serfdom now, no ineffaceable mark of caste; he lives in an age when luxury is attainable by the most ignorant, by means of money; in an age when information is abroad in the air; when the incessant friction of man against man, the quick modes of transit and communication, offer opportunities for crime, and especially organized crime. To win money or power by any means other than that of slow, patient industry is the temptation that besets him at every turn. Civilization has put her aids and appliances into his hands without teaching him how to use them, and they become murderous weapons; and now civilization demands for her own sake what is to be done with him? How is he to be tamed and softened and brought to look at the world and God with clear rational comprehension of his relations to both? The time of his imprisonment is the only opportunity when society can work her wholesome regenerating will upon him; he is there unable to avert discipline, be it wise or foolish; he has proved the bitterness of evil-doing, and, whether remorseful or not, has learned that its wages are misery; he has reached, in short, a halting-place in his journey, where he is forced to look upon the two paths before him and to choose between them. Instruction or discipline from society to the free man must necessarily be infrequent, irregular, and unauthorized, but the convict is in the grasp of society as helpless as a child in its mother's hands. "He cannot choose but hear." The period of his imprisonment is the golden opportunity, therefore, to supply him with the moral truths which are lacking in his training: to teach him, through his daily habits, by the very necessities of his body for food and warmth, that labor—steady, faithful labor—is the only means by which comfort can be made certain and the respect of his fellow-man insured.

To this end we would strenuously urge that productive labor should be made sure and constant in every prison as a positive reformatory measure, and that the criminal shall be taught to regard it as a relief and a reward for meritorious conduct, rather than as a compulsory infliction; that the prisoner be taught some trade or handicraft (if he have not already skill in one), in order to qualify him for gaining on his discharge an honest livelihood; and, also, that he be given as far as practicable the elements of practical learning, accompanied always with such moral and religious instruction as shall give vital power to all knowledge.

In conjunction with this general scheme of training, that the treatment of each convict in detail should appeal to his higher rather than his lower nature, and develop the saving principles of self-respect and the recognition of a constant overruling power.

The proceeds of the labor of the convict to be used first to defray the expenses of the state on his behalf. In the New England States, where the contract system is generally used, the excess of earnings of the convicts over their expenses was $39,000, in 1871, Massachusetts reporting an annual excess ranging as high as $20,000 per annum. In Ohio the excess amounts to $40,000 per annum. When such gains as these are attainable, while the price paid *per capita* for contract labor is but from fifty to eighty cents a day, there would be, it is reasonable to conclude, a much larger surplusage if the prisoners were working with the knowledge that they were themselves to be the gainers by their industry. After the indemnity of the state from their earnings, we therefore suggest and respectfully urge that the remaining sum be appropriated—

1. To the convict's family, if such aid be necessary.

2. To form a sum in reserve for the use of the convict himself on his discharge. Many discharged prisoners are tempted to crime from the lack of means to support life until they can obtain work. It is almost impossible (with the prison ban upon him) for the discharged prisoner to find employment, and he is driven to steal by the actual necessity for food. The surplus of his own earnings would be a sure preventive of this

immediate peril. Nor do we perceive the justice of applying the product of the convict's labor to the service of the state, beyond the sum which indemnifies it for his maintenance. The punishment inflicted on him for his misdemeanor is imprisonment for a stated time and such hardships of lodging, fare, &c., as may be deemed suitable. To appropriate his earnings during that time (beyond the sum requisite for his maintenance) is to impose a fine upon him, in addition to the punishment of the body,—a fine not contemplated by law or embraced in his sentence.

Changes in the primitive and remedial systems such as we suggest are of necessity dependent upon you for execution, and once enforced will directly affect the condition of the convict without influence from the agents who are deputed to enforce them. But there is much of the treatment of the criminal, the mental and moral regimen which he shall receive from day to day, which depends wholly on the character, convictions, or even mood of his keeper. Laws devised with the profoundest knowledge of human nature and the broadest humanity, and schemes tempered with the tenderest charity, can be converted into cruelty by an unjust, vindictive, or even coarse jailor. Greater care should therefore be exercised in the choice of these officials; a certain standard of culture and moral attainment should be established by which their fitness for their duties may be measured.

Political usefulness, popularity, or brute strength are scarcely to be regarded as qualifications for the post of guardians over hospitals filled with the mentally and morally unsound,—invalids whose ailments are of the soul, and which require even wiser and more skillful and humane treatment than those of the body.

The appointment of women of discreet and cultured minds as visitors and supervisors of the female wards of our prisons, jails, and reformatory schools would, as we believe, tend much to their improvement. We do not conceive that this point requires argument other than those which will readily suggest themselves to every thoughtful mind.

The tenderness of nature, the intuitive sense of justice and fitness which characterize women, qualify them to detect disorder and discrepancies in the administration of any scheme of reform, while a certain tact and gentleness of expression enable them to approach the weak and erring with peculiar success. We owe our own improved method of dealing with crime and insanity largely to the counsel and suggestion of one good woman, and there are many others employed in practical work of prison reform in Europe with the most positive and enduring effect. There are many questions concerning the control and treatment of women prisoners, of which inspectors of an opposite sex can take but superficial view and incomplete cognizance. It is conceded that the prisoners should be under the management of a matron, and if it be proper that such control be accorded to women of inferior mental status, it is assuredly just and proper that the supervision of their labors should be placed in the hands of women of high character for intelligence and humanity.

We would call your attention, finally, to the successful labors of the Prison Reform Association, which had its birth in this country, although greater progress has been made in foreign countries in the wise and humane treatment of crime and pauperism than in the United States, and a larger amount of research and practical experiment have there been brought to bear on these difficult problems.

The formation of this association, for whose existence and development all praise is due to Dr. E. C. Wines, was the first step towards concentrating these separate discoveries and researches, giving them a world-wide publicity, and, by the force of union, endowing these hitherto scattered efforts of a few philanthropists with the dignity of a science and the authority and power of an international movement.

The conventions in London, Cincinnati, Baltimore, and St. Louis included men (eminent for their philanthropy) of widely-differing nationalities. The majority of members, too, were men employed for years in the management and supervision of prisons or institutions of reform, and the controllers of widely-extended schemes for the amelioration of the extreme conditions of humanity, whether those conditions be induced by crime or poverty.

The association, therefore, brings to the elucidation of these problems not only the most earnest, almost religious enthusiasm of the work of rehabilitating their fallen brethren, but a clear and long-tested knowledge of the most practical methods of accomplishing this work in both its outline and detail.

The reformatory scheme of work proposed by the members of this International Congress is, briefly:—

"Penal laws and institutions to be brought into fuller accord with reason and humanity.

"Police systems to be rendered so efficient that few criminals can escape detection and punishment.

"Crime capitalists to be hunted, dispersed, and crushed. Preventive agencies to be made so comprehensive and perfect as greatly to diminish the number of criminals.

"The mass of adult criminals to be brought to a healthier condition of mind and habit, and restored to the walks of useful industry."*

The association is, however, a council, not an executive body; a parliament without constituencies, unless we call such the weak and degraded of mankind, for whom it labors.

It can design and submit schemes of reform, but it remains for the governments of countries and of states to make them of practical benefit. The results of the conferences of this association are already apparent in many European states. In Switzerland, the congress in London aroused public attention to penal reform and effected a change in the constitution by which capital and corporal punishments were abolished.

A house of correction, a society for the care of discharged prisoners, an asylum for neglected and vicious children have been introduced in different cantons, while, in two, a modification of the Crofton plan has been adopted in their penitentiaries.

In Sweden radical changes in the penitentiary system have been made in accordance with the advanced views of the congress.

Discharged prisoners' associations have been formed, and two reformatory schools founded, modeled after

* Prison Congress, St. Louis, page 44.

the admirable institution at Mettray. To these last the royal family and nobility have contributed liberally.

In Italy an institution for the education of prison officers has been founded.

It was to his school for prison officers, it will be remembered, that Demetz owed his signal success in the reform of criminals.

In Holland a modification of the cellular system and other progressive measures of reform are now before the legislature.

In France an earnest interest in penal and preventive reform has been awakened by the congress.

Throughout the civilized world attention has been aroused and the minds of sincere, practical, and thoughtful men turned towards the most vital of all the problems which affect the well-being of humanity.

In the United States, where the movement originated (but which, as we have said, lags behind several other nations in her application of the best modes of reform), the endeavor of the association is at present to secure the erection of a national prison, to which shall be removed the convicts sentenced by United States courts, and where the association will be enabled to illustrate the highest and most successful system. Such a prison would offer an example which would doubtless be speedily imitated by the several States and by other governments.

It is in accordance with the general progressive movement in this reform throughout the world that we address you on the subject of the aid you have heretofore extended to the reformatory and other charitable institutions of the Commonwealth. Pennsylvania, through her late Constitutional Convention, has taken a retrogade step in this matter. The whole of her reformatory and charitable institutions, with the exception of the Eastern and Western Penitentiaries and the State Lunatic Hospitals at Harrisburg and Danville, are deprived of State aid unless it is given to them by a two-thirds vote of your houses. We appeal to you to support them liberally as heretofore; an appeal which we have little doubt will prove effectual. When nations which we have been accustomed to regard as but half-civilized urge the movement of reform, Pennsylvania will assuredly not resign herself passively to the government of the already encroaching forces of ignorance and crime.

We here present a descriptive table of the number of the several classes of "criminals" in the State. The statement may be relied upon as accurate:—

POPULATION OF THE CRIMINAL CLASSES.

The estimated population of the State on September 30th, 1874, is three million eight hundred and twenty-one thousand seven hundred and fifty-seven, and the following statement will exhibit the number of convicts in the penitentiaries, Allegheny county workhouse, and county jails or prisons; the number of persons under sentence of justices of peace; number awaiting trial and otherwise in prison on September 30th, 1874, the aggregate forming part of the above-estimated population:—

	Males.	Females.	Total.	Aggregate.
Convicts—In State penitentiaries, .	1,053	10	1,063	. . .
Workhouses, ...	134	9	143	. . .
County jails, ...	787	90	877	. . .
Total of convicts, ...			. . .	2,083
Otherwise in prison—In county jails for payment of fines and costs, &c., ...			. . .	67
Summarily convicted—In county jails, under sentence of justices of peace, ...			243	. . .
In workhouse, under sentence of justices of peace, ...			354	. . .
In house of correction, under sentence of justices of peace, ...			593	. . .
Total summarily convicted, ...			. . .	1,190
Awaiting trial in county jails, ...			. . .	449
Total in prison September 30th, 1874, ...			. . .	3,789

As above stated, the number of convicts in the penitentiaries, workhouses, and county jails on September 30th, 1874, was 2083, or one to 1835 of the population; 67 were in county prisons under sentence of court for payment of fine and costs, &c.; these can hardly be considered as convicts, and are not, therefore, included with them; 1190 were in prison, summarily convicted under sentence of magistrate or justices of peace, for disorderly conduct, breaches of peace, &c. The number awaiting trial on September 30th, 1874, was 449.

As the most powerful and direct method of combating these forces in society, we entreat your brief consideration of the subject of neglected and destitute children. (See Education, page 76.)

CARE OF THE INSANE.

INSANE HOSPITALS.

GENERAL REMARKS.

WE have shown, in a previous report, the "census" statistics of the insane in each county of the State, the total number in 1870 being stated at three thousand eight hundred and ninety-five; the ratio, one insane to nine hundred and four inhabitants. This enumeration, indeed, is not accurate—the fact being sufficiently proved by the impossible discrepancy which appears in a comparison of the several counties—the ratio varying from one in two thousand to one in twelve thousand, in places where there are no asylums for their reception. The general ratio is, of course, reduced by computing the insane in asylums, hospitals, &c. But erroneous as the statement is, falling short of the reality, it is sufficiently suggestive. It manifests the unhappy fact that the State makes provision for about one-fourth only of these hapless wards—to which, if we add the number cared for in incorporated or private hospitals, it will appear that at least five-eighths of these are in almshouses, or uncared for in any institution whatever. What the condition of the insane is, as a general rule, in the poor-houses of the State, we set forth clearly in our earliest report; and although there has been since then a manifest improvement in their condition and treatment, in several of the county establishments, it is impossible, from the circumstances which characterize the whole arrangement, discipline, and government of such institutions, that these invalids can be otherwise than grossly neglected and foully wronged; for *at the best* they are merely confined in places of detention, under the guardianship of a respectable overseer, who is wholly ignorant of their disease, and of the means necessary for its alleviation or its cure. We say, *at the best*. We hesitate to describe the reverse of the picture. It would exhibit a scene of as cheerless and uncomforted misery as the most bitter misanthrope could desire to look upon. It is hardly fair to claim that we have passed beyond the ignorance and barbarity of the middle ages, in our consideration and care of this class of unfortunates, so long as we suffer the glaring abuses which are prevalent in our midst to continue unredressed.

It is inconceivable to every reflecting mind, that abuses can be heaped upon the defenseless victims of this saddest of disorders, who should rather be the objects of the most spontaneous sympathy, and the most willing kindness and consideration. The fact that the chances of exposure are too remote to be estimated, and, as in the case of the child and the brute, that resistance is impossible, no doubt gives impunity to the foul wrong-doing which the insane frequently suffer. But the most fruitful cause of this evil is the incompetency of those who are set over them. It is an evil almost irremediable, under the present system of appointments in the county almshouses. It generally happens that these are based solely upon political considerations. Some useful partisan must be rewarded, or in some way helped, and he is given an office, the duties of which he feels in no wise called upon to discharge; having earned its perquisites by political services before he received it, and feeling his position secure, he is quite naturally led to neglect his trust, by ignoring its most essential requirements. Unfitness of the highest measure is the character of such appointments generally; and the victims in this case are a class of defenseless invalids, whose circumstances appeal with especial urgency to every sentiment of humanity and justice. This mode of appointment should be abolished, rather than extended, and we earnestly invoke the action of your honorable bodies to revoke all legislation which favors it. The institutions established by the State and the counties at so great a cost, and supported from year to year by large expenditure of the public funds, extracted often by onerous taxation, should be managed after a principle which will secure those objects, to accomplish which they were respectively founded. Wherever this does not obtain, just so far have waste and failure been realized instead of gain and success. This may not always be apparent to the general observation, for we are not quick to scrutinize matters of this nature; but the results will not be questioned if the premises are well-founded, and it needs but slight investigation to establish the verity of our report in this behalf. The same danger exists, though much more remotely, in establishments specially designed for the reception and cure of the insane; and we consider it to be the solemn duty of the superintendents of all institutions for this class, *to know*, from patient investigation and inquiry into the antecedents of the applicants, that none are employed for nurses or attendants who are not adapted to the service, by the characters they possess for patience and forbearance and strict conscientiousness. They should also take pains to instruct them in their duties, and should know they are fulfilled. We think that a clear responsibility rests upon the directing head of every institution, *to know* that his subordinates fulfill their proper duties. If the appointments are not allowed to them, it would seem that the danger of ignorance and incompetency is greater, and, therefore, closer scrutiny becomes essential. But superintendents should have the authority, at least, to nominate their subordinates. They know better than others the requisites for the office; and the responsibility would be felt and authority more readily maintained.

Inattention to these requirements has subjected institutions of hitherto high repute to severe public odium, not in our own but in other communities, and it is a just cause for condemnation. We shrink at the recital of occasional cruelties visited upon malefactors, even where insubordination or other grievous misconduct has merited punishment; and philanthropy is expending itself largely in contriving schemes of punishment for crime, by which the offender may be saved from wanton cruelties; but for these, innocent victims of a providential dispensation,—the chief causes of whose mental derangement have been "anxieties, domestic griefs, reverses of fortune,"—the trust of the general public in the effective and humane protection provided in any asylum where they may be placed, seems fixed and unwavering. We believe that the State and private institutions of this Commonwealth are commendably free from the reproach we have suggested. We are familiar with their workings. We know the direction of all of them with entire familiarity, and we respect the earnest humanity and high intelligence which characterizes them; but we cannot too firmly impress even upon these the supreme necessity of insisting, for themselves and for those to whom they owe their appointment, upon the employment of subordinates of every degree who have the ability and the disposition to carry out the instructions which they receive from their superiors. The very fact that seclusion from the public eye is the characteristic of these institutions should be the strongest influence with high-minded and conscientious men to interpose the broadest shield of gentleness and humanity between their wards and the slightest injustice. Insanity should have a better and a truer name than madness. To "mistake ideas for truths" does not mean so much as this; and although such perversion not infrequently influences the patient to dangerous violence, it is equally true that this irritation may be tranquilized and subdued by quiet, firm, judicious gentleness. Scarcely any are wholly insane. There exists somewhere, and almost invariably, a phase of their intellect which is not clouded, and their delusions do not even unfit them always for the ordinary duties of life.

We think we have a right to present this class of defectives in a favorable light. The general view exposes them unfairly to the public eye; and that eye is too well satisfied to look complacently upon the house of detention in which they reside as the *summum bonum* for all their needs. Houses of detention, simply as such, misrepresent the real demand of an enlightened public mind, in relation to all classes of unfortunates. They ignore the principle of the dignity of the human *person*, which should govern the consideration of these classes. This discrimination is lost whenever the thought prevails that the chief good to be attained is to restrain—to save the public, in some sort, from inconvenience or damage or depredation. This should surely be looked after and secured; but its complete attainment may be better accomplished by considering, at the same time, the duty of humanity in the care and custody of every class of defectives. There are noble examples and exponents of this theory, in this age, in all parts of the civilized world, and nowhere more devoted to its realization than in our own country and in our own State; and we believe that a very large number of the insane in this Commonwealth are not only skillfully, but tenderly treated. But this is not so in many of the county poor-houses. They have neither the accommodations nor the medical care which are suited to their wants. They are, for the most part, wholly uncared for. Beyond the mere provision of sustenance, often unfit and insufficient, they are kept immured in cells (sometimes naked and often in indescribable filthiness), or tied to their cots, or intimidated by fear of punishment, to save the trouble and expense of adequate oversight. They are in the hands of attendants as unfit to minister to them as they would be to govern a vessel in a hurricane; and so they are stranded or wrecked for want of good and skillful management. The condition of such as these is little better than the sad lot of the same class whose misfortune it was to exist during what we call the "middle ages"; and, indeed, to the time when Pinel set the splendid example of liberating from mechanical restraints the inmates of the Bicêtre hospital, at Paris,—one of whom had been in chains for forty years,—and which was the first great step in the amelioration of the condition of the insane. But are not the ignorance and stolidity and want of principle which so often characterize the attendants who *now* have charge of the insane, or perhaps their inaptitude and inexperience, practically equivalent to the barbarous practices of the same class who were their custodians in the dark ages? It is true they are not now "chained in the lowest dungeons," but they are confined, and often bound, in loathsome rooms. They are not "systematically beaten with the lash, by direction of the most approved authorities," but they are often punished by a process much more painful and fatal, and frequently upon the slightest provocation. They are not "exhibited for money, like wild beasts," but they are brought forth from their beds at midnight to dance and make grotesque displays for the entertainment of the guests of their custodians. They are even statedly assembled, once a week, to amuse the public at a maniac's ball.

The following case will stand for one of many similar performances at county poor-houses; and, as recent testimony proves, in establishments of higher pretensions. It is the case of a maniac, whose condition there was so alarming that his removal to an insane hospital was ordered. The physician of the latter institution states that the patient was brought to the hospital in a cart, with his limbs restrained. He was feeble, but greatly excited. His condition at the time of admission was so distressed that the usual practice of bathing and re-clothing was dispensed with, and, after administering a sedative, he was put to bed. As soon as it could be done, an examination was made, and numerous injuries to his person were apparent; but his exhaustion increased, and it was impossible to ascertain the whole extent of his injuries. On the eighth day the patient died, when an autopsy was made, and the sternum and nine ribs were found to be broken; accumulations of pus were discovered in various places, and extensive bruises of the most serious nature. Such was the condition of this insane man, poor, perhaps, and friendless, but, nevertheless, a man and a citizen, when transferred from an almshouse to a State hospital.

We cannot better express our own opinions on this theme than by quoting the strictures of a journalist upon recent abuses, fully proved in a neighboring institution:—"One of the noblest results of civilization has undoubtedly been the care and protection extended to the insane. There is something so touching in the spectacle of human beings deprived of their reason that every one of right feeling must extend to them the deepest sympathy. This sympathy brought about the establishment of hospitals where the insane could be properly cared for and sheltered from the dangers that beset them. It was hoped that through the instrumentality of these institutions these unfortunates would escape the neglect and brutality to which they were exposed. This, at least, has been the popular idea in connection with the guardianship of the insane provided for by the public. But, however humane may be the intention of the community in creating these refuges, the brutality of the persons selected as 'attendants' entirely neutralizes the benevolent motive and turns them into places of torture, from which death is looked on as a welcome release by the sufferers. It would be idle to waste words on the brutes in the shape of men, who are capable of inflicting torture and suffering on their fellow-creatures. So long as the present vicious system is continued, the abuses will go on unchecked; and it is only when some act of cruelty has been followed by fatal results that public attention will be directed from the whirl of business and politics and for the moment visit the offense with a generous indignation."

It is a matter of history that even Egypt of old knew and fulfilled her duty better towards these unfortunates, and that her "priests" provided faithfully for their comfort and enjoyment. Music, games, and recreations,—in short, whatever modern ingenuity has devised to charm the diseased mind, was in vogue in this "earlier age." And in ancient Greece one of the most distinguished alienists recommended that bodily restraint should be avoided; that none but the most violent should be restrained.

We conclude this part of our report on this subject

by presenting the wise conclusions of another, which may well be entertained and realized by those who have responsibilities to discharge in relation to this interesting and serious matter:—

"The patients of an asylum for the insane should be surrounded by *experienced attendants*, allowed the greatest liberty, and treated with the utmost amount of indulgence compatible with their safety. The free use of their limbs and abundant exercise in the open air tend to carry off the superfluous energy and excitement of the malady. Everything which can employ and interest a healthy mind, and which is apart in its character and association from the morbid thoughts of the patient, ought to be brought into exercise for his recovery—judiciously adapted to each case; for the insane hospital should be the isolation and safety of the dangerous; a retreat and home for the hopeless and incurable; a hospital for their restoration to mental and physical health; a house for mental, moral, and physical education; an industrial establishment, where the busy crafts of artisans and gardeners and all the homely employments which can occupy the heads and hands of men and women, are called into systematic and daily activity. Everything should be avoided which would give the idea of a prison. They should be made to feel themselves happy and contented in the prosecution of some purpose which carries their mind away from the subject of their disease, and which is adapted to their capacities, their natural tastes, or the peculiar phase of their malady. The qualifications of the medical superintendent—and every insane asylum should have such an officer—are, indeed, of the rarest kind, but they are indispensable. He must unite benevolence with firmness. He must be good and humane and, also, just and inflexible—courageous and calm, tempering firmness with severity and kindness with decision and impartiality. He must have the tact to govern others with ease, to acquire their confidence and esteem, and, at the same time, to command their ready obedience and respect. Combined with these general qualifications, he must be skilled in his own profession in all its departments, so as to give the advantage of enlightened professional skill to the medical treatment of his patients."

These requisites seem difficult to command; but if the natural elements are not wanting, the rest may be acquired. And the same principle and the same rule should apply here which we have insisted upon in our notice of a different class of institutions. Almost the whole hope of successful management of any one of them depends upon the suitableness of the directing head of the establishment. The power which appoints this officer should see to it that he understands and appreciates his work and its responsibilities. In such case there is small chance of his subordinates being ignorant or neglectful of their duties.

The law of commitment to an insane asylum would seem to need revision. If it were carried out according to its spirit, it might be sufficiently protective of the rights of the citizen, of which it behooves us to be strictly jealous. This law provides "that insane persons may be placed in a hospital for the insane by their legal guardians, or by their relatives or friends in case they have no guardians, but never without the certificate of two or more reputable physicans, after a personal examination, made within one week of the date thereof, and this certificate to be duly acknowledged and sworn to or affirmed before some magistrate or judicial officer, who shall certify to the genuineness of the signature and to the respectability of the signers."

In the first place, the medical test is clearly insufficient. If the two "reputable" physicians were in good repute as alienists, there would be reason in submitting to their judgment the liberty of a citizen. But it is well known that insanity is the most unfamiliar of all maladies; that there is no chair in our schools for instruction in this branch of medical science; that it has always been a special study, and that not one in a hundred of the "reputable physicians" know anything about it, which should entitle them to the authority conferred on them by the law. Still, we have instances where commitments have been made by doctors *by diploma*, who never had a patient of any sort to prescribe for, unless dentists be physicians, or chiropodists be classed with surgeons.

We would not cater to the sensational apprehensions of careless thinkers on this subject. We do not believe that in our State there is at this time much real danger, in this behalf, to the freedom of any sane person; for we happen to be favored with enlightened experts in each of the important institutions, private and public, of the State, who would undoubtedly take means to redress a wrong perpetrated either by ignorance or design. Still it is necessary to provide for contingencies, and if the medical test is even uncertain, the importance of amending it will be admitted without reserve, for the authority is final when the requirements of the law are even formally complied with, and the "adjudged" lunatic must be received into the lunatic wards.

The legal examination is equally unreliable. There is no evidence received in behalf of the restrained person. The charge is almost uniformly taken for granted, and the "lunatic" almost never seen by the magistrate. The reason is that the magistrate is quite unable, of himself, to pass judgment on the case, and he does not embarrass himself by the attempt.

We would, under these circumstances, recommend that a lunacy commission, in each county, be appointed by the officers of the medical society in conjunction with the superintendents of the State hospitals for the insane, which shall be substituted for the "two reputable physicians" required by the present law; and that the magistrate be held to a penalty unless he complies literally with the provisions which are set forth for his action in the premises. In the counties where medical societies are not organized, that the commissioners be appointed by the superintendents alone. In cases of sudden and violent mania, temporary detention in a hospital should be provided for,—the requirements of the law to be complied with within reasonable time thereafter.

Safe as we may fairly regard ourselves, it should be our aim to improve, by the example of our legislation and our practice under it, the insufficiency of what prevails in other States as well as to add to our own security. We may thus effectually bar the personal liberty of every citizen against unjust invasion.

It is a superstition resulting from ignorant credulity, which *takes for granted* every accusation of lunacy, and which regards the disclaimer of the accused as added evidence of his mental alienation.

Provision being made for present security, in obvious cases of mania, it cannot be denied that the doubtful should be held in suspense until adequate judgment be pronounced ; especially when the accused denies the charge and demands investigation by an arbitrament capable of pronouncing an intelligent decision. The most perverted and chronic criminal can claim this right, and the bare possibility of mistake should secure it for those whose liberty may be innocently lost.

We called the attention of your honorable bodies to the condition of the insane poor in the first words we addressed to you.

We did not speak in terms of reproach of the public or the legislature, because there had been, until then, no official commission, expressly delegated by your own authority, to investigate their condition and make suggestions of amendment. We then recommended that the insane should be always under the care of a medical superintendent ; that no recent case be admitted into an almshouse ; that the State hospitals be adequately extended that all might be provided for. But we are concerned lest the unwillingness of the last legislature to appropriate the money needed to complete even so much of the hospital for the insane at Danville as would utilize the expenditures already made there, and, what is more important, open a door for the reception of the large number of insane demanding admission, indicates a serious unconcern in relation to this class of unfortunates, or a want of appreciation of their claims upon the State's attention. We earnestly renew our request to your honorable bodies to furnish, with as little delay as possible, the hospital room urgently needed for the accommodation of all the insane of the Commonwealth, excepting only those who are received into private hospitals, or cared for by the larger cities, who propose to provide for the insane of their particular localities.

We are prepared, upon a call of either branch of the legislature, to report upon the whole subject, stating the numbers and condition of this class; how they are now circumstanced; what proportion are probably chronic and what curable cases; what additional accommodations are needed, and, if required, a scheme for realizing the demand which is made upon the State for the complete fulfillment of this imperative duty.

It is a question with those who make the subject a particular study, whether the incurable insane should or should not be separately provided for, and many specialists have given their opinion that the interests of the class, as a whole, would be better maintained by associating them in general hospitals for the insane. It is not our intention to discuss this question at this time; what we declare now, we are entirely clear about, namely, that it is a reproach to the boasted liberality, humanity, and civilization of our honored State, that such of her unhappy children as we refer to, should be consigned to the hopeless wretchedness which they suffer, and that it becomes us, without delay, to apply an effectual remedy. It may be well, in this connection, to set forth the measures which the great State of New York has adopted to relieve this crying evil, and by which it is certain that every insane man, woman, and child will, within a reasonable time, be provided with a hospital home, furnished with every requisite for its intelligent administration and management. The fixed policy of that State is to separate the chronic insane poor from the recent and curable cases.

A select committee of the senate, appointed for this purpose, made report in 1856 as follows:—"That as insanity is a disease, which, in all its forms and stages requires special means for the care and treatment of its victims, the policy of the State to provide for their safety, comfort, and care, when possible, is as wise as it is humane. The duty of the government, thus to provide for its insane, is acknowledged in all civilized countries.

"That the State should make ample and suitable provision for all its insane not in a condition to reside in private families.

"That no insane person should be treated, or in any way taken care of in any county poor or alms house, or other receptacle provided for, or in which paupers are maintained or supported."

It is a well-established principle that the insane cannot recover amid the ordinary circumstances and influences of home, but they must be removed from familiar associations and scenes to others which are new and strange to them. This disease, instead of being a malady necessarily consigning its victims to despair of recovery is, under favorable circumstances, the most curable of diseases.

Authorities upon the statistics of insanity state the results of proper hospital treatment at about seventy-five per cent. of recent cases in favor of recovery. It is stated in a memorial to the legislature, emanating from high official authority and medical experience on the subject, that it may be expected that one in every one thousand six hundred and ninety persons in Pennsylvania will yearly become insane, and that under an adequate system of treatment three-fourths of these will annually recover, and the remainder become hopelessly incurable. That, in the absence of such a system, not over seven per cent. would recover, and the remainder sink into hopeless incurability. The perfect accuracy of the estimate is not material, it is sufficiently correct to sustain our argument. The calculation can be readily made as to how the pecuniary interests of the State would be affected in the two cases, and whatever modification was made in the interests of the insane would proportionally advance the interests of the State, so that it can be easily inferred that the insane become a public burden because of the neglect of timely medical treatment. There is nothing more true than that the State or the county must pay for the support of the sufferer during life, unless suitable provision for cure and treatment induce timely restoration. It is, therefore, no more than the common wisdom that is applied to the ordinary business of life, to take such measures as will give them the best opportunity of restoration that the age affords.

Assurances such as these, which could not fail to impress the mind of every intelligent man to conviction, induced the New York Legislature to pass an act instituting a commission to investigate the condition of the insane poor in the various poor-houses, almshouses, and insane asylums, and other institutions where the insane are kept. The condition of the insane poor in the counties of New York was, in a word, pronounced "deplorable," and their report was the origin and base of what is called the Willard asylum for the insane, taking its name from the author of the report. The law in reference to this subject was passed in 1865, and its title declares it to be "an act to authorize the establishment of a State asylum for the chronic insane poor."

The intent of the law was further stated to be the removal of every insane pauper from every county poor-house to the Willard asylum, or to the State lunatic hospitals,—to the latter the recent or curable, and to the former the chronic or incurable cases.

There has been no retreat from this determination on the part of this great Commonwealth; but an extensive hospital has been built on a farm of about five hundred acres, admirably located for health and beauty, and the most liberal appropriations have been continuously made by the legislature for the full development of the policy and intent of the law, by which every one of the insane poor shall, in due time, be properly provided for.

The policy of separating the curable from the chronic need not enter into discussion. The point is, to furnish hospital accommodations for this class, and the legislature can investigate the subject through a separate commission, or through the agency of this board. Since the existence of the Board of Public Charities of the State of New York, viz., since 1868, it has been the organ of communication with the legislature. Its last report on this subject declares that no further provision need be made for founding a new insane hospital; that when those now in course of construction are completed, in accordance with the plans, provision will be secured for every insane person in the Commonwealth of New York. State of Pennsylvania, go and do likewise!

PLEA FOR THE INSANE.

Insanity in its relation to legislation and jurisprudence, as well as to mental, moral, and medical science, to its characteristics and the mode of determining its presence, as well as the method of treatment for its cure, to the best means of protecting society against its violent or mischievous assaults, as well as to the claims upon our humane regard and sympathy, is a subject of great difficulty, but, at the same time, of commensurate interest and importance.

It is not easy to give a clear definition of insanity, and when we attempt it, the danger is that we run into one extreme or another, and either allow none to be insane but the raving maniac, or make all insane who commit anything foolish or wrong. But we need not attempt a definition here.

Whenever the condition of the raving maniac is so far approximated, and the reason so far disordered or dethroned, that the apprehension of the distinction between right and wrong is lost, either wholly and in all relations, or partially and in relation to some particular subjects, then insanity so far exists as to demand to be specially recognized by the administration of justice, in the means to be provided for the protection of society, and in determining the treatment due to those who are its subjects.

The diagnosis of such cases we may leave to experts, and the determination of the facts to the proper officials, judges, or juries. We have nothing here to do with the question of insanity as it is presented to the psychologist or to a petit jury or to a commission *de lunatico inquirendo*, or to a board of medical examiners. In the cases to which we propose to call attention, we assume the fact of insanity to be established, and then, looking at the insane man afterwards, we inquire what is to be done.

But we must protest, at the outset, against a certain form of mistaken feeling which, we suspect, may very generally exist; we refer to the disposition to regard all persons who, being charged with crime, are acquitted on the ground of insanity, as at least highly suspicious characters, to be classed with criminals without reserve, because it happens that the greatest criminals so often seek to evade the punishment due to their crimes by setting up the plea of insanity.

But this sweeping generalization is no more reasonable—especially in the case of the poor, who have no powerful friends to work for them, and cannot pay liberal fees for an elaborate defense—than it would be to regard all men as criminals and suspicious characters who are charged with any crime, however clearly their innocence may be demonstrated; for this plea of insanity is, by no means, the only plea which is abused for the protection of knavery and violence.

As to the specious modern plea of moral insanity, either it must be absolutely rejected, or, to be consistent, all administration of penal jurisprudence must be abandoned. Any insanity that can be recognized in law, must include a derangement or loss of the *rational* faculties, and by such derangement or loss it must be measured. A "moral insanity" which consists merely in an abnormal violence of vicious propensities, or of some particular vicious propensity, while yet the light of reason remains unabridged, and the conscious moral judgment is clear and distinct, is only another expression either for diabolical wickedness, or for the ordinary condition of human temptation.

But, waiving all such discussions, the subject which we desire to present to the practical consideration of the legislature is this: *What public provision should be made for the care and treatment of the insane, especially of the insane poor*, including those who have been convicted of crime or charged with its commission?

In order to a clear exposition and apprehension of the subject which we thus desire to present, it will be advisable, and even necessary, to analyze it, and to distribute the insane into their several classes, with reference to the end we have in view,—to the public provision to be made for their safe-keeping, care, and treatment. With this view, the insane may be distributed into three different classes:—

1. Those who have done no violence or public harm—the ordinary insane. These, again, fall into

two sub-classes:—1. The harmless, or those from whom no harm is feared. 2. The harmful—those with manifestly dangerous and destructive propensities.

2. Those who have done harm—have committed crime—while sane, but (1) have become insane before trial or conviction; or (2) have become insane after conviction,—"insane convicts" in the strict legal sense.

3. Those who, having done harm—having committed acts of violence or mischief—have been acquitted of crime on the ground of insanity.

And first, of the insane who have done no harm. Among these, the insanity may vary in character and degree from some simple special hallucination down to complete *dementia.* It may include both sexes and all ages; may proceed from a variety of causes, moral and physical, may be recent or may have become chronic, may be more or less violent or dangerous, may be curable in various degrees, or may be absolutely incurable. These varieties may call for various medical classifications and modifications of treatment, all of which we leave to medical men to arrange and determine. The classification which more directly concerns us, viewing the subject in its relation to the demand for legislative interposition or State aid, is—

1. Those who have the means of support, and

2. Those who are dependent and destitute.

The first class can be cared for, either at home by their friends, or at private asylums established for the purpose. The only occasion for legislative interposition in their behalf is, to see that they have proper guardianship to secure them in the possession and right use of their property. And the only occasion for such interposition for the protection of the community in this regard is, on the one hand, to see that friends, who undertake their guardianship, do not neglect it to the peril of the community, or abuse it to the detriment of the sufferer; and, on the other hand, to provide lest by the criminal collusion or interested misjudgment of relations and physicians, any sane person should, under certain circumstances of helplessness or exposure, be condemned to the living death of incarceration in some private hospital for the insane,—a fate next in horror to that of being buried alive. As to what legislation is required in relation to this class, we have only to refer to the suggestions presented in our last report.

But, however important the claims of this class may be upon the public consideration, they are as nothing in comparison with those of the other class of the harmless insane, viz., the destitute and dependent.

To these and their sad fate we beg once more, respectfully, but most earnestly, to urge the serious and special attention of the legislature. In our former reports, we have not overlooked the claims of these helpless victims of the sorest of human maladies; but, in the discharge of our official duty, we have repeatedly, though hitherto, perhaps, without sufficient fullness and emphasis, presented those claims to the consideration of the legislature, and we now beg to refer to our former statements and suggestions on this subject.

In our report for 1870:—"More especially do we wish to denounce the cruel wrongs which the insane suffer who are inmates of almshouses. These institutions are generally wholly unsuitable for their care or even detention; or, if suitable, are presided over by persons who are entirely ignorant of the needs of this class of the sick and infirm, and whose administration is based on the crudest ideas of mental disease; it is limited to the discovery of the most available methods of preventing them from harming anything or any person but themselves. We could instance the most glaring abuses, not as we believe intentionally inflicted, but the result of incapacity and ignorance. The time has gone by when a disturbed imagination or a disordered intellect should be held to have converted its human victim into a distempered brute, whose home should be akin to the sty or the stable, and whose lightest restraint should be perpetual incarceration within the limits of a cell. These wrongs demand prompt redress. No hospital for the insane should remain without the constant supervision of a medical superintendent. The stewards of almshouses are never selected from any consideration of the needs of the insane."

The report was also accompanied with the following formal resolutions of the board:—

"*Resolved*, That the Board of Public Charities, having witnessed the evils which result from the connection of insane asylums with almshouses, and believing that a wrong is done to the insane by classing them with paupers, hindering the public from estimating aright their claims to sympathy and remedial treatment, disapprove of such an alliance, and believe that the best interests of this afflicted class of people and the duty of the State, concur in the establishment by the State, within a reasonable time, of sufficient accommodations for the maintenance and treatment of all the insane who may not be cared for in private hospitals.

"*Resolved*, That in the judgment of the board all superintendents of hospitals of the insane should be members of the medical profession."

In 1871 the following from our general agent was laid before the legislature:—

"In some of our prisons cases of insanity are found which ought to be transferred to hospitals established for the maintenance and treatment of this class of persons. In the course of my inspection of these institutions, as will be seen by a reference to my report, instances of this character have been noticed. It occasionally happens that insane persons have to be, at least temporarily, committed to a prison; but few cases can arise where this necessity exists for any great length of time. If they have been arrested for a crime, the law has made ample provision for a proper disposition of them without a protracted confinement in a county jail, and the sooner they are removed therefrom the better, whether their incarceration is the result of crime or merely for the purpose of safe-keeping. All the better feelings of humanity, as well as a sound philanthropy, concur in this sentiment.

"Among the various defects in our poor-houses

none are to be more deplored than that which relates to the provision made for the insane. Scarcely one can be mentioned which is not deficient in this particular. The sexes, as the custom is in the other departments, are frequently allowed to mingle together; few have suitable accommodations for their comfort, and even in the best of them there is a lack of sufficient attendance. New buildings have been erected in several counties with a view to increased facilities for the support of this class, but even here, in some cases, persons have been selected who have no experience and but little qualification for the duties to which they have been assigned.

"The attention which I have given to this grave subject induces me to believe that all cases of an acute character should be placed in one of the public institutions which have been established in the State, city, or county, with a view to their treatment. To place a recent case where no suitable medical treatment or other proper attendance can be had, is either simply to leave it to nature or facilitate its passage into a chronic condition. To render an institution suitable for the successful management of such cases, nearly all the means essential for such a purpose are wanting. A proper construction of the building, where a favorable classification of the inmates can be maintained; where all the modern improvements for in-door comforts and amusements and out-door exercise and recreation, and where competent medical and other attendance can always be procured, are necessary to attain the great object in view—a restoration to health and a sound mind.

"For the most part all that can be expected in our county almshouses is to secure such provision for the chronic and incurable insane as will meet the demands of a Christian humanity. To confine them in close and badly-ventilated apartments, with scarcely any of the comforts which an enlightened philanthropy would suggest—a condition in which they are too often found—manifests such a failure of duty as to bring odium and shame upon the civilization of the age.

"In New York, a State institution was established in 1865, under the name of the Willard Asylum for the Insane, for the reception, care, and treatment of the chronic insane poor, who were then provided for in the several county poor-houses in the State. This institution is reported to be in successful operation. Whether the plan of separating this class of insane from the more acute and hopeful cases, and keeping them in different institutions, is best adapted to the successful treatment of the insane population, is a question much discussed among experts of the present day. The medical superintendents of our insane hospitals, after a full and able discussion of the subject, came to the conclusion that such a classification would be detrimental to the interests of both classes. With such able authority against such a measure, I am not prepared to endorse the action of the New York Legislature, but prefer to leave the subject for further experience, and the candid consideration of philanthopists."

As to the statistics in regard to this class of unfortunates, this board hereby renews the offer made last year:—"We are prepared, upon a call of either branch of the legislature, to report upon the whole subject, stating the numbers and condition of this class, how they are circumstanced, what proportion are probably chronic and what curable cases, what additional accommodations are needed, and, if required, a scheme for realizing the demand which is made upon the State for the complete fulfillment of this imperative duty."

But as to the number of helpless sufferers, these dependent wards of the State, we may say beforehand, and without reference to statistics, that, if the number is some thousands, their moral claim upon the State, as a matter of simple duty on her part, is multiplied so many thousand fold; and if the number is small, there is the less excuse for shrinking from the performance of that duty—for making proper and complete provision for the care and treatment of them all.

If these persons are to be allowed to live among us, if they are not to be left, some to starve and perish, and others to spread their mischief far and wide, it is for the interest of the State that public provision should be made for their detention and maintenance; and if they are to be detained and supported at the public expense, it is for the interest—the palpable pecuniary interest—of the State that they should have appropriate and comfortable accommodations, kind supervision, and the most patient and skillful curative treatment. This may be demonstrated in a few words. We may take two facts as well ascertained, and we believe they are admitted without a dissenting voice, first, that under care and skillful treatment, as in our best hospitals, about seventy-five per cent. of recent cases of insanity will be cured in the first six or twelve months; second, in poor-houses not more than seven per cent. will be cured in the first year. Assuming these premises, and making the expense of each patient in the hospital twice what it would be in the almshouse, the gain in the first instance, under hospital treatment, is simply enormous. But this is not all. There are likely to be more cures afterwards under the skillful treatment than under the other. But suppose there were not, and that all the remaining cases were incurable, there would remain, on one side, ninety-three incurables to be maintained for life, and, on the other, twenty-five; and if the ratio of expense were still double, the result would be in favor of hospital treatment as fifty to ninety-three. That is to say, the latter method would be a continual saving to the State for many subsequent years of more than forty-six per cent. per annum. Nor is this all. It must be remembered that the greater part of the insane poor owe their poverty to their insanity, and not their insanity to their poverty; and that, in losing their power to support themselves, they have lost, also, in a very large proportion of cases, the power to support families more or less numerous, who thus become dependent upon the public for their maintenance. The restored maniac resumes not only the enjoyment of a man's consciousness but of a man's activity—the power of self-support; and not only of this, but of supporting by his industry those dependent upon him; and every man who, by his enterprise, skill, and labor, supports himself and family, contributes also to the support of other men and their families. Such are the economical advantages accruing to the State from a proper treatment of the insane poor and their consequent restoration to mental health.

But these unfortunate persons have claims upon the State higher far than mere considerations of economy. They are her wards, and she is bound by the dictates of simple justice and imperative duty to secure to them that humane, watchful, and patient care, and that skillful treatment which will give the best promise of their speedy restoration. If she choose to put them out of the way, like noxious beasts, or to let them alone to starve and die, she might say that charity and philanthropy were no part of her mission, and ask who made her their keeper. But when she has laid her hand upon them, put them in places of restraint and detention, and taken control and charge of them, *she has made herself their keeper*, and has bound herself so to treat them as shall most conduce to their future well-being as well as to her own.

As to their actual condition in our county poor-houses or prisons, we do not propose to weary the patience or offend the sensibilities of the honorable members of the legislature by the renewed recital of the more than three-times-thrice-told tale of the woes and sufferings of this sorely-stricken class of our fellow-citizens. That the story, with all its touching and terrible details, ranging from the intensely sad to the unspeakably horrible, should have been so often repeated, and yet the evil remain to so large a degree unremedied, instead of exciting our impatience, should rouse our shame, and provoke us to immediate and energetic action. The story can never grow old or worn, as long as the subject-matter itself remains a fresh and living reality. There is but one voice in this case. No intelligent person has ever made a general visitation of the prisons and almshouses of this State without being startled and almost overwhelmed by the forlorn and hopeless, and sometimes horrible, condition of their insane inmates. Those who some years since made a similar visitation in the State of New York, pronounced their condition "deplorable," and that State forthwith determined to apply an effectual remedy. The impression made upon this board by similar visitations in our own State, have been laid before the legislature in our reports from year to year. The shocking and sickening revelations, so graphically set forth in the memorial of Miss Dix, presented to the legislature of 1845, are not yet obsolete. There have been some improvements since made in some of these places. In the Philadelphia almshouse, since then, there has been a great reform; and in several other counties, well-constructed hospitals for the sick and insane have heen built; but, with one or two exceptions, there is no special medical supervision or paid attendance at all. But in most parts of the State that condition remains now substantially the same as then. Indeed, without a total revolution of the system, it is impossible greatly to improve it. There may be grave faults in the management in these poor-houses, some of which might be remedied, and others are probably incapable of remedy; but the great cause, the fundamental cause of the evil, is in the system itself. If the administration was made as perfect as human infirmity allows, if the best superintendents or wardens and the most faithful attendants were secured, while the evil might be mitigated, it would remain substantially the same, until the system itself is changed. The remedy is not reform, but revolution.

We take leave to insert here the report made in the course of the present year by a member of this board, of his personal inspection of one of our county poor-houses:—

"With respect to the strictly pauper department of this almshouse, it bore a resemblance to other establishments. There was a scene of listless idleness and uselessness, without any superintending care. My attention was particularly directed by the general agent to the hospital for the insane, which was a separate building, upon the same ground with the other departments of the almshouse. I found these inmates suffering for the want of almost every attention and consideration which are necessary to make life, even to the strong and hardy, tolerable. They have sufficient food, such as it is, at stated intervals, and the cells they occupy are furnished generally with a rough bed and bed-clothes. These cells, too, are *tolerably* clean, for the cleaning of an establishment such as this can be done without much difficulty, because there is always a sufficient number of paupers to do the work. Where the insane patients are considered violent or even disagreeable, it often happens that their cells are either neglected, or forcible measures are resorted to for the purpose of overcoming their interference, while their cells are being cleaned by the paupers. Though the board had previously called the attention of the directors of this institution to the imperfect ventilation of the insane hospital, I found that even the means available for correcting the cause of this complaint had been very imperfectly attended to. The consequence was that the atmosphere of most of the cells had become so vitiated and offensive that any person accustomed to the open air would necessarily have fainted upon remaining within the apartment for a moment of time. The inmates seemed to have become used to this noxious atmosphere, and they did not complain of it. On the contrary, the only complaint on their part was that made by an old woman, when her window was lowered a little to admit the fresh air.

"The responsibility for this chronic neglect of these classes begins with the public and ends with the humblest attendant of the institution. So lost to all sense of decency have the insane of this hospital become, by reason of the failure on the part of those in authority to encourage a proper appreciation of self-respect among the inmates, that their habits are precisely like those of a brute. Consequently many of them are kept naked in their cells, from which they are drawn out each morning to be cleaned and their rooms put in order. The filthiest part of the litter—for their bedding consists wholly of straw—is then removed and its place supplied with a similar quantity of the fresh material, when they are returned to their disgusting dens, there to pass another period of solitary wretchedness in an atmosphere whose odor exceeds in offensiveness anything which the imagination can conceive. Through the gradual enfeebling of the higher attributes of their natures, some of these people come to be regarded by the other inmates as mere animals, and the young girls of the establishment look upon these naked men simply as they would look upon a horse or a hog. I am told that frequently two of the young female inmates of this insane hospital are called upon to clean these men each morning as they are drawn out from their cells."

The following statement of the condition of the insane in another poor-house, is given on the well-sustained authority of another member of the board:—

"In February last, a visit was paid this almshouse, and an insane inmate was seen,—a young woman over twenty years of age, whose whole dress consisted of a thin chemise with short sleeves, a single skirt, and a pair of shoes. When brought before the visitors a borrowed cloak was thrown over her shoulders. She was blue with cold and utterly filthy in person. Her cell had the appearance of having undergone a recent hasty washing, but was pervaded with an odor loathsome in the extreme. On the day of this visit the thermometer fell to fourteen degrees.

"In March another visit was paid to the institution by several gentlemen in a body. Only one portion of the building was visited, which is supposed to be devoted exclusively to women. In one cell was a young woman, the one already referred to. Her cell was without any furniture whatever, her bed consisted of one blanket, her clothing a ragged chemise open to her waist, and one scanty skirt and a pair of shoes. She was indescribably unclean, and alive with vermin. Her cell reeked with a sickening odor, the result of a total absence of all conveniences of cleanliness. She shivered with cold, while in the presence of her visitors, the thermometer standing, at the time, several degrees below the freezing point.

"Opposite to the cell, which we have very faintly described, was another. The short day had already faded into dusk, and as the light was thrown through a little aperture in the door, it fell upon two wretched women, both of whom were absolutely without a single garment to cover them. One of the poor creatures sat crouching in the corner with a small blanket drawn across her shoulders, while the other was crawling on all fours on the floor, without even this poor apology of any remnant of human decency! There was not a particle of furniture in the cell; and there, on this wintry March night, in an atmosphere which the witnesses declare to have been utterly horrible, were these two human beings, brought down far below the level of our domestic brutes.

"In an adjoining cell the visitors found a man lying on an old mattress, the only sign of furniture which they saw in either of the rooms inspected. They were informed that the inmate was a woman, but upon one of the gentlemen calling to him, he sat up, and it was seen that it was a man. The attendant, with some confusion, explained that he must have been brought in while he was away.

"We found the female insane department in a shocking condition; so bad that it would be impossible to give a description of the place on paper. In some cells there were two or more women confined, some without any clothing, lying on the floor without mattress, carpet, or anything else, except an old Government blanket. The place had a horrible, putrid odor.

"We examined one woman who was quite young. I was afraid to go near her, as she seemed covered with vermin. We were all much shocked by the visit, and I think I shall remember it as long as I live."

And the general agent reports the following amongst many similar instances of abuses and neglect in the same establishments :—

"Insane totally neglected morally, physically, and medically; less attention is given to them than would be given to the lowest animals ; four are, incapable of self-care, confined in filthy cells; one, a female, has great neighborhood notoriety, from sad incidents connected with her history; known as an intelligent, esteemed, and attractive young lady, the daughter of a well-known inhabitant of the neighborhood, she fell a victim to the arts of the seducer. Insanity is alleged to be caused by her disappointment. This occurred twenty-one years ago. The sad case is rendered still more painful by her present forlorn condition. A bed of straw upon a damp, dirty floor, into which the external light can find no entrance, is the only furniture. A seat, a chair, or a bench, has apparently never been furnished; the consequence of which is, that the muscles of the lower extremities, from the cramped position in which she was always found, have become permanently contracted, so that the only movement of which she is capable is one similar to that of a frog."

"An unusually large number of insane, many of chronic form, but quite a number of strongly-marked cases, who were confined and had been chained to the floor until released by my direction. A young girl of seventeen years of age, confined in a gloomy cell, since removed, by my request, to the State hospital, where she is gradually being restored."

"Twenty-two insane, twelve are kept in close confinement, some in chains; one always chained to the ceiling to prevent him from tearing his clothes; some entirely nude; at least six with straw litters; not one of the twelve was ever removed into the open air. All confined in apartments opposite each other, a narrow corridor extending between them. The effect of this close proximity was to make the day and night hideous with the distressing shrieks and yells of the wretched and maltreated madmen.

"Eight insane, one of whom hand-cuffed, one hoppled; one female confined to her room."

"One hundred and thirty-five inmates, four blind, one palsied, seven idiots; seven cells in the basement, with insane in each, in a revolting condition."

"Twenty insane; of these about eight were confined, not to their uncomfortable cells only, but restrained by iron fetters, long after the necessity had passed away. These were removed at my instigation, and the doors of their cells were opened, to give them the benefit of the open air and exercise, with decided improvement in their condition."

There are two difficulties in the way of checking these and similar abominations: one is the unwillingness of the directors of the poor to make expenditures for the comfort and well-being of the classes committed to their charge. They employ a steward, whose principal requisite is that he shall be a good farmer, and whose attention must be given mainly to the farm of the institution, which may be, in extent, from one hundred to four hundred acres. As a consequence, the care and supervision of the human beings over whom this "steward" is placed are lost sight of, to a great degree, in the apparently more important business of the farm, and are generally committed to the oversight of the paupers themselves. This is one evil. The other is apparent in the very unsuitable arrangement and construction in which the most helpless inmates—we mean the insane—are placed. In these structures it is a rare thing to find the sexes at all adequately separated, and, generally, they have no airing grounds, or even yards, to which the patients can repair and refresh themselves during the day. Therefore they must remain in seclusion within their cells, from the beginning to the end of the year, existing in an atmosphere of great impurity, and constantly deteriorating in their mental and physical condition.

In order to make the work of the board effective, a certain amount of executive power should be granted to it, as has recently been conferred upon the New York Board of Public Charities by the legislature of that State. The public seem to be satisfied with *houses of detention.* To get the various classes of unfortunates out of sight seems to be the main object. The consequence is, that, as a general rule, the prison is better than the poor-house as a receptacle for the insane.

We may lay it down as a principle, at length become too plain to be controverted, indeed, as a point admitted on all hands, that poor-houses are not, and cannot be made, fit places for the care and treatment of the insane. That they may receive proper treatment with any hope of recovery, they must be placed in hospitals or asylums, especially constructed and fitted up for their accommodation, with cheerful scenes within and cheerful scenery around, with skilled medical supervision and carefully selected and well-trained attendants; none of which conditions can be commanded in, or in connection with, an ordinary county poor-house. In connection with so large an establishment as the Philadelphia almshouse, where are gathered nearly one-half of all the pauper population of the State, a separate hospital of the required character may be provided and supported; and we commend the humane and earnest spirit which is engaged in two or three of the larger communities, as, for instance, Berks and Lancaster counties, in making adequate provision for their insane. But in connection with the smaller almshouses of the several counties, and still more in connection with the township arrangements for the care of the poor, such separate hospital accommodations are out of the question. They will never be established, and, if they were, they could not be maintained.

It will naturally be asked here, whether the State has not already established one or more general hospitals for the care of the insane, with a view to meeting this precise difficulty? She has; and established them, professedly, for this very class of the insane whose case we are now considering,—for the insane poor, the insane who had been or are liable to be gathered into the almshouses, or sent for safe-keeping to the prisons, in the several counties. The State has established these hospitals at no little expense; but a very small percentage of the "poor" insane are now in them; the great mass still remain in their former wretched, forlorn, and hopeless quarters, a spectacle of misery or a butt of derision; and an element of disturbance and irritation to the rest of the inmates. To the hospital at

Harrisburg there were committed by the public authorities and courts during the year 1872, sixty-one poor patients; and one hundred and thirty-eight "paying" patients were sent there by "friends." And of the four hundred and eight remaining on December 31st, 1872, there were one hundred and seventy-nine supported by "public authorities," and two hundred and twenty-nine by "friends of patients." Again, of the one hundred and sixteen patients committed to this hospital during the nine months ending September 30th, 1873, eighty-four were "paying" and only thirty-two public or indigent insane patients.

Now it is manifest from the memoral of Miss Dix, in response to which the State hospital was established, and by the express words of the law of 1845, coeval with its establishment, that the original design of the hospital was what that of any such hospital ought, in all reason, to be,—to provide for the insane poor.

The law, section twenty-five, declares that, in order of admission the "poor" shall have precedence of the "rich," defined throughout the act "paying patients," and while the finances of the State do not permit ample provision for all cases of insanity, recent cases shall have precedence over cases of long standing. If, under this law, the whole capacity of the hospital were devoted to the "poor," no objection, perhaps, could be made to sending away the incurable, after a reasonable period of trial, to make room for recent cases; although it does not appear that such was the intention of the law, which seems to have merely laid down a "rule" to govern the order of admission to vacancies as they should be found to exist. But how should it happen that a majority of the inmates of this State institution should be "paying patients"?

How happens it that during the year 1872 sixty-nine per cent. of the patients admitted were paying patients, and only thirty-one per cent. public patients, and of those admitted during the nine months ending September 30th, 1873, the paying patients should increase to seventy-two per cent., with corresponding reduction of public patients to twenty-eight per cent.? Again, that at the close of the year. 1872, this hospital should be occupied with fifty-five per cent. of paying patients, and at the end of September 30th, 1873, with fifty-six per cent. of the same class?

It is said that the incurables are sent away to make room for recent cases. But upon what authority? And, besides, if those sent to the hospital by their friends are recent and curable cases, in a larger proportion than the others, how comes it that a smaller percentage of these are discharged during the year? Or, if they are incurable in a large proportion than those committed by the public authorities, why are they not sent away in still greater proportion than the others, instead of being discharged in still less proportion? Or, rather, why are they not *all sent away;* or rather kept away, as long as any of the others remain unprovided for? We understand that, as a general rule, those committed to this hospital by the county authorities, if not "speedily" cured, are sent back to the helpless and hopeless life-doom of the poor-houses. On the other hand, it is evident that "paying" patients may stay as long, apparently, as their comfort and the convenience of their friends require, and their means suffice for their support. Now we cannot but regard all this as a gross public wrong. The State has erected hospitals, *not for the "rich," but for the "poor;"* or, for the rich, only when the poor should all be provided for. There is no need, even if it were right, that the State should erect hospitals at the public expense and out of the public taxes, for the accommodation of the rich; they can or they will provide hospitals for themselves, including persons of moderate means as well as of considerable wealth. We maintain that the entire capacity of the State hospitals should be appropriated to the poor patients, before any such are refused admission or sent away under any pretext whatever. The hospital at Dixmont, though a *private* charitable corporation, and only aided by the State, comes much nearer to our idea of the duty and the intention of the State in this regard than that at Harrisburg. At the former, there remained, at the close of the year 1872, only one hundred and seventeen private patients out of a total of four hundred and forty-six; and on September 30th, 1873, only 23.89 per cent. of "paying" patients, or one hundred and eight out of a total of four hundred and fifty-two.

And again, of the one hundred and sixteen patients received into the State hospital, at Harrisburg, during the nine months ending September 30th, 1873, eighty-four, or nearly three-fourths, were "paying" patients; while for the same period out of one hundred and seventy-three patients admitted to the hospital at Dixmont, only seventy-two, or about two-fifths, were "paying" patients. In other words, 30.79 per cent. more *private* patients were received into the State hospital for the "insane poor," at Harrisburg, than into the private hospital for the insane (aided by the State) at Dixmont.

It may be said, and perhaps with truth, that in many cases the friends of insane patients who can furnish the smaller sum required at the State hospital for their support would not be able to meet the heavier charges of a private asylum; and that, therefore, such insane patients must be thus admitted at the hospital or sent to the poor-house. This idea seems highly plausible and might at first receive favor from inconsiderate persons. But upon reflection it clearly appears unsound in theory; and upon experience it proves highly objectionable. If these patients are *poor* why should precisely this class of poor patients have precedence of those who are still poorer? And if they are rich, as by the terms of the statute all "paying" patients are, then the law expressly gives the poor the precedence over them. Besides all these middle measures of giving public aid to the poor are found in practice to be dangerous and liable to great abuses on the part both of the recipients and the almoners of the public bounty. This case has proved itself in our judgment no exception to the general rule.

It may be suggested that it has been thought well to have some *paying* patients in order to give respectability to the institution.

We can scarcely listen to the suggestion with patience or answer it with calmness. If all the poor were already provided for and accommodated the suggestion might pass, although we should not make it. We should never propose that the State should tax herself to furnish hospital accommodations to the rich in any case, whether by way of gratuity or of profitable speculation. But that is not the case. The poor are not all enjoying the care and treatment of the hospitals; and shall they by the hundred and the thousand continue to languish into idiocy or rave out their miserable lives in the cells of prisons with malefactors and felons, or in the more foul and wretched and hopeless receptacles of county poor-houses, in order that the hospital, which receives a few score of them, may be respectable, and its superintendents and officers may not find themselves in charge of an institution of mere paupers?

But, finally, it may be said, as a partial explanation of the great comparative rapidity with which the poor who are committed to the hospital are sent away, that a large part of them—those committed by the courts—are persons charged with crime who have been acquitted on the ground of insanity. Under the present law this explanation must to a certain extent be accepted; but as these persons do not fall under the general class of the insane now under consideration, viz., those who have done no harm and are free from any charge of crime, their case is reserved for consideration in the sequel.

In the class of harmless insane we include, it will be remembered, all those who are legally charged with no acts of mischief, violence, or crime; as well, therefore, those from whom such acts may be apprehended as those who, from their apparently gentle and inoffensive habits, are the objects of no such fear. Whether there be any of the insane so entirely harmless that they can be trusted with absolute confidence, needing no special watch or restraint, some have doubted, and we need not decide or discuss the question; for, in our clear judgment, there is no good reason why those who may need greater degrees of watchful care and restraint should not be treated in the same establishments with those who may need less, especially as the distinction is merely one of varying degrees. Even those who exhibit the greatest developments of insane cunning for mischief or are subject to the fiercest paroxysms of violence or even of homicidal impulse, may be kept, with proper classifications and internal arrangements, in the same institution with patients of the greatest gentleness and quietness of temper and demeanor. At all events, the proper hospital, with its more skillful superintendence and its more varied and thorough appliances, is, of all others, precisely the place for the former class; for in poor-houses they can scarcely be kept at all, except as wild beasts, and prisons are not places to which justice or humanity can doom the innocent and helpless madman, however violent or dangerous. Yet are not such poor, defenseless unfortunates, if adjudged too dangerous to go at large and pronounced not curable, habitually sent to rave and rot in the foul dens of a poor-house or in the dungeons of a prison, there to be classed with robbers and murderers?

The importance of having the State hospitals for the insane subjected in this and in other respects to the supervision of some party not connected with the immediate management, so that the rights of the poor may be more surely, steadily, and systematically protected, we reserve for fuller consideration further on. But we cannot omit to observe here, that the State hospitals for the insane poor were not devised originally at the suggestion of *experts*, but upon the pains-taking investigations and earnest petitions of Miss Dix and other benevolent persons; and it is highly reasonable that their management, particularly as regards the receiving and discharging of patients, should be placed under the visitorial power of disinterested parties, concerned only in securing the good to be derived from them for the defenseless insane poor. It is not to be supposed, however, that, under any management, sufficient provision has yet been made in our State hospitals for all the insane poor in the Commonwealth.

Such provision ought to be made with all possible dispatch. To propose to make it is no wild or visionary or extravagant scheme. It can be made in Pennsylvania as well as in New York. As we have already shown, if we are to take care of the insane poor at all at the public expense, the most economical method, irrespective of the demands of humanity, is to gather them into well-managed hospitals, instead of leaving them to linger out a miserable existence, hopeless of restoration, in prisons and poor-houses.

We proceed now to consider the case of the two other classes of the insane.

II. Those who, while sane, have committed acts of violence or crime, but have either

1. Become insane before arraignment, and so have never been tried; or,

2. Have become insane after conviction—insane convicts.

III. Those who were insane at the time of committing such acts, and who, therefore, have been acquitted of crime on the ground of their insanity. These fall into various sub-divisions to be mentioned hereafter.

The two classes (1) those who stand charged or convicted of committing acts of violence or mischief *while sane;* and (2) those who, although charged with crime for the commission of such acts, have been acquitted on the ground of insanity at the time of their commission, we place together, not to identify or confound them under any such denomination as "criminal insane," but rather in order the more emphatically to contra-distinguish them.

We begin with the case of the first of these classes; and the question is, what disposition is to be made of the insane who stand charged with, or have been convicted of, crime. And first of those who may, with some propriety, be called "the criminal insane," *i. e.*, those who are charged with the commission of crime while sane, but who have become insane before arraignment; and who, consequently, have never been convicted or tried. Their case is a somewhat delicate one in a legal as well as a moral point of view. According to legal principles, it would seem that their detention cannot be regarded as a punishment, for they are not to be presumed guilty because they are charged with crime, nor until they are found guilty upon trial and proof; but in their present condition they are not capable of pleading, and, of course, cannot be put upon their trial. Both as accused and as dangerous persons, they may properly be kept under detention and restraint; but neither in fact nor in feeling are they to be classed with felons or looked upon as tainted with crime, or as suffering a penalty. The fact of their present lunacy may be ascertained and established without the intervention of a jury, by the court itself, or by a commission appointed for the purpose; but their having committed the criminal acts laid to their charge, and having committed them in a sound state of mind, can be ascertained and determined only by the intervention and verdict of a jury; and any investigation or inquiry in that direction, instituted without such intervention, and without a hearing of the defendant, must necessarily be merely *ex parte*. And it is but the natural course of things, when a poor, friendless man, in his squalor and raggedness, is arraigned before a court, under the charge of some atrocious crime, accompanied by the confident allegation that, whatever may be his present mental condition, he was sane up to and at the time of the commission of the acts charged against him—it is but the natural course of things, that such a man is easily believed and presumed to be guilty; and as society must at all events be protected from his violence, whether sane or insane, he is consigned, side by side, with the convicts and felons, to the safe-keeping of a prison cell.

But surely this ought not to be so—in all reason it ought not to be so. The State owes it to her own self-respect, to her own sense of justice, if not to her sentiments of humanity, not to consign to the odium and punishment of crime, one of her citizens whose guilt has never been duly ascertained. What then shall be done with such persons? That is a serious question, and we shall endeavor to answer it. But, for the present, we only say, what is clear in the face of the matter, that they ought not to be placed in prison, or in any department of a prison; and they ought to be placed where they not only will be effectually restrained from doing harm, but where they will have the best curative treatment, and the best prospect of being restored from their fearful malady.

The case of insane convicts—that is, of those who become insane after conviction and while undergoing the punishment of crime—is different from the foregoing in several important particulars. For these the question of guilt is presumed to have been duly ascertained, and that they are suffering a just punishment, but in the midst of it the mind loses its balance, and they become lunatics. Supposing this point to be ascertained and admitted—and the feigning of madness is pretty easily detected—then they are no longer responsible beings; they are no longer proper subjects of prison discipline. It is utterly unreasonable and unjust, as well as inhuman, to continue to inflict punishment on a maniac, who neither knows the reason, nor the end, nor the idea of rightful punishment. It is as absurd as to inflict indignities or violence upon the dead body of a criminal; it is even more malignant, for the dead body has no sense of pain, but the maniac has.

Besides, the State owes it to these helpless beings, who, while under her enforced control and guardianship, have been smitten down with the most terrible of maladies—owes it to them as a mere matter of right,—to give them the most skillful and promising curative treatment in her power, to save them, if possible, from confirmed and permanent mania or imbecility. To suffer a convict to become, from neglect, an incurable lunatic is worse, unspeakably worse, than to dismiss him, at the expiration of his sentence, bereft of sight or hearing, or crippled by loss of limbs, or under some chronic bodily disease, in consequence of a reckless neglect of the proper medical care and treatment at the proper time. These irremediable losses and disabilities formed no part of his sentence.

The State is bound, so far as she reasonably can, to discharge the convict, at the close of his term of punishment, in at least as good a condition—mental, moral, and physical—as that in which she received him. And, for failing in this, it will not do to seek an excuse in the small number, or the unworthy character of those who may suffer the wrong. The State, the very fountain of justice, she who takes it upon herself to punish wrongs, is bound to do no wrong even to one, and that one the meanest and most undeserving of her citizens. If there are but few convicts who need surgical or medical treatment, whether for bodily or mental diseases, so much the less excuse is there, at least on the ground of economy, for neglecting them.

Nor is this all. Even of those who are strictly insane convicts in the legal sense, and it is of those only we are now treating, *i. e.*, of those who have been convicted of crime, as having been sane both at the time of the commission and the conviction, but being found insane afterwards,—even of these it would be easy to show that by far the larger number were probably insane before conviction, and even at the time of the commission of the alleged offense. It is the rich and respectable offender, who has friends and money, who can fee lawyers, who can procure and array a crowd of witnesses in his behalf, who can protract his trial, clog the wheels of justice, and make interest by his audacity—it is he who too often escapes from merited punishment under a mistaken verdict of insanity. But the poor friendless man, who has been seized in some terrible act of atrocity, though committed under the impulse of actual insanity, is swiftly arraigned; and, having nobody of any consideration or influence who personally cares for him to stand by him or advise him; without testimony, and, from his very unsoundness of mind, perhaps, neither caring nor knowing how to procure it; the evidence against him ample and clear, his defense provided by the court being merely professional and perfunctory, and, of course, under such circumstances, both hasty and imperfect, he is forthwith convicted and sentenced to the penitentiary or the gallows. That this is no fancy picture, but a familiar matter of fact, is established by an abundance of proof. The uniform testimony of those who have charge of jails and penitentiaries is, that almost all the so-called insane convicts under their charge were insane when brought to prison, and so were almost certainly insane when tried, and probably so when they committed the offenses for which they were convicted.

Dr. Compton, in charge of the State Lunatic Asylum of Mississippi, says:—"My own experience with insane criminals leads me to feel rather charitable towards them. I have had only three, and there have been circumstances connected with each of these cases which lead me to think they were insane before committing the crime."

Of the eighteen prisoners reported insane in the Eastern Penitentiary in 1852, the inspectors declare that "three had been placed in the penitentiary for safe-keeping only, and not for crime, and had already been confined in its cells—one nearly three, one over three, and one over seven years! Eleven of the remaining fifteen were more or less insane when they were received into the penitentiary, two of the others became so a few months after, one a year, and one about four years after his reception. It will thus be seen that a large proportion were insane in a greater or less degree when first sentenced to the penitentiary, and all but one or two of the rest developed it shortly after. The observation and experience of the inspectors have convinced them that the commission of crime is more frequently connected with mental disease than courts and juries (far less the public) suspect: hence the necessity of a prompt removal of all, who are found to be thus afflicted, to a place where proper treatment may restore them to mental health, and, as a consequence, to moral rectitude." Nor did this state of affairs cease at a later period. In their report for 1862, the inspectors repeat that "there are yearly received into this penitentiary insane convicts, insane or of diseased mental condition, on their admission." And again, in 1863:—"The inspectors again ask the legislature to require the State Lunatic Asylum to take insane convicts, or to make an appropriation for their medical treatment in the penitentiary. When so many convicts are known to be insane on reception into this prison, this course is wise, humane, and necessary."

There are now about twenty of these "insane criminals" in the two penitentiaries, all of whom, according to the reports of the wardens, were insane or imbecile when received there. We insert here the report of Mr. Townsend, warden of the Eastern Penitentiary, made on this subject in October last, and also that of Captain Wright, warden of the Western Penitentiary, made on November 24th.

REPORT OF WARDEN TOWNSEND.

"E. S. PENITENTIARY, October 24th, 1873.

"*To George L. Harrison, Esq.*,
"*President of the Board of State Charities,*

"DEAR SIR:—I sent you a list, some time ago, of eleven persons confined in this penitentiary who were more or less insane. Since that time one has died, and one was pardoned by the governor of the State, leaving now in confinement nine. The one who was pardoned is now an inmate of an insane asylum. The nine who remain were all noted on our physician's book as '*insane*,' or '*mentally unsound*,' at the time of admission. One was sent here *twenty-three years* and *ten months* ago, charged with assault and battery with intent to kill, and sentenced, not for a term of years, but for safe-keeping; he is a harmless imbecile. One was sent here from Luzerne county for ten years, on a charge of burglary and larceny. The object seemed to be to rid the neighborhood of a troublesome fellow. One sent from Northampton county for ten years on charge of rape. One from Bradford county, charged with child-murder, holding his own child under water, to see the effect of it, thus proving the insanity of the act; his sentence is twelve years. A woman from Luzerne county, for shooting her husband, sentenced to eleven years and eleven months. She is very crazy, and not a fit subject for penitentiary discipline.

"One woman on several charges of larceny, sentenced to nine years. This woman has been an inmate of an insane asylum. One from Luzerne county, for 'injury to railroad.' He piled lumber on the road to see how it would be scattered by the engine (a crazy man's trick). One from Philadelphia, for aggravated assault and battery, sentenced to seven years, very weak-minded on admission, and easily provoked to violence. One from Philadelphia, for wife-murder, sentence ten years; insane on admission. These individuals have received such care and attention as we were enabled to give them, but we have no accommodations for insane patients—*no* rooms larger than the ordinary cells. They have had such medical care as our resident physician was able to give them, but we have no suitable nurses, nor places for any. I consider it very improper, very unkind, very cruel, to send insane persons to a jail or penitentiary. It is almost certain to fasten the malady upon them, until it becomes irremediable. A hospital, with hospital appliances, is the only place for these poor stricken ones.

"I think that a hospital for the insane should not be

connected in any way with a prison, but be entirely separate, and under separate administration.

"Could not a part of the Danville Asylum be thus used?

"Hoping these interrogatories are sufficiently answered, I remain, very truly and respectfully, thy friend,

"EDWARD TOWNSEND,
"*Warden.*"

Report of Warden Wright.

"Allegheny, Pa., November 24th, 1873.

"*Geo. L. Harrison, Esq.*,
"*President of Board of Public Charities*,

"Dear Sir:—In your letter of 17th of October, you request that I give you my views on the subject of the treatment of the criminal insane confined in penitentiaries and jails.

"The subject has often been referred to in the annual reports of this penitentiary, and the inspectors, in their report for 1844, say:—'If, in the present pecuniary embarrassment of the Commonwealth, you cannot erect and endow a State asylum for the insane, we must urge upon you the propriety and necessity of authorizing us to establish, within the prison walls, a hospital for the reception of the limited number of demented convicts which may unhappily come under our supervision. The occurrence is rare that they become so after they enter the penitentiary; but, in many instances, they are sent here after the commission of crime, because there is no other barrier to protect society from their demoniac depredations. There is a convict of this character now immured in one of our cells, for such is the sentence of the law. He came here in this lamentable condition.' In the report for 1857 it is said, 'convicts are often sent here whose proper destination should be the State Lunatic Hospital. Why they are sent here, whether for the purpose of supposed relief to the treasury of the county from which they come; from culpable ignorance of the law regulating the State Lunatic Asylum, or from the suggestion, flattering to us, that we will take good care of them, and that society at large will be exempt from the dangers incident to a too close proximity to madmen; it is a practice alike contrary to the policy of the law and the dictates of humanity.'

"I have thus far made up, as briefly as practicable, from our own reports, evidence that insanity has proven no bar to conviction and confinement in the penitentiary, and do not doubt further evidence could be given showing that harmless imbecile prisoners have been received and discharged without further record than such as was given to other prisoners.

"As having a direct bearing upon the views expressed in a former report, that prisons are often used as asylums, the following extract from the report of the warden of the Eastern Penitentiary, for the year 1871, bears pertinent testimony:—'Men are frequently sent to this penitentary who are not fit subjects for its discipline. During the year four men were received who were quite insane when admitted; one in unsound mind; and four of weak intellect. One of these insane prisoners died of tetanus, resulting from injuries inflicted upon himself shortly after his reception, and another committed suicide in one month after he came here. Of the nine hundred and eleven confined in 1871, twelve were insane when admitted; four of unsound mind; two feeble-minded, and thirty-six of weak intellect, bordering on idiocy.'

"In the annual report of the Eastern Penitentiary for 1872, it is stated that two hundred and twenty-six convicts were received during the year, of whom one was of unsound mind, four were weak-minded, fifteen were dull, and two doubtful, making nearly ten per cent. of impaired intellect. Of the two hundred and seventeen convicts discharged, one insane died, two were weak-minded, and thirteen were dull, being nearly seven and a half per cent. of the discharged impaired in intellect.

"Under the provisions of the act of 1852, four prisoners were removed in December, 1859, of whom the physician of the prison states:—'It would be absurd to assert that no case of insanity ever occurred in this prison; but to show the probable effect of the discipline in these cases, I will refer to their condition on admission:—No. 1419, general good health, but appears to be of unsound mind; circumstances had led to the belief of insanity before he was brought to the prison. No. 1485, general good health. No. 1987, good health, but owing to his inability to speak English, his mental condition was not recognized, but I now have no doubt he was insane when admitted. No. 2094, insane.'

One of the above-noted prisoners, No. 1485, was returned to the prison exactly three months after his transfer to the hospital, of whom it is afterwards entered that he died in the prison, insane, in January, 1862, after an imprisonment of ten years and nine months. The physician notes in his official report, 'upon his return here, he was decidedly insane.' (Dixmont Hospital was not then open.)

"The physician's record of insane prisoners as given to your board, and printed on page fourteen of report for 1870, in brief, shows that one prisoner died in 1862 (previously noted as received in good health in 1851), and seven others were received from 1863 to 1868; five were sent to Dixmont by order of the governor, and two were discharged insane. All were insane or of feeble intellect when admitted.

"The physician notices eight cases of the various forms of insanity under treatment in 1871, who are stated to have been received insane; four were transferred from the Eastern Penitentiary; one had been in several insane asylums; one when received was a mental and physical wreck (since dead); one had been held in jail a long time, owing to uncertainty, is still confined, a complete imbecile; one had been unsound as to his mental health. He was sent to Dixmont, where he remained for several years. None of the cases originated in this prison. The report for 1872 contains further mention of the four cases remaining over from the preceding year.

"The records of jails and other institutions within the Commonwealth, if culled from the official reports to your board, would furnish abundant evidence of the need for a change in the present method of treatment of the criminal insane.

"I doubt not you will recommend some important changes, and whether you favor the erection of a State asylum for the 'criminal insane,' or endeavor to meet the present exigency by procuring the setting apart of a wing in one or more of the existing State lunatic hospitals, I trust you will arrive at a satisfactory solution of this important question, and submit a plan wise in its details and ennobling in its humanity.

"Very respectfully,

"EDWARD S. WRIGHT,

"*Warden.*"

We pass now to the consideration of the third class of insane persons, viz., of those who, having committed acts of violence or mischief, are acquitted of crime on the ground of insanity.

Here we presume that those persons who commit such acts under a partial aberration of mind or a monomania or a sudden impulse, which did not destroy or disable the power of rational moral judgment; or under a temporary delirious excitement, resulting from their own deliberate action, and the cause of which was under their own control, as in a fit of intoxication, are not to be regarded as properly insane, and should not be acquitted of crime on that ground. But acts committed in a state of proper insanity—that is to say, when the whole rational faculty is so deranged that the moral judgment, the power of discrimination between right and wrong, is, by the visitation of Providence, utterly blotted out or partially paralyzed; such acts, however destructive or atrocious, cannot, without great impropriety and even absurdity, be denominated crimes; and those who so commit them cannot be classed among criminals. An "insane criminal" as an expression intended to describe a person as having committed a crime while in a state of insanity, is a contradiction in terms.

How the facts are to be ascertained in these cases or what are the proper evidences, is not a point which concerns us at present; such questions belong to courts, juries, and experts; but *if* the facts have been ascertained and adjudicated; *if* there is admitted to have existed in the person arraigned such a general mental derangement as obliterated the moral judgment, or any other mania which involved the loss or subversion of the moral judgment and control, in relation to those acts to which the impulse or propensity points, whether such be judged and found curable or incurable, and whether the lunatic be adjudged dangerous or harmless; then such acts cannot be reckoned crimes, and the person who has committed them cannot, without gross injustice and inhumanity, be regarded or treated as a criminal. And such is presumed to be the case of all those who are acquitted of crime on the ground of insanity. Yet, under our laws and the administration of justice (!) in this Commonwealth, numbers of these innocent and pitiable sufferers *are* so regarded and treated,—especially those who are tainted with the sin of poverty as well as the crime of insanity. This is, at the present moment, one of the foulest blots upon the escutcheon of our State,—a blot which, instead of being in process of gradual effacement, has been made darker and deeper by our more recent legislation. All the improvement and tendency to improvement in this respect which resulted and promised to result from the just and merciful laws of 1845 and 1852, have been retracted and reversed by the law of 1861.

The cases of insanity to which we now refer may be variously classified; but the law fixes its attention chiefly on that form of mania which is more or less dangerous and requires more or less restraint for the protection of the community as well as for the safety of the patient.

And that the case may be brought clearly and in one view under the eye of the members of the legislature, we may be excused for here reciting somewhat at large the present provisions of our laws on this subject as they stand in the statute-book.

Proceedings Against Criminal Lunatics.

Act of 1836.

(At the time this act was passed there was no State hospital for the insane, and for want of such institutions they were sent to the penitentiaries and jails.)

Section 58. In every case in which it shall be given in evidence, upon the trial of any person charged with any crime or misdemeanor, that such person was insane at the time of the commission of such offense, and such person shall be acquitted, the jury shall be required to find specially whether such person was insane at the time of the commission of such offense, and to declare whether such person was acquitted by them on the ground of such insanity, and if they shall so find and declare, the court before whom the trial was had shall have power to order such persons to be kept in strict custody, in such place and in such manner as to the said court shall seem fit, at the expense of the county in which the trial was had, so long as such person shall continue to be of unsound mind.

SEC. 59. The same proceedings may be had, if any person indicted for an offense shall, upon arraignment, be found to be a lunatic by a jury lawfully impaneled for the purpose; or if upon the trial of any person so indicted such person shall appear to the jury, charged with such indictment, to be a lunatic; in which case, the court shall direct such finding to be recorded, and may proceed as aforesaid.

SEC. 60. In every case in which any person, charged with any offense, shall be brought before the court, to be discharged for want of prosecution, and shall, by the oath or affirmation of one or more credible persons, appear to be insane, the court shall order the prosecuting attorney to send before the grand jury a written allegation of such insanity, in the nature of a bill of indictment, and thereupon the said grand jury shall make inquiry into the case, as in cases of crime, and make presentments of their finding to said court; and if said grand jury shall affirm said written allegation, they shall endorse the same thereon, thereupon the court shall order a jury to be impaneled to try the insanity of such person. But before a trial thereof be ordered, the court shall direct notice thereof to be given to the next of kin of such person, by publication or otherwise, as the case may require. And if the jury shall find such person to be insane, the like proceedings may be had as aforesaid.

SEC. 61. *Provided*, That if the kindred or friends of any person, who may have been acquitted, as aforesaid, on the ground of insanity, or in default of such, the guardians, overseers, or supervisors of any county, township, or place, shall give security in such amount as shall be satisfactory to the court, with condition that such lunatic shall be restrained from the commission of any offense, by seclusion or otherwise; in such case it shall be lawful for the court to make an order for the enlargement of such lunatic, and his delivery to his kindred or friends; or, as the case may be, to such guardian, overseer, or supervisors.

Act April 14th, 1845.

SECTION 8. The admission of insane patients, from the several counties of the Commonwealth, shall be in the ratio of their insane population: *Provided*, That each county shall be entitled to send at least one insane patient.

SEC. 9. Indigent persons and paupers shall be charged actual cost, &c., payable by counties.

SEC. 10. The courts of this Commonwealth shall have power to commit to said asylum any person who, having been charged with an offense punishable by imprisonment or death, shall have been found to have been insane in the manner now provided by law, at the time the offense was committed, and who still continues insane, and the expenses of said person, if in indigent circumstances, shall be paid by the county, &c.

SEC. 12. The several constituted authorities having care and charge of the poor of the respective counties, districts, and townships, shall have authority to send to the asylum, such insane paupers under their charge as they may deem proper subjects, and they shall be severally chargeable with the expenses of the care and maintenance, and removal to and from the asylum of such paupers.

SEC. 14. That if any person shall apply to any court of record within this Commonwealth, having jurisdiction of offenses, which are punishable by imprisonment, for the term of ninety days or longer, for the commitment to said asylum of any insane person within the county in which such court has jurisdiction, it shall be the duty of said court to inquire into the fact of insanity in the manner provided by law; and if such court shall be satisfied that such person is, by reason of insanity, unsafe to be at large, or if suffering any unnecessary duress or hardship, such court shall, on the application aforesaid, commit such insane person to said asylum.

SEC. 15. In the order of admission, the indigent insane of this Commonwealth shall have always precedence of the rich [in another place "paying patients"], and—— recent cases shall have precedence of those of long standing.

Act May 4th, 1852.

Whenever, in the opinion of the inspectors of the Eastern Penitentiary, any of the prisoners therein confined shall develop such marked insanity as to render their continued confinement in said penitentiary improper, and their removal to the State Lunatic Hospital necessary to their restoration, it shall be the duty of the said inspectors to submit such cases to a board composed of the district attorney of the county of Philadelphia, the principal physician of the Pennsylvania Hospital for the Insane, at Philadelphia, and the principal physician of the Friends' Insane Asylum, at Frankford, in Philadelphia county, and in case a majority of them cannot at any time when required attend, a competent physician or physicians to be appointed by the Court of Quarter Sessions of the County of Philadelphia, in the place of such as cannot attend, upon whose certificate of insanity or the certificate of any two transmitted to the governor, and if by him approved, he shall direct that said insane prisoners shall be by said inspectors removed to the State Lunatic Hospital, there to be kept and properly provided for at the cost and charge of the county from which they were sent to the penitentiary, and if at any time during the period for which any such insane prisoners shall have been sentenced to confinement in the Eastern Penitentiary, they shall, in the opinion of the trustees of said lunatic hospital, be so far restored as to render their return to said penitentiary safe and proper, then the said trustees shall cause the said prisoner to be returned to the Eastern Penitentiary, due notice to be given to the clerk of the court of quarter sessions of the county from which such prisoners were sent to the penitentiary of all such removals or transfers.

Act April 8th, 1861.

SECTION 1. When application shall be made under the fourteenth section of the act of April 14th, 1845, to which this is supplementary, to any court of this Commonwealth, for the commitment of any person to the Pennsylvania State Lunatic Hospital, it shall be lawful for such court either to inquire into the fact of insanity in a summary way, &c.; and in all cases, it shall be lawful for the several courts to use their discretion in sending insane persons to said hospital, or cause them to be confined elsewhere, as the said court may deem the case to be curable or otherwise.

SEC. 2. No person shall hereafter be sent to the said lunatic hospital, under the tenth section of act April 14th, 1845, or any other law of this Commonwealth, who shall have been charged with homicide, or having endeavored or attempted to commit the same, or to commit any arson, rape, robbery, or burglary, and have been acquitted of any such offenses on the ground of insanity, or been proceeded against under the fifty-ninth or sixtieth sections of the act of 1836 (see above), where the court trying the same shall be satisfied that it will be dangerous for such lunatic to be at large, on account of having committed or attempted to commit either of the crimes aforesaid; but such persons shall be confined in a penitentiary or the prison of the proper county.

SEC. 3. In every case where a lunatic has been or shall be committed to said hospital, after an acquittal of any crime on the ground of insanity, or after an investigation in court under the fifty-ninth and sixtieth sections of the act June 13th, 1836, or on account of its being adjudged dangerous for such lunatic to be at large; and in all cases where any lunatic has been or shall be removed from either of the penitentiaries, or any prison of this Commonwealth, under the order of a judge or of any court, it shall be lawful for the trustees of said hospital, with the aid of the superintending physician, to inquire carefully into the situation of the lunatic, and if a majority of the board, including the physician, shall be satisfied that there is no reasonable prospect of a cure of the insanity being effected by a retention of the lunatic in the hospital, they shall, at the expense of the proper city or county, cause him or her to be removed to the prison of the proper county, or the penitentiary from which he or she was sent.

Thus it appears that before 1845, before the erection of a State lunatic hospital, (1) persons tried and acquitted of crime on the ground of insanity, (2) persons indicted for an offense and found to be insane when brought up for trial, and (3) persons charged with some offense and brought before the court, to be discharged for want of prosecution, but being found in a state of lunacy—provided they have no friends—were to be sent to the penitentiary, the county jail, or, if the county authorities should give the required guarantees, to the county poor-house—as the court should judge most proper.

By the act of 1845 and the establishment of the State Lunatic Hospital, this state of things was at once and in prospect greatly improved. This alleviation was obtained upon the memorials of Miss Dix and other philanthropic citizens, backed by the following representation from the judges of the criminal courts:—

The memorial of Miss Dix to the legislature, dated February 3d, 1845, contains the following certificate from members of the judiciary in relation to the imprisonment of "insane criminals," Miss Dix prefacing its introduction with this paragraph:—

"Next, after private families and poor-houses, the insane will be found in the jails and penitentiaries. On this subject the opinion of some of your jurists has been so explicitly declared, that I feel it but justice to the cause to give this expression of their sentiments place here."

"PHILADELPHIA, March 5th, 1839.

"The want of an asylum for the insane poor often occasions painful embarrassments to the courts when the defense in the criminal charge is insanity fully sustained by proof. Although the jury may certify that their acquittal is on that ground, and thus empower the court to order the prisoner into close custody, *yet that custody can be in no other place than the common prisons,*—places illy qualified for such a subject of incarceration. We cannot doubt that the ends of justice would be greatly promoted if such an asylum as the petitioners contemplated were established with proper regulations, and the courts were authorized to commit to it all persons acquitted of crimes on the ground of insanity.

"(Signed) EDWARD KING,
"ARCHIBALD RANDALL,
"J. RICHTER JONES,
"*Judges of the Court of Quarter Sessions.*
"JAMES TODD,
"J. BOUVIER,
"R. T. CONRAD,
"*Judges of the Criminal Sessions.*
"CALVIN BLYTHE,
"*Judge of the Twelfth Judicial District.*"

Miss Dix adds:—"It is believed that all the judges of the courts of the Commonwealth of Pennsylvania, having criminal jurisdiction, would coincide in the above opinion."

But by the act of 1861, now in force, the benefits which had been secured, or which it was hoped would be secured, and which the judiciary thus earnestly desired might be secured, have been substantially anuulled and frustrated; for, as to the subsequent act of April 20th, 1869,—an act intended to guard the commitment to, and secure a proper discharge from, private hospitals,—it will be seen immediately, that it simply provides for the mode of procedure in one particular case, viz., in *discharging* a person who has been acquitted of crime on the ground of insanity, at the time of its commission, but who is alleged now to be sane. It provides for his "confinement," and then prescribes how the question of his sanity shall, before his discharge, be adjudicated. It is, in fact, legislation for the sane and not for the insane. (See Judge Brewster's "opinion," further on.)

Under the first section of this act (1861) a person, a man or woman, though free from the taint or charge of any crime whatever, having committed no act of violence or mischief,—a poor, pitiable, harmless lunatic,—may be sent to jail for indefinite incarceration; and if, upon summary examination, such person is thought to be more probably incurable, it is more than suggested to be the DUTY of the court to send him to prison. And, if once sent there, his case is remediless, unless he can get through the provision of section three, and we shall see what probability there is of that.

Under the second section, no person charged with committing or attempting to commit certain heinous crimes, and acquitted of the charge on the ground of insanity, shall, if the court judge it dangerous for him to be at large, be sent to the hospital at all, but he *shall be confined in the penitentiary or the prison of the proper county;* that is to say, the only option left to the court is, either at once to discharge such a person and let him go at large, or to commit him to a hopeless imprisonment,—hopeless, we say, unless he can run the gauntlet of section three.

Under this third section—and this is the key to the right understanding of the present state of our whole legislation on the subject—any lunatic who, (1) upon trial, has been acquitted *of any crime whatever*, and however slight, or (2) who has been indicted for *any offense*, and upon being brought up for trial has been found insane, or (3) who, when brought up to be discharged for want of prosecution, is found insane, or (4) who, though *never charged* with any crime or any act of violence or harm, has been adjudged dangerous if allowed to go at large,—any lunatic of either of these four classes, who has thereupon been sent by the order of any court to a State hospital for the insane,—as well as any lunatic (5) who, by the order of the governor, or by any provision of law, has been removed from any penitentiary or jail to the said hospital, may, upon, the judgment of the trustees and superintending physician of said hospital, that there is no reasonable prospect of a cure of his insanity, be by them, and by their sole and uncontrolled authority, consigned to a helpless and hopeless imprisonment in the penitentiary or the county jail. (Perhaps we ought to remark, by the way, that the last words of the section, "from which he or she was sent," may seem to confine the exercise of the power of the hospital authorities to the fifth class of persons before described; but as in that case the four other classes would have been enumerated in the section without any enactment in regard to them, it is presumed the act should be interpreted as extending the same power of removing the parties from the hospital to prison, to all those four classes of cases also; and so we believe it has always been interpreted. But perhaps it is to the credit of those who drew the act that there should be marks of *haste* in its composition.) It is clear, however, that this act contains no authority for sending any patients, however incurable, to the county poor-houses; they can be sent back only to the prison or the penitentiary.

We must ask your indulgence, gentlemen of the

legislature, if we find ourselves compelled to speak harshly, or even disrespectfully, of the law of the land. We are addressing legislators and not a jury. But what a law is this! Is it possible that the members of our subsequent legislatures,—is it possible that you, gentlemen, have been fully aware of its extraordinary, of its atrocious, provisions? a law which, we are constrained to say, in the terrible coolness of its barbarous enactments, in its disregard not only of all the claims of humanity and justice, but of the simplest civil rights of every citizen, is, so far as we can find, without a parallel in the legislation of any other State of this Union, or of any Christian or civilized community in the world. By this law, not only are persons, men and women who are admitted and solemnly adjudged to be innocent of all crime, men and women who have never even been charged with any act of violence or harm, liable to be hopelessly incarcerated,—incarcerated professedly for life (for they are pronounced *probably incurable*, and this is their only crime); incarcerated in the common jail or the penitentiary, incarcerated in the society of felons, incarcerated where they can have no proper care or treatment; not only this, but such persons liable to be so incarcerated, not upon the verdict of a jury of their fellow-citizens, or the examination and sentence of any court of justice, but upon the dictum—the sole, peremptory, uncontrolled, and irreversible dictum—of whom? The dictum of the trustees and superintending physician of a State hospital, a tribunal unknown elsewhere to the Constitution and laws of the State; whose rescript overrides and reverses the solemn sentences of all the criminal courts of the

Commonwealth, and holds, in respect to them, the character of a judgment of a supreme court of errors and appeals; and the *appeal* to this court is made by the court itself,—and even this is not all, but the court is the party interested to be rid of the care and burden of the poor speechless and defenseless victims, whose cases are to be passed upon!

Can anything be added to the extraordinary character of such a law? Shall it be allowed any longer to disgrace our statute-book, and tarnish the fair fame of our beloved and honored State?

No man, no one of us, gentlemen, can be sure that he will not become a helpless lunatic to-morrow. But does every citizen of Pennsylvania know that he is liable, without any fault of his own, to be sent at any time to the common jail, for life-long detention, by the sole and irrevocable authority and sentence of the superintendent and trustees of a State lunatic hospital? And that in spite of, and in reversal of, the contrary judgment and sentence of every court of justice, which may have passed, or which by law can pass, upon his case!

We beg here to disclaim, once for all, intending any personal reference to or reflection upon the estimable gentlemen who have the charge of the State hospitals for the insane. We doubt not they are honorable and conscientious men; but they are *men*. The constitution of such a court of review must, we think, be admitted to be an anomaly in our legislation, and no less an anomaly that interested parties, however honorable and trustworthy, should be empowered to decide in their own case. And perhaps it is worth observing that, while a lunatic may be thus summarily removed from the hospital to the prison, by the simple fiat of the hospital authorities alone, a lunatic could not so readily be removed from the penitentiary to the hospital. For this purpose the law of 1852 presented a complex process. In order that a lunatic might be removed from the penitentiary to the hospital, the law provided that not only the inspectors of the penitentiary—honorable and conscientious men—should judge the continued confinement of such lunatic in the penitentiary to be improper, and his removal to the State lunatic asylum necessary to his restoration, but the case must also be submitted to a board composed of the district attorney and either two superintendents of insane asylums or a competent physician or physicians to be appointed by the court of quarter sessions. Nor was their certificate of approval sufficient to secure the object; but that certificate must be transmitted to the governor, and, if he approved, he might order the removal. So careful was the law in that case to guard the process against abuse.

But we may be asked why should we cavil at what may be considered a theoretic anomaly, while it accomplishes the best results, and is the shortest and best way of accomplishing them? We answer by asking in return, what have been the results? Have the courts, by them, been encouraged to send lunatics to the hospital, or, on the contrary, have they found that this is too often a roundabout way of sending them to prison? But why is it that for more than twenty years the law has existed for sending certain lunatics from the penitentiaries to the hospital, and yet the experiment of doing so has been tried in the eastern district of the State but once,—indeed, has not been tried at all in that district for full twenty years past? Is it said that lunatics so transmitted very soon make their escape? But if the hospital is by law to receive such lunatics, some part of it ought manifestly to be so constructed and arranged as to be suitable for their safe-keeping, as has been done without difficulty or opposition in the hospitals of several other States. Have the hospital authorities sought to provide such construction and arrangements, in order that the ends of the law might not be defeated? Or, have they not rather sought and obtained the counter-provisions of the law of 1861, authorizing them to send all such lunatics back to prison? Since which time it has been hardly thought worth while to commit any such to their care. Indeed, it has been trumphantly said, on apparently good authority (see Journal of Insanity, October, 1873, page 214), that, after the first experiment, *i. e.*, before the law of 1861, as well as since, the board of trustees of the State Lunatic Hospital, at Harrisburg, declined receiving any more cases. That is to say, the board of trustees decided the question by their *sole* and ultimate authority—commission or no commission—law or no law. We do not vouch for the fact, but it has been publicly so stated, without dissent, in the presence of the superintendent of the lunatic asylum. We presume the refusal, if made, was a mere declaration and not an act; but the statement, however interpreted, is highly suggestive. The act of 1852 is still the law of the land; a law whose ends are eminently politic, just, and humane; but can the authorities of the State hospital be counted upon as ready cordially to concur in carrying out the provisions of that law, for the accomplishment of those ends?

The views of the judges of our criminal courts and of the Supreme Court of the State, upon present legislation in regard to the insane poor and the insane criminal, will appear in their petitions to the legislature, which we here introduce:—

"*To the Legislature of the State of Pennsylvania:*

"The judges of the criminal courts being greatly embarrassed under the law of 1836, in the disposal of persons charged with crime, who were acquitted on the ground of insanity, being obliged to commit them to 'close custody'; the jails and penitentiaries being alone open to them, memorialized the legislature in 1839, in behalf of the establishment of a hospital for the 'insane poor,' and denounced the commitment of the irresponsible insane to the prisons of the State. By such influence and other humane and rightful effort, the legislature, in 1845, established the State Lunatic Hospital at Harrisburg, under a law which gave proper protection to the rights of the 'poor' and the 'criminal insane.' This legislation satisfied the judges who bore the responsibility of disposing of such persons, and was also a clear exponent of the public mind on the subject.

"By more recent legislation, namely, by the act of April 8th, 1861, the courts, having jurisdiction of such cases, are forbidden to send them to the State hospitals, however irresponsible for crime, unless 'speedily curable,' *if they are deemed dangerous persons to be at large;* and in every case where a lunatic may have been sent to the State hospital, *after an acquittal of any crime on the ground of insanity*, the authorities of such hospital *may send such persons to a penitentiary or jail,* at the expense of the county where he belongs, unless they deem the case 'speedily curable.' Substantially the same provisions are contained in the act of April, 1863, relating to the western part of the State. The undersigned, regarding the provisions of the acts of 1861 and 1863, above cited, as an obstruction to the ends of justice; and, being greatly embarrassed in our administration of such causes, respectfully beg that the legislation be repealed, or such amendments made as will relieve from unjust and injurious imprisonment with felons the irresponsible class referred to, and which will also protect the 'insane poor' in their rights, and enable the courts to comply with the laws, without violating a sense of right or a sentiment of humanity.

"The act of April, 1863, in relation to the commitment of the insane to the Western Pennsylvania Hospital, provides for the return of insane criminals and persons acquitted on the ground of insanity, to the jail or penitentiary, if deemed incurable.

"Jos. Allison,
"Jas. R. Ludlow,
"Wm. S. Peirce,
"Thos. A. Finletter,
"Edward M. Paxson,
"*Judges of Court of Quarter Sessions, Philadelphia Co.*
"F. H. Collier,
"James P. Sterrett,
"Edwin H. Stowe,
"*Judges of Court of Quarter Sessions of Allegheny Co.*"

"We concur in the foregoing recommendation.

"GEO. SHARSWOOD,
"HENRY W. WILLIAMS,
"JOHN M. READ,
"DANIEL AGNEW,
"ULYSSES MERCUR,
"*Judges of Supreme Court.*

"November 28th, 1873."

We turn to another description of the insane—to those who, without any charge or suggestion of crime, have, either as dangerous or simply as helpless lunatics, been placed in the county poor-houses. These may by law be committed by the county authorities to the State hospitals for the insane. How many of them have been so committed? Does the management of these hospitals encourage and stimulate the authorities to send them there? They need encouragement and stimulus; for, as experience too constantly shows, those authorities are extremely liable to be led by the considerations of a false and short-sighted economy, to endeavor to make a cheaper provision for the care and maintenance of their insane than that furnished by the hospital. Are those whom they actually commit sent back to them again, with a charge for the expense of both transfers? If so, by the authority of what law are they sent back? What law provides that the authorities of the hospitals may send any of their patients, or allow any of their patients, however violent or incurable, to be taken to a county poor-house? Yet the simple fact is that while there are some five hundred of the insane poor in our hospitals, sent from the county almshouses, there are more than twice that number raving or languishing in our county poor-houses, an incarceration much better fitted to make a sane man mad, than a madman sane. And of the two, if there is less disgrace, there is also, in a majority of cases, less chance for comfort, and no better chance for recovery, in the poor-house than in the prison. So that it may be said upon a deliberate calculation, to be better, as regards comfort and a prospect of restoration, for an insane person to be convicted of crime, and sentenced to the penitentiary for a definite time, than, as an innocent lunatic, to be imprisoned in the poor-house. But we may add that the great and irremediable defect in both the prison and the poor-house, but especially in the latter, is the want of proper attendance and of skillful medical care. These poor creatures are not expected to recover. They are given over to utter hopelessness.

And now, what is to be done? To this question we would address ourselves with the full appreciation of the many and formidable difficulties with which the subject is encompassed. But we believe that there is no thoughtful person, who has made himself practically acquainted with the facts, that does not fully concur in the judgment that no poor-house can be a proper receptacle for the insane. We shall enter into no argument, therefore, to show that all the insane poor now gathered in the county poor-houses should, as soon as possible, be provided for in State lunatic hospitals, and transferred to them, to be there supported as the law may direct, unless any particular county has population enough, and insane poor enough, to render it advisable and feasible to establish and maintain a separate hospital for itself, with the full appointments and provisions for the best and most skillful care and medical treatment of the inmates, with a view both to their comfort and their care, as well as to the safety of the community.

As to the other, less numerous, class, who have been committed by the courts (or by the hospital authorities) to the jails or the penitentiaries, including (1) those who, having been charged with the most heinous felonies, have been acquitted on the ground of insanity; (2) those who, on the same ground, have been acquitted of any offense whatever, and however slight; (3) those who have been indicted for any offense, and, upon being brought up for trial, have been found insane; (4) those who, when brought up to be discharged for want of prosecution, have been found insane; (5) those who, though never charged with any act of crime or harm whatever, have been judged dangerous if allowed to go at large; as well as (6) those who, having been convicted of crime, committed while they were presumed to be sane, have since become lunatics,—in regard to all these, it seems now to be universally conceded that the jail or the penitentiary is not the proper place for their cure and detention.

The practical question then is, what other provision is to be made for them?

The act of May 4th, 1852, had, as we have seen, provided that any of the prisoners confined in the Eastern Penitentiary, being found insane (thus, insane convicts as well, but not insane convicts only) might, by a certain process, be removed to the State Lunatic

Asylum. In their report of the year following, the inspectors of the penitentiary inform us that of eighteen persons proposed by them as candidates for removal, eight had been so transferred by order of the governor, and they add:—

"The inspectors cannot omit this opportunity of again calling upon the general assembly, should the means provided for this object be found in any way inadequate, either in the terms of the law authorizing the removal, or in the provision for the safe-keeping in the lunatic hospital, not to halt in the good work until it is carried into full effect. Let it no longer rest upon the fair fame of Pennsylvania, who claims to be foremost in the work of penitentiary reforms, that insane men are imprisoned in the cells of her penitentiary for long years or for life. * * * Surely, in this enlightened Christian age and country, the cells of the penitentiary should cease to be the abode of human beings without moral perceptions or responsibilities to fit them for the salutary effects of either penitentiary punishments or moral reform. The inspectors have gone more fully into this subject than they otherwise would have done, from the fact that a State hospital has been put into operation by the legislature for this enlightened and benevolent purpose. Its establishment has been long needed."

In their report for the next year (1854), the inspectors remark that "the eight persons before alluded to were the first so removed since the opening of the prison, twenty-five years ago, as until last year no institution existed in Pennsylvania, as in other States, for the reception and treatment of persons who, though insane, required punitive restraint. No other cases have since occurred requiring removal from the penitentiary. The State Lunatic Hospital is an establishment of the highest utility,—its purpose approved by the most enlightened benevolence and sound policy. Every humane mind cannot but hope that it will be fostered and encouraged for the accomplishment of benefits to an increasing class of unfortunate people." They then proceed to a class who are sometimes included among the "criminal insane," in the following terms:—"As yet no complete provisions have been made for the reception and treatment of those insane who are sentenced to restraint of their liberty, because the fact of their unsound mind renders them irresponsible for the crimes charged against them. There are now four prisoners in the penitentiary thus confined; their dangerous character, arising from homicidal mania, rendering them unsafe, unless under a cautious restraint. As they are in the penitentiary not as convicts, but here retained because of no other place of equal security, it is difficult properly to treat them for the confirmed malady under which they labor. The time will come when, in the State hospital, provision can be made for this class of insane."

Nearly twenty years have elapsed, and these poor, wretched beings are still in jails and almshouses.

The inspectors making the report in 1853 were John Bacon, Richard Vaux, Hugh Campbell, Singleton A. Mercer, and Charles Brown; in 1854, Messrs. Bacon, Vaux, Mercer, Andrew Miller, and Charles McKibben.

Then came the law of 1861, which empowers the

trustees and physician of the State Lunatic Asylum to send insane persons, committed to the hospital by the courts, or removed to it from the penitentiary, back to the penitentiary from which they were sent, or to a prison to which they were not committed by the courts, when there appeared no reasonable prospect of a cure. The result is, that it is found a useless expenditure of pains and money, in many cases, for the courts to send to the hospitals insane men acquitted of crime, and always for the penitentiary to remove thither its prisoners or insane convicts, while authority resides in the hospital forthwith to send them back again. In anticipation of this result, the inspectors of the Eastern Penitentiary, in their report of the following year (1862), "respectfully suggest to the legislature that provisions by law be made *requiring the State Lunatic Asylum to take insane persons convicted of crime into that institution.*" And, in 1863, "the inspectors again ask the legislature to require the State Lunatic Asylum to take 'insane convicts.'" The inspectors in 1862 and 1863 were Richard Vaux, Samuel Jones, M. D., Alexander Henry, Thomas H. Powers, and Furman Sheppard.

It is plain that these gentlemen, as well as the inspectors of 1853 and 1854, judged it to be the wisest and most desirable plan, in this as in other States, that provisions should be made for the criminal insane and even for insane convicts in connection with the State hospital rather than with the State penitentiary.

We append here, without comment, as the documents tell their own story very clearly, the communications to this board from the inspectors of the Eastern and Western Penitentiaries, requesting its intervention with the legislature for the modification or repeal of the obnoxious laws against the rights of the insane which now disgrace our statute-books.

"NOVEMBER 26th, 1873.

"*To the Board of Public Charities:*

"The inspectors of the State Penitentiary for the Eastern District of Pennsylvania have heretofore in their reports called the attention of the legislature to the deplorable condition of the insane committed to the custody of that institution, and have suggested legislation which would relieve us from the pressure of a duty which we could not fulfill in providing for them proper care and medical treatment, and which also would provide for these defenseless and, for the most part, irresponsible persons, a more rightful and suitable abode than a prison. We now most respectfully appeal to the legislature, through your board, to so amend the legislation of the act of April 8th, 1861, as will give effect to the former representations of the inspectors, and place the class of the 'poor insane' and the 'criminal insane' in the more just and favorable position which they occupied under the law of April 14th, 1845, which established the State Lunatic Asylum at Harrisburg.

"RICHARD VAUX,
"THOMAS H. POWERS,
"ALEX. HENRY,
"CHARLES THOMSON JONES,
"JOHN M. MARIS."

"*To the Board of Public Charities:*

"The inspectors of the Western Penitentiary desire to call the attention of the legislature, through your board, to the necessity of further and fuller provision by law for the care and protection of the indigent and criminal insane.

"In many of the annual reports of this penitentiary, attention has been directed to the fact that insane persons have been convicted of crime and sent to prison. The following, from our report for 1867, briefly states the facts in the case, and in its conclusions, we trust, will receive your earnest co-operation:—

"We would ask the attention of the legislature to the great necessity there is for such legislation as will secure to the insane convict a place in some State institution where he may be properly cared for. By special amended enactments of the law on this subject, no insane convict who has been committed to prison on the higher grades of crime, can be transferred to the hospital at Dixmont, 'unless by the verdict of the jury in the case there is reason to believe that a cure of such insanity may be speedily effected.'

"If this institution is intended only for the benefit of the *curably* insane, what is to become of the ill-fated wretch who has no helper, and whose reason is declared to be 'clean gone forever.'"

"We hold that it is the duty of the State to make some speedy provision for his relief, either by the modification of existing laws, or the enactment of such statutes as will guarantee to him a humane and Christian protection.

"T. H. Nevin,
"Robert H. Davis,
"John Dean,
"George A. Kelly,
"Ormsby Phillips,
"*Inspectors.*"

In like manner the secretary of the Massachusetts Board of State Charities, in his report for 1871, recommends, and in that for 1872 renews the recommendation, that a special "receptacle or institution be provided for insane convicts, and for insane persons who, in a state of insanity, have committed or are disposed to commit violent acts;" for which he gives his reasons at large, and then adds, "it is submitted that the construction of such a receptacle may perhaps be wisely made a part of the plan for a new hospital at Worcester. It can be made a separate building, surrounded by a wall, sufficiently removed from other buildings to avoid any unpleasant associations, and yet near enough to have the benefit of the general superintendence of that institution."

That is to say, as the secretary immediately adds, the project of a new and (totally) separate institution for the class referred to, is sure to start some vexed question, with which it would not be well to embarrass the desired improvement. The "convict insane" would give to it its distinctive character, and then any proposition to admit to it others, not "convict insane," who could be better provided for in it than elsewhere, would be resisted, as affixing to them the repute of a criminal class. Nor is it likely that it would, with its peculiar character, as well as it smaller numbers, be provided, in the long run, with a corps of officers equal in skill to those whose services are commanded by the other hospitals. "For these and other reasons, it is better that provision should be made for the insane, who have committed or are predisposed to homicidal or violent acts, in buildings or apartments, properly arranged and provided with means of security, in connection with some one of the lunatic hospitals."

So much from the secretary. The board itself, in its first report, had said, "there is still another class, the 'criminal insane,' for whom special provision should be made. Formerly they were kept in the prisons, confined in cells; but more recently they have been placed in the State hospitals. It is generally thought that this class of the insane should not be allowed to mingle with those who are free from crime, but should have apartments built expressly for their accommodation. The most appropriate plan for an asylum, designed for this class of insane persons, would probably be at one of the State hospitals."

The same subject was again referred to in their fifth and sixth reports; and again it is added, if a proper building for "insane convicts" and others predisposed to violent acts should be provided *in connection with one of the State lunatic hospitals*, "power should be given to this board to transfer from the other hospitals to the one where such provision is made, persons of the class referred to." "From the other hospitals," observe—not "from the prisons,"—in Massachusetts there are no "insane criminals," nor "insane convicts" in the prisons.

We have referred to the injurious and wrongful effects of the act of 1861, and we have seen the earnest counter-recommendations of the inspectors of the Eastern Penitentiary and other just and honorable authorities. We have ourselves already pointed out the disastrous consequences of that act; and now, to confirm our position, we beg leave to insert here the results of the experience and research, and the carefully-drawn statements of Judge Brewster on this point, conveyed to us in a letter dated October 10th, 1873.

"No. 214 West Washington Square,
"Philadelphia, October 10th, 1873.

"*To Hon. George L. Harrison,*
"*President of the Board of Public Charities,*

"Dear Sir:—Your communication of August 14th, in reference to 'insane criminals,' was duly received and acknowledged.

"With your permission, the examination of the authorities which you desired was postponed until a recent date.

"I have considered with some care the question you propound, and the several acts of assembly to which you referred me. I was induced to do this, not only because of the respect due to your letter, but also because of the peculiar interest which ever attaches to the subject of the treatment of persons afflicted with the peculiar and distressing calamity of insanity.

"Your favor refers me to a passage which is to be

found in a communication addressed by your board to the public.

"As you invite a statement of my opinion as to its accuracy, it is proper that I should quote it at length; it is in these words:—

"'The sad and anomalous condition of "insane criminals" under the provisions of the act of 1836, relating to this class, did not satisfy the public mind, little as the public mind takes cognizance of such matters, and it found in Miss Dix such an exponent of its wishes as led to the legislation of 1845, which established the State Lunatic Hospital at Harrisburg, at which provision was made for the reception of this class of the insane in community with the other patients. So largely did this feature interest the public, that it was the common thought that this institution was created for the special care of this class. The act of 1861 practically nullified this legislation, and since then a great wrong has been imposed upon them, which this board is endeavoring to remove. Very many of them are consigned to the public jails. While wholly irresponsible in the eyes of the law, they are dealt with by the law as convicted criminals. We maintain that, under the law of 1861, the wisdom and humanity of our able and excellent judges are not competent to make any other disposition of them.'

"You ask me to give my 'professional opinion upon the accuracy of the statement' just quoted.

"Save for your request, which implies that some one has ventured to doubt the correctness of your narrative, I should not have supposed it possible that it needed confirmation.

"My first impression was decidedly in favor of its entire truth, and my subsequent examination of the law has confirmed my original conviction.

"By the act of June 13th, 1836, it was provided that upon the acquittal of a defendant in a criminal case 'upon the ground of insanity,' the court should have the 'power to order such a person to be kept in strict custody, in such place and manner as * * * should seem fit * * * so long as such person should continue to be of unsound mind.' (Act of June 13th, 1836, section 58, P. L., 1836, page 603.)

"The like proceedings were authorized if the defendant were upon arraignment found to be a lunatic and even where he was about to be discharged for want of prosecution.

"Prior to 1841 there was no place in which such unfortunate persons could be 'kept in strict custody,' except prisons and penitentiaries. The private asylums were evidently not contemplated by the law, and were probably under no obligation to receive any person sent to them by the courts.

"March 4th, 1841, Governor Porter approved an act 'to establish an asylum for the insane of this Commonwealth.' This statute reflects great credit upon the gentleman who drafted it and upon the legislature and the governor who passed and approved of it. It established 'a public asylum for the reception and relief of the insane of this Commonwealth.' The governor was to appoint three commissioners to purchase a site and to erect a building for the accommodation of three hundred patients and necessary offices, at an expense not exceeding $120,000.

"The eighth section of said act was designed to remedy the evil you refer to as existing under the statute of 1836. It provided:—

"'That the proper courts of this Commonwealth shall have power to commit to said asylum any person who, having been charged with an offense punishable by imprisonment or death, shall have been declared by the verdict of a jury or otherwise, to the satisfaction of the court, to have been insane at the time the offense was committed and who still continues insane.'

"The prior act of 1751 had contained no such provision. The act of 1841 removed the blot upon our system of confining insane persons as criminals.

"So far as I have been able to discover, there was no change in this system for many years. It evidently met with the support of the people. By act approved by Governor Shunk, April 14th, 1845, a hospital was established at Harrisburg (P. L., 1845, page 442).

"The tenth section of this statute repeats the humane provision of the act of 1841.

"March 18th, 1848, Governor Shunk approved the act incorporating the Pittsburg Hospital. (P. L., 1848, page 218.) By a supplement to this charter, approved by Governor Pollock, May 8th, 1855 (P. L., 1855, page 512), the provisions of the act of 1841 were extended to that institution.

"Provisions for the removal of insane persons from prisons and penitentiaries were repeated by the acts of May 4th, 1852 (P. L., 1852, page 552), and March 24th, 1858 (P. L., 1858, page 151).

"So the law stood from 1841 to 1861. During those twenty years the courts and all classes of citizens were satisfied with the propriety, justice, and necessity of these laws.

"April 8th, 1861, a statute was approved which prohibited the commitment to the Pennsylvania State Lunatic Asylum of any person charged with certain crimes enumerated. It, however, contained a humane proviso which left the power of commitment with the courts where they were satisfied that there was 'reason to believe that a cure of insanity might be speedily effected' (P. L., 1861, page 249). But a subsequent section authorizes the trustees and the superintending physician to reverse the order of the court, for if they are 'satisfied that there is no reasonable prospect of a cure' * * * 'they may in all cases cause the patient to be removed to the prison of the proper county or the penitentiary from which he or she was sent.'

"It is therefore unfortunately true, as stated by you, that the act of 1861 practically nullifies the humane legislation of former years, and that since 1861 a great wrong has been imposed upon a class of unfortunate persons who, although not responsible to the law, are yet subject to confinement in prisons and penitentiaries as felons. These views are not affected in any wise by the act of April 20th, 1869 (P. L., 78), for the officers of the State asylums are not embraced within its provisions. The act of 1861 stands unrepealed.

"I am, very respectfully, yours,

"F. CARROLL BREWSTER."

In a large number of our sister States constitutional provision has been made to secure appropriate legislation in behalf of the insane; but in order to bring the whole subject more fully before the legislature, in all its bearings, or, at least, in a great variety of points of view, we take leave to introduce here the legislative provisions of a number of States as to insane persons, charged or convicted of crime; premising that we have examined the constitution and laws, together, of thirty-three States (all that we have been able to reach), in relation to the insane, and in all cases their rights have been tenderly protected and the legislation in behalf of the class to which we are now directing your attention, with the single exception of Pennsylvania, is invariably of the most humane character.

Legislation of other States in relation to Insane Criminals.

Arkansas.—A person that becomes insane or lunatic after the commission of a crime or misdemeanor, shall not be tried for the offense during the insanity or lunacy.

If, after verdict of guilty and before judgment pronounced, such person becomes insane or lunatic, then no judgment shall be given while the insanity or lunacy shall continue.

If, after judgment or before execution of the sentence, such convict becomes insane or lunatic, if the punishment be capital or corporal, the execution thereof shall be stayed until the recovery of such convict from such insanity or lunacy.

Connecticut.—That section two hundred and forty-three of the act concerning crimes and misdemeanors be amended by erasing from the fourth line thereof the words the "common jail," and inserting in lieu thereof the words "the General Hospital for the Insane of the State of Connecticut."

Georgia.—It shall be the duty of the physician to the penitentiary of the State, when he discovers that any one of the convicts in said penitentiary has become lunatic or insane, to certify the same to the principal keeper of said penitentiary, and it shall be the duty of said principal keeper, upon the receipt of such certificate, to transfer said convict to the lunatic asylum of this State, and shall send together with such convict a copy of said certificate, together with the day on which the term of service of such convict will expire in said penitentiary, and the county from which he was sentenced.

Louisiana.—Whenever any person arrested to answer for any crime or misdemeanor before any court of this State shall be acquitted thereof by the jury, or shall not be indicted by the grand jury, by reason of the insanity or mental derangement of such person, and the discharge or going at large of such person shall be deemed by the court to be dangerous to the safety of the citizens or to the peace of the State, the court is authorized and empowered to commit such person to the State Insane Hospital or any similar institution in any parish within the jurisdiction of the court, there to be detained until he is restored to his right mind or otherwise delivered by due course of law.

Maine.—When any person is indicted for a criminal offense, or is committed to jail on a charge thereof by a justice of the peace or judge of a police or municipal court, any judge of the court before whom he is to be tried, when a plea of insanity is made in court, or he is notified that it will be made, may in vacation or term time order such person into the care of the superintendent of the insane hospital, to be detained and observed by him till the further order of the court, that the truth or falsity of the plea may be ascertained.

When the grand jury omits to find an indictment against any person arrested by legal process to answer for any offense by reason of his insanity, they shall certify that fact to the court; and when a traverse jury for the same reason acquits any person indicted, they shall state that fact to the court when they return their verdict; and the court by a precept stating the fact of insanity, may commit him to prison or to the insane hospital till restored to his right mind or delivered according to law; *but he shall only remain in prison till provision can be made for him at the hospital and then removed thereto.*

When an inmate of the State prison becomes insane, the warden shall notify the governor of the fact, and he, with the advise of counsel, shall appoint a commission of two or more skillful physicians to investigate the case, and if such inmate is found insane by their investigation, he shall be sent to the insane hospital until he becomes of sound mind; and if this takes place before the expiration of his sentence, he shall be returned to prison; but if after, he shall be discharged free. The expenses of the commission, removal, and support shall be paid by the State.

Minnesota and Wisconsin.—When any person so indicted or informed against for an offense, shall on trial be acquitted by the jury by reason of insanity, the jury, in giving their verdict of not guilty, shall state that it was given for such cause, and thereupon, if the discharge or going at large of such insane person shall be considered by the court manifestly dangerous to the peace and safety of the community, the court may order him to be committed to prison, or may give him into the care of his friends, if they shall give bonds with surety, to the satisfaction of the court, conditioned that he shall be well and securely kept; otherwise he shall be discharged.

Oregon.—If the defense be the insanity of the defendant, the jury must be instructed, if they find him not guilty on that ground, to state that fact in their verdict, and the court must thereupon, if it deems his being at large dangerous to the public peace or safety, order him to be committed to any lunatic asylum authorized by the State to receive and keep such persons, until he become sane or be otherwise discharged therefrom, by authority of law. (General Laws, Oregon, page 469, section 170.)

New Jersey and New York.—When a person shall have escaped indictment or have been acquitted of a criminal charge upon trial, upon the ground of insanity, upon the plea pleaded of insanity or otherwise, the court being certified by the jury or otherwise of the fact, shall carefully inquire and ascertain whether his insanity in any degree continues, and if it does, shall order him into safe custody, and to be sent to the asylum.

If any person in confinement, under indictment or under sentence of imprisonment, or for want of bail for good behavior * * * shall appear to be insane, the judge of the circuit court of the county where he is confined shall institute a careful investigation, call two respectable witnesses, physicians, and other credible witnesses, invite the prosecutor of the pleas to aid in the examination, and, if he shall deem it necessary, call a jury, and for that purpose is fully empowered to compel the attendance of witnesses and jurors, and if it be satisfactorily proved that he is insane, said judge may discharge him from imprisonment, and order his safe custody and removal to the asylum, where he shall remain until restored to his right mind, and then, if the said judge shall have so directed, the superintendent shall inform the said judge and the county clerk and prosecutor of the pleas thereof, whereupon he shall be remanded to prison, and criminal proceedings be resumed, or otherwise be discharged.

Persons charged with misdemeanors and acquitted on the ground of insanity may be kept in custody and sent to the asylum in the same way as persons charged with crime.

New York.—An act to organize the State lunatic asylum for insane convicts passed April 8th, 1858.

SECTION 1. The building now being erected on the prison grounds at Auburn, for an asylum for insane convicts, shall be known and designated as the "State lunatic asylum for insane convicts."

[After defining the method of administration, the statute proceeds:—]

SEC. 8. Whenever the physicians of either of the State prisons of this State shall certify to the inspectors, that any convict is insane, they shall make immediately a full examination into the condition of such convict, and shall cause such convict to be examined by one of the physicians of the State Lunatic Asylum, at Utica, and if satisfied that said convict is insane, or that there is probable cause to believe such convict to be insane, they shall order the agent and warden of the prison where such convict is confined forthwith to convey such convict to the State Lunatic Asylum for insane convicts, and to deliver the said convict to the superintendent thereof, who is hereby required to receive said convict into the said asylum, and retain him there so long as he shall continue to be insane; and no convict who has been committed to said asylum as insane shall be discharged from said asylum by reason of the expiration of the term for which he was sentenced, unless the relatives of such convict shall produce to said superintendent satisfactory evidence of their ability to maintain such convict, and shall execute and deliver to said superintendent an agreement in writing that such convict shall not be a charge upon any public charity, if such convict shall continue to be insane at the expiration of the time for which such convict was sentenced.

Act May 21st, 1873.

No person, association, or corporation shall establish or keep any asylum, institution, or house of retreat for the care, custody, or treatment of the insane, or persons of unsound mind, without first obtaining a license therefor from the Board of State Charities: *Provided*, That this section shall not apply to any State asylum or institution or to any asylum or institution established or conducted by any county, or by any city or municipal corporation.

The said board may revoke the license of any asylum or institution, issued under the provision of this act, for reasons deemed satisfactory to said board; but such revocation shall be in writing and filed, and notice given in writing to the person, association, or corporation to whom such license was given.

Act June 7th, 1873.

If any inmate of any such almshouse, when admitted, is insane, or thereafter becomes insane or of unsound mind, and the accommodations in said almshouse are not adequate and proper, in the opinion of the said secretary of the State Board of Charities, for his treatment and care, the said secretary may cause his removal to the appropriate State asylum for the insane, and he shall be received by the officer in charge of such asylum, and maintained therein until duly discharged.

Ohio.—If any person in prison shall, after the commission of an offense, and before conviction, become insane * * * an examining court may be called in the manner provided in the act entitled * * * and if such court shall find that such person became insane after the commission of the crime or misdemeanor of which he stands charged or indicted, and is still insane, the court shall proceed and the prisoner shall, for the time being, and until restored to reason, be dealt with in like manner as other lunatics are required to be after inquest had: *Provided, however*, That if said lunatic be discharged, the bond given for his support and safe-keeping shall also be conditioned that said lunatic shall, when restored to reason, answer to said crime or misdemeanor and abide the order of the court in the premises; and any such lunatic may, when restored to reason, be prosecuted for any offense committed by him previous to such insanity.

If any person, after being convicted of any crime or misdemeanor, and before the execution in whole or in part of the sentence of the court, become insane, it shall be the duty of the governor of the State to inquire into the facts, and he may pardon such lunatic, and commute or suspend, for the time being, the execution in such manner and for such a period as he may think proper, and may by his warrant to the sheriff of the proper county, or warden of the Ohio Penitentiary, order such lunatic to be conveyed to the asylum and there kept until restored to his reason. If the sentence of any such lunatic is suspended by the governor, the sentence of the court shall be executed upon him after such period of suspension hath expired, unless otherwise directed by the governor.

Rhode Island.—If upon examination a judge is satisfied that the person thus imprisoned is insane or idiotic, he shall have the power to order the removal of such prisoner from the State prison or jail aforesaid, to be detained in the State asylum for the insane, if he can be there received, or if not in the Butler hospital.

Such order of removal shall be for and during the term of said prisoner's sentence, and be directed to the sheriff of the county in which such prisoner stands committed.

Any person removed as aforesaid, upon restoration to reason may, by an order of either of the judges of the Supreme Court, in his discretion, be remanded to the place of his original confinement, to serve out the remainder of his term of service.

Massachusetts.—The physician of the State prison, as chairman, with the superintendent of the State Lunatic Hospital, shall constitute a commission for the examination of convicts in said prison alleged to be insane. Each commissioner shall receive for his services in such capacity his traveling expenses and three dollars a day for each day he is so employed.

The commission shall investigate the case, and if, in the opinion of the majority of them, the convict has become insane and his removal would be expedient, they shall so report, with their reasons, to a judge of the Superior Court, who shall forthwith issue his warrant under the seal of that court, directed to the warden, authorizing him to remove the convict to one of the State lunatic hospitals, there to be kept till, in the opinion of the superintendent and trustees thereof, he may be recommitted consistently with his health.

When a convict in the prison appears to be insane, the warden or inspector shall give notice to the chairman of said commission, who shall forthwith notify the members thereof to meet at the prison.

New Hampshire.—The governor, with the advice of the council, may remove to the asylum, to be there kept at the expense of the State, any person confined in the State prison who is insane.

South Carolina.—Any judge of the circuit court is authorized to send to the lunatic asylum every person charged with the commission of any criminal offense, who shall, upon the trial before him prove to be *non compos mentis*, and the said judge is authorized to make all necessary orders to carry into effect this power.

Tennessee.—That section 5488 of the code of Tennessee be so amended as to read, whenever the physician reports to the keeper of the penitentiary that any convict is insane, and ought on that account to be removed to the lunatic asylum, the keeper shall cause such insane convict to be removed accordingly, there to remain until discharged by the physician of said lunatic asylum.

Texas and Iowa.—If any person charged with or convicted of any criminal offense, be found to be insane in the court before which he is so charged or convicted, said court shall order him to be conveyed to and retained in the State Lunatic Asylum, and he shall be received and retained, until removed by the order of the court by which he was committed to the asylum.

If any person after being convicted of any crime or misdemeanor, and before the execution in whole or part of the sentence of the court, becomes insane, it shall be the duty of the governor of the State to inquire into the facts, and he may pardon such lunatic or commute or suspend for the time being the execution, in such manner and for such a period as he may think proper, and may by his warrant to the sheriff of the proper county, or warden of the Iowa Penitentiary, order such lunatic to be conveyed to the hospital and there kept until restored to reason.

As before said, the State of New York has made provision for the care in hospitals of all her insane poor. For this she is to be commended; in this to be imitated. But the hospital or asylum referred to in the foregoing statutes as that to which "insane convicts" and others are to be sent, is a lunatic asylum established by a statute of 1858, on the prison grounds at Auburn, expressly for this object. In this, her *purpose* is most laudable; but the propriety of her *course* is most questionable, as will more fully appear in the sequel.

This board had the honor, last year, of causing to be prepared and laid before the senate the draught of a bill "to provide for the care and keeping of the criminal insane of this Commonwealth—including those who may be acquitted of crime on the ground of insanity." And the proposition was, in general terms, that a department, a wing, or a distinct building surrounded by a wall, of the hospital now under construction at Danville, should be so planned, arranged, completed, and organized as to make it fit, suitable, and convenient for the care, keeping, and treatment of the classes of insane persons referred to. It may be proper to say that the board had chiefly in view the more numerous class,—those who were in prisons with criminals, without ever having been convicted of crime; and that they made their recommendation, so far as regards the less numerous class, the strictly "convict insane," on the assumption, which we have shown may fairly be made, that the vast majority of such convicts were really insane, or, at least, in the incipient or latent stages of insanity, at the time the acts charged against them as crimes were committed.* They

---

* Report in relation to the insane convicts in the Eastern Penitentiary on February 24th, 1873, by Edward Townsend, warden. Number this date, 12.

W. W.—Confirmed lunatic on admission.

M. L.—Imbecile in mind on admission.

T. R.—Unsound mind on admission.

A. N.—Unsound mind on admission.

I. B. H.—Imbecile on admission.

G. V.—Decidedly imbecile when admitted.

M. V. B. S.—Very weak-minded on admission, since insane.

Dora S.—Insane on admission and remains so.

Mary S.—Insane on admission and had been an inmate of an insane asylum.

M. McG.—Very feeble-minded on admission.

E. L.—Weak-minded, bordering on lunacy, when admitted.

P. L.—Insane on admission.

Report of Edward S. Wright, warden of Western Penitentiary, on the same subject, made at the same time. Number of insane convicts in penitentiary, 8.

Prisoner No. 3324, mental health impaired on admission.
" " 3720, " " "
" " 3750, " " "
" " 3958, " " "
" " 4006, " " "
" " 4008, " " "
" " 4019, " insane on admission.
" " 4030, " " "

were cases of this sort, or this was the aspect of the cases we had in mind, and for which we sought relief; the others, the ten per cent. or so, we regarded as simply exceptions, which, at all events, should not vitiate the rule. We proposed but did not urge the bill; and, through misunderstanding, and in consequence of opposition from interested parties, it was lost.

At the late meeting in Baltimore of the Association of Medical Superintendents of Hospitals for the Insane, it was openly stated by a member from Pennsylvania that "that measure was defeated (I suppose) by the efforts of certain members of this association," and the statement was not contradicted. (See Journal of Insanity, October, 1873, page 236.)

This meeting of medical superintendents was a notable one. Believing that the case of the proposed law just referred to had not been fully understood, and wishing to have the subject freely and thoroughly ventilated, we addressed to the president of this association the following communication:—

"PHILADELPHIA, May 28th, 1873.

"*Dr. J. S. Butler, President of Convention of Medical Superintendents for the Insane,*

"DEAR SIR:—The morning papers inform me that the important humanitarian body over which you preside has assembled, for the consideration of the interests of the insane, in convention at Baltimore. On other like occasions, the commissioners of this board have been honored with an invitation,—to be represented, of course, in presence merely; but still we are glad to be apprised of your meeting by public announcement, and venture to address you on a subject of great interest to this board, and one which, we think, has escaped any authoritative action of your body.

"We refer to the subject of the care of the 'criminal insane.' We are led to refer this matter to you *for action*, because of an unsuccessful effort made by this board to have a precedent established by the Legislature of the State of Pennsylvania, to construct a department for this class *upon the grounds of the Hospital for the Insane at Danville, Pennsylvania*, for the reception and treatment of (for the most part) the irresponsible insane, who are now incarcerated in the penitentiaries and jails of this Commonwealth.

"It is true that we did not press this matter upon the legislature, believing that the simple proposition should be sufficient for favorable action; but as the higher advice of representatives from this State in your convention prevailed to defeat the measure which we proposed, we feel justified in asking you to take such definite action as will have like influence in protecting the class who are committed, in this State, at least (I am glad to say not in all other States), to the miseries of a felon's doom.

"In noticing this subject I beg your permission to venture on a few observations on this subject, and in doing so I express the mind of every member of this board.

"It is a fact patent to all of us, that multitudes of irresponsible criminal insane are now in prisons of many of the States, and it is equally true that the influence of the body known as the Association of Medical Superintendents of American Institutions for the Insane has exercised a most potent and salutary influence in shaping the legislation of the several States in behalf of this afflicted class of their citizens.

"Believing that your influence will avail to check the enormous wrong which the class we refer to suffer, we ask your intervention in their behalf, and urge you to set forth a distinct and definite policy which shall satisfy its demands.

"We know that in Great Britain there are two asylums for the specially criminal insane; one at Broadmoor, not far from London, a distinct institution, with accommodations for from five to six hundred inmates; and one at Perth, Scotland, under penal jurisdiction, but in charge of a special superintendent.

"We know that on the continent of Europe there is no special provision for the criminal insane; it being held by the most distinguished alienist physicians, and so proclaimed in many works on psychological subjects, that insanity should level all distinctions; and, as Dr. Manning reports, that 'the great gulf which separates the convict from the honest man is bridged over by insanity; that when sick in body, the prisoner should be kept within his prison and treated for his malady, but when sick in mind, the prison should be opened and the badge of the convict be forgotten.'

"In this view, the well-known humanitarian, Miss Dix, concurred.

"We also know that in these United States there is an asylum for insane convicts at Auburn, New York, intended originally for the reception of such as became insane when convicts, but more recently for those, also, who have been acquitted on the ground of insanity. We know of no other special provision made for this class, unless it be in jails. In the State of Pennsylvania there are not, we think, over ten per cent. of the number who are now confined in the penitentiaries and jails who, on the report of the wardens and prison-keepers, were not insane when sentenced, and of this small percentage some, of course, were mentally imbecile or in the incipient stage of insanity when the crime was committed. The law holds them to be 'irresponsible,' and still they are held as felons by the act of the law. As has been well said, 'the courts fail to detect the disability for want of a proper defense or because the mental disease is still latent.' The jails thus receive these forlorn 'wards of the State,' forsaken by man; not, we believe, by God. We could enumerate instances of marked cruelty in individual cases, but we point only to the injustice which must inevitably oppress them, when subjected to the treatment of prisoners in the State and county jails. Their lightest affliction being perpetual incarceration without the slightest consideration of their sufferings or their needs. This is the case certainly in Pennsylvania.

"There will be no dispute as to the impolicy as well as the wrong-doing of such 'proceedings.' These 'irresponsible' citizens are, as if often said, 'wards of the State.' Surely no official of the State, no private citizen, who is the head of a family, would overlook the claims of his own children. They would extend the solace and the help all the more for their infirmities.

"In the year 1871 the Massachusetts Board of Public

Charities addressed communications to the superintendents of the lunatic hospitals of that State, requesting their views on certain points. That which concerns this board is the inquiry as to the *provision* which should be made for the class to whom we refer. It is highly honorable, in our judgment, to the intelligence as well as to the humanity of each of these distinguished gentlemen, that neither recommended that a hospital for the 'criminal insane' should be an appendage or an appurtenance of a prison, or built at all on prison grounds. On the contrary, although one of them, to relieve the urgency of the case, admits that he has recommended the fitting of a lunatic ward in the State prison, to be placed under the special care of the prison physician, still he declares 'there would be but little objection, aside from sentiment, to the treatment of lunatic convicts in a properly constructed hospital for the insane, where they would not mingle indiscriminately with the other classes of patients.' Another says, 'I would not advocate making it an adjunct of the State prison, or any penal institution.' The last, after recommending that a distinct institution be established for the reception of this class, says, with the knowledge that they are provided for [in Massachusetts] in the State lunatic hospitals, 'if the superintendents and trustees of any State lunatic hospital, and the general agent of the Board of State Charities, concur in the opinion that a patient of said hospital ought to be removed to said building, he should be so removed. This is the alternative to care and treatment in a general hospital for the insane: in Pennsylvania [it would be] from a prison to a hospital.

"As the result of the investigations of this intelligent commission, and the views forcibly presented by the eminent alienist physicians of their own State, viz., Drs. Godding, Earle, and Bemis, this cautious board has recommended in their present report, just issued, *the establishment of a hospital for the 'criminal insane,' to be placed near enough one of the other State hospitals for the insane to be under the same administration.*

"This board concurs in the principle which underlies this recommendation, as well as in its practical wisdom, for as to the latter, it cannot be expected that any one State will incur the expense of an independent establishment for this class and the cost of its proper oversight and maintenance. As has been already stated, there is but one in England whose population approximates to our own (that of the United States). As to the former, there is no *moral ground* upon which the separation of the two classes can be based. It is simply the ground of disagreeableness, to those who conduct the institution, to a small proportion of the patients, and to some of their friends. It is 'sentiment,' and this we admit should be religiously regarded in the consideration of every provision for the insane. Let it not be overlooked in behalf of the class we are now considering! We say sentiment only, for the scheme proposed to our legislature provided for a separate and secure building, separately enclosed with suitable walls, *but to be under the supervision of the superintendent of the general hospital*, on the same premises.

"Believing that our views have been clearly conveyed in this communication, and excusing its crudeness by the obvious necessity of haste, I beg most respectfully to commit the subject to your thoughtful determination and action; and I trust that they may be so enlightened as to reflect honor upon your body and yourselves individually—not merely for the present, but for all time.

"I am, most respectfully, yours,

"GEO. L. HARRISON,

"*President.*"

When the association entered upon the consideration of this letter, the following resolutions were offered:—

"WHEREAS, The proper disposal of that class of the insane, whose criminal acts require their seclusion and confinement, is a matter on which this association is requested to express an opinion.

"1. *Resolved*, Therefore, as the opinion of this association, that neither jails and penitentiaries nor ordinary hospitals for the insane are proper receptacles for this class of persons; but that they should be cared for in establishments designed expressly and solely for them.

"2. *Resolved*, That under no circumstances should 'insane convicts' be associated with other insane persons, believing that such an association is not calculated to improve the condition of the latter, and that the best interests of the former require a special management, and architectural arrangements of a peculiar kind, both very different from such as are adapted to the needs of other classes of the insane.

"3. *Resolved, also,* That the example of the State of New York, which has thus provided for its 'criminal insane,' as they are usually called, be commended to imitation by other States, either singly or collectively."

We take the liberty of reproducing here some of the most noteworthy utterances which this discussion called forth in the association, as they are published in the Journal of Insanity, before cited.

Dr. Shew, superintendent of the general hospital for the insane, Middletown, Connecticut:—"If the resolutions refer to persons who commit acts which would be considered criminal, were they not insane, I cannot concur in all the resolutions. Many of the patients received in our hospital commit those acts, and are sent to the hospital because they are dangerous to society,—dangerous as insane persons. It seems to me that there can be but one opinion, and that is that insane criminals should be separated entirely from patients in hospitals. First, because of the dangerous influence upon other patients; secondly, because of the odium which it brings on the institution, and the unpleasant feeling which the friends of the patients have in supposing or believing that their loved ones are associating daily and hourly with criminal persons.

"In practical experience I have not found that 'insane convicts' are particularly objectionable in themselves—not so much as Dr. Shurtleff and Dr. Curwen have." [Dr. Curwen has not given his remarks in the official publication.] "Three years ago the Legislature of Connecticut passed a law requiring the trustees of the hospital at Middletown to receive all insane convicts after a proper examination, which was specified, and a commission appointed. We had no separate provisions, and were obliged to receive them in the hospital proper, *and place them in association* with the other patients. Since that time twelve insane convicts have been transferred from Wethersfield to Middletown; two of that number have escaped; one of them feigned insanity; arrangements had been made to transfer him to Wethersfield, but he escaped the very night before the transfer was to be made. Of the ten others, seven have been among the most valuable farm laborers, harmless, industrious, and peaceable, and yet positively insane; much less dangerous than many of the chronic patients. One of the number has been very valuable the past few years, in sharpening the tools used by the stone-cutters in the erection of the two wings, saving the cost of one skilled mechanic. It was his trade and occupation before being sent to prison. None of the seven who have been employed ever attempted to escape."

[*Why, then, was it that in the case of the eight insane convicts sent to the Harrisburg institution, five managed to escape?*]

"They are generally liked by the patients, and are not more troublesome than others. The friends of the patients ['paying' patients, doubtless] object to the association, and in my report last year I called the attention of the legislature to that fact, and asked that an appropriation be made for a separate building, distinct from the main hospital, a cottage simply, to provide for the insane convicts. * * * During the present year, we hope to have a building for the *accommodation of twenty persons*, in which we will provide for all the insane convicts. There have been only three transferred from Wethersfield each year."

Dr. Shew then—assuming that the population and resources of some of the States, and the number of their insane convicts, may be such as to warrant the construction in each of an entirely separate hospital for their accommodation, with all the best appointments for their proper care and treatment—proceeds to express, in that case, his preference for having such a hospital, intended exclusively for the insane convicts proper, erected on the grounds of the State prison, rather than on those of a general hospital; but otherwise, and for other States, he clearly prefers such an arrangement as he has described at Middletown.

Dr. Compton, of Mississippi:—

"The third resolution, I think, I would amend, because that condemns the action of my own State in this matter. It declares that under no circumstances should insane convicts be permitted to associate with other insane persons, believing that such association is not calculated to benefit the insane, &c. I would be very decidedly against the first part of the resolution, that, 'under no circumstances should they be associated.' *I would take them into my asylum rather than let them remain in the penitentiary or jail. In the absence of the proper provisions I would take them out of the penitentiary and jails and put them into my asylum.*"

Dr. Earle, of Northampton, Massachusetts:—

"I would put the convict insane in a separate institution, independent of all other institutions. I would put in the same place those who have been tried for crime and acquitted on the ground of insanity; then those incendiary and homicidal patients who never had been tried for crime. I would make the provision that they should be removed to that institution, but not unless it was decided by the superintendent of the hospital and the Board of State Charities and its agents; all these authorities must concur before a man who had committed a criminal act, and had not been convicted of crime, should be removed (not from the common hospital to the penitentiary or prison, but) from the common hospital to this institution. This applies only to the incendiary and homicidal class, because our most dangerous patients are not convicts, and have never been tried for crime and acquitted on the ground of insanity."

Dr. Grundy, of Athens, Ohio:—

"In endorsing the action of the State of New York, we go further than my amendment would contemplate, because we endorse this course. They have done very well in providing a hospital for insane convicts, but with those insane convicts they send persons who are compelled to mingle with them, whose acts of violence were committed in their diseased condition. It is urged that this is a matter of expediency, because the hospitals are not able to contain them for various reasons. If the hospitals are not properly constructed make them so. If special arrangements are required for violent patients, have those special arrangements made." The doctor then goes on to speak with more kindness than respect of boards of State charities; but with this we have nothing to do.

Dr. Smith, of Fulton, Missouri:—

"I must also object to that part of one of the resolutions which endorses the New York law. Those conversant with this law inform us that one of its provisions requires that all acquitted on the ground of insanity shall, in the discretion of the judge, be sent to the same institution designed for convicts." [And he might have added, standing as a department of the State prison.] "Such a provision as this I cannot endorse. * * * *Endorsing this law would be equivalent to endorsing the punishment of the insane, because of the acquittal of crime;* the penalty of assigning them to a position most repulsive to their feelings and those of their friends, and one that would not only retard but often prevent recovery." [What would the doctor have said of sending them, *as we do*, not to a common hospital, but to a common prison?] "*We have patients in our institution, who, prior to admission, committed terrible deeds, and no doubt there are such in most hospitals for the insane.* We have fathers who killed their wives and children, and a mother who killed her husband; all under the influence of delusions in regard to different members of their families. These patients have been as orderly, quiet, and pleasant as any in our building; have shown no tendency to violence, and exerted no injurious influence over others."

The resolutions were amended and finally passed as follows, and were transmitted to us at the response of the association:—

"WHEREAS, The President of the Board of Charities of Pennsylvania has requested that this association should express its opinion in regard to the proper disposition of insane convicts: therefore,

"*Resolved*, That neither the cells of penitentiaries and jails, nor the wards of ordinary hospitals for the insane, are proper places for the custody and treatment of this class of the insane.

"2. That when the number of this class in any State (or in any two or more adjoining States which will unite in the project) is sufficient to justify such a course, these cases should be placed in a hospital specially provided for the purpose; and that until this can be done, they should be treated in a hospital connected with some prison, and not in the wards nor in separate buildings upon any part of the grounds of an ordinary hospital for the insane."

The published report of the debate, from which we have made the foregoing citations, as containing important medical opinions bearing on the subject in hand, would have been more complete and fair, as well as less liable to misunderstanding, if the letter from this board which called it forth had not been suppressed. It would then have appeared that both the debate and the final action of the association failed to grasp the precise points presented in the letter. They treated the subject with reference to an ideal standard, rather than with reference to the actual laws and practice of Pennsylvania in the case.

The whole debate and the final action were eventually narrowed down to the case of "insane convicts" exclusively, instead of taking into view all the classes of the "criminal insane," so called, which were presented for their consideration.

It is instructive, however, to compare the resolutions finally adopted with those originally proposed.

1. Both sets of resolutions agree—and so did, apparently, every member of the association, in the most emphatic manner—in the fundamental principle, that neither the cells of jails and penitentiaries, nor the wards of ordinary hospitals for the insane, are *proper receptacles for the custody and treatment* of that class of the insane whose case was under consideration.

2. The resolutions adopted confine themselves to the care of *insane convicts as such*, a portion only of the cases submitted for consideration, while the original preamble included the "proper disposal of that class of the insane whose criminal acts require their seclusion and confinement." Precisely what class was intended to be thus described might be doubted, but if simply "insane convicts" were intended, it was a very circuitous way of saying so.

3. It is not expressly and positively declared, in these as in the former resolutions, that, under no circumstances, should "insane convicts" be associated with other insane persons; but merely that they should be treated "*in a hospital specially provided for the purpose.*"

It is left an open question whether or not other special classes of insane persons may be treated in the same specially-provided hospital, *i. e.*, supposing such hospital not to be on prison grounds, and, at the same time, not a department of any ordinary hospital for the insane.

4. The commendation of the New York plan of sending other insane persons besides convicts to a hospital connected with a State prison, is carefully avoided.

5. A separate hospital for this class—separate from prisons as well as ordinary hospitals—is proposed as the proper and desirable plan, provided it can be had.

6. Until such a hospital can be had, it is proposed, as an imperfect, temporary, and unsatisfactory substitute,—but as much better than giving "insane convicts" no special or remedial treatment at all,—that they, *i. e.*, *the strictly "insane convicts" as such, and by themselves*, should be treated in a hospital connected with some prison, rather than on the grounds of any "ordinary" hospital for the insane.

The conclusions thus reached, as far as they go, would be quite in harmony with the views of this board, except, perhaps, in the last-mentioned particular; and, on that point, there might be no substantial disagreement when the case is narrowed down to the precise circumstances contemplated, and the precise expressions employed. *It is, in terms, an undesirable alternative which is thus presented.* We think, and we shall hope to show, that it is neither reasonable nor necessary to resort to such an alternative at all.

The plan of two or more States joining in the erection or support of a hospital for insane convicts is not new. Such a plan was proposed and drawn out at large by Dr. Edward Jarvis, of Massachusetts, in

1857, in a very able and suggestive paper on the "criminal insane." We cannot but regard all such propositions as simply futile. No two or more States will ever combine in building a common hospital for their "insane convicts;" nor will any one State ever provide such a hospital for the use of other States. In reference to such joint action, the case of insane convicts is very different from that of the blind or deaf-mutes or the ordinary insane. We may therefore dismiss such suggestions as visionary and illusory. And the fact that *United States* convicts are received into the convict-prisons of several of the States, in the absence of a national prison, furnishes no parallel at all to the expedient suggested, of one State taking charge of another State's convicts. It may be quite possible, and fair, also, for a child to accommodate a parent in an emergency, and impracticable and unreasonable to extend like assistance to a fellow-child. But let it be observed, in any case, that we make no *objection* to the joint action of several States in the premises: we only express a decided opinion that it will never be brought about.

It remains, then, for each State to make provision for herself. We must consider the subject in this point of view, if we are to give it any *practical* consideration at all. No one State—not even New York or Pennsylvania, has such a number of *insane convicts*, in the strict sense of the term, as would warrant the erection and equipment of a completely separate hospital for their exclusive care and treatment,—such a hospital as should furnish them the best supervision and attendance, and nothing less ought to be furnished them. The number of such convicts in this State is probably not many more at any one time than could be accommodated in Dr. Shew's "little cottage" attached to his hospital. For it is to be observed that the magnitude of the existing evil in this particular case consists not so much in its numerical extent as in the principle involved, and in its ramifying connections.

The State has no right to offset economy against an injustice or against inhumanity; but she has a right, in doing justice, to study economy; and she is likely more fully to meet the demands of justice and humanity on the whole and in the long run, when she makes her plans with a far-seeing and systematic economy, than when she indulges in spasmodic extravagance.

It may be assumed as another settled thing, that the State will never establish an entirely separate hospital, separate from all connection either with prisons or with ordinary hospitals, *for the exclusive accommodation of twenty or thirty "insane convicts,"* and provide it with all the appointments of a complete hospital for the care and treatment of the insane. This plan may be dismissed as equally visionary and illusory with the other.

But it is not to be forgotten that, besides the strictly insane convicts, there are other analogous and closely-bordering classes of insane persons yet to be provided for in this State:—(1.) Those who have been convicted of crime, but have served out their sentences and continue insane; and of these, there may be nearly as many as of the others. (2.) Those who have been charged with crime, but found insane before trial or sentence; these are a class as numerous, probably, as the insane convicts, and yet they are not insane convicts. (3.) Those who have committed terrible acts of violence or destruction, as homicide, arson, burglary, &c., and have been acquitted on the ground of insanity, but who, for the safety of the community, must be kept under the most watchful and perhaps rigorous restraint, as well as provided with the most skillful curative treatment. All these classes are now in our jails and penitentiaries or poor-houses, or are by law liable to be there, and other classes besides them;* and their case is be provided for as well as that of the strictly insane convicts. And even if a special hospital should be provided for insane convicts, in connection with some prison or penitentiary, and on the prison ground, rather than in connection with one of the State lunatic asylums, and with the imperfect appointments and supervision which must needs characterize such an

* The following facts are reported by the general agent of this board under date November 1st:—

Insane frequently sent to prison, sometimes as many as eight or ten at a time, who are kept until the court decides what disposition to make of them.

One lunatic sentenced November 13th, 1868, for ten days, to enter bail for good behavior. In default of bail he has been confined ever since. The cause of his detention is the want of suitable accommodations in the county almshouse.

Eight insane were sent to this prison in 1872, all of whom were transferred to the county almshouse.

One lunatic confined since last winter, was sent here from the poor-house for safety, not being able to keep her at the latter.

One "criminal insane," confined nearly six years under a "charge" of arson.

One man charged with having stolen a horse was acquitted on the ground of insanity, but is still confined.

One committed for threat to kill.

One man not charged with crime committed for safe-keeping.

Insane frequently committed.

One charged with attempt to shoot suffers under mental disorder.

Insane frequently committed.

establishment, considered as a mere department of the prison, we will not ask now whether this is all that is due to the "insane convicts" themselves; but we do ask whether those other classes of insane persons ought to be sent to such a hospital, to associate with the insane convicts in a department of a prison? Either that, or left in the cells of the jails and penitentiaries or poor-houses, *where they are.* But it is asked, why not send them, in such a case, to the ordinary lunatic hospitals? We answer by asking why they are *not* uniformly sent there now? or why, when sent there, they are exposed to be remanded to the prison cells?

It may be said that this very class of "criminal insane" *are* in the hospitals, and that the "returns" to this board, from these institutions, present this fact continually. We have not denied or disputed the fact. We have not found fault with the little good that is done; but only with the great wrong-doing which so completely obscures and over-shadows it. The law should declare the rights of every citizen, and vindicate them uniformly and without exception, especially the rights of the poor and defenseless.

In fact, the whole question is narrowed down to these points:—

1. It is agreed on all hands that neither prisons nor ordinary hospitals, with the ordinary arrangements, are fit places for the custody and treatment of "insane convicts."

2. The co-operation of several States in establishing or maintaining a special hospital for that purpose is out of the question.

3. It is equally out of the question for one State—for this State—to provide for the exclusive use of this class of insane an entirely separate institution, with the proper hospital equipment and superintendence.

4. Their special hospital, therefore, if they are to have any, must either be upon the grounds of a prison and an appendage to it, with the imperfect and insufficient supervision of the prison physician, the attendance of prison overseers or keepers, and the atmosphere of prison associations, or upon the grounds of some State hospital, so as to be under the same supervision of high and appropriate medical character, the same attendance and the same curative influences; though, while a department of the hospital, it may be made as completely secure, and kept as separate from it as may be thought best;—to be denominated, not "the convict department," or "the criminal department," but simply "the special department of such a hospital." This remains the only practical alternative.

If the former course is chosen, the patients will not be secured *that degree of skillful treatment and of humane and careful attendance* which is their due, and without which there is small prospect of their recovery; and, what is perhaps more, it would be utterly unjust and outrageous to retain those other classes of the insane,—if placed in the same hospital with the convicts,—not only in connection with those convicts, but in association with the scenes and the character and the odium of the penitentiary. Even that might, indeed, be an improvement upon their present condition; but in principle and in fact, the wrong inflicted upon them would be the same; they would still be consigned to the penitentiary. Either this, we say again, or they must be sent to ordinary hospitals.

If, on the other hand, the latter alternative is chosen, then *this special or separate department of the hospital, instead of being regarded as properly intended for insane convicts, may and should be regarded as intended chiefly, and in the first instance, for the accommodation and safe-keeping of the three (and perhaps other) classes of insane persons above described; and the far less numerous class of insane convicts may be regarded as being admitted, in the character of insane, to a higher position than, as convicts, they could claim;* and meantime, the infamy of incarcerating innocent and helpless men and women in the criminal's dungeon would be done away, while the ordinary hospitals would be relieved from the charge of some of the insane, who require the most special and expensive arrangements for their safe-keeping. *It would not be that the insane of these other classes would be thrust into a convict hospital; but convicts would be admitted to a hospital intended for other classes. And even this need not continue, and should continue no longer than till the State should feel justified in establishing a totally separate hospital for the insaue convicts themselves.* If, till then, it be thought a wrong to these other classes of lunatics, that convicts, though insane like themselves and equally irresponsible, should be thrust upon their society at all, we answer that among these classes as little of actual association or intercourse might be allowed, even within this separate department or wing of the hospital, which they would occupy in common, as might be thought advisable. At all events, to be obliged to be associated with insane convicts in a common hospital is *small ground for complaint*, in comparison with being thrust into association with felons, sane as well as insane, in a common prison. As to the inmates of the other departments of the general hospital, on whose grounds this special and separate department would stand, for us or for their friends to think of any hardship or degradation to them in consequence of their *separate connection with this department*, is, surely, nothing less than the most superlative extravagance or sentimental fastidiousness; especially when it is remembered that the whole hospital is furnished by the liberality of the State for the accommodation of poor and destitute insane people; people, too, who would, otherwise, be miserably and hopelessly languishing in poor-houses and prisons.

And besides, the objection to making the provision we have suggested for the criminal insane, so called, in a separate department on hospital grounds, leaves only the alternative of keeping them in *direct association* with unoffending insane in the poor-houses, where they are constantly sent; so that, as these are not "paying" patients, it would seem that they are to be left out in a discussion of the subject, and their rights are not to be considered. Let us not continue, as a State, to inflict, by the wholesale, upon our helpless fellow-creatures, the most outrageous wrongs, waiting until we can be sure of doing right with the most mathematical precision, or after the nicest and most perfect ideal and sentimental model. Let us not strain out the gnat while we unhesitatingly swallow the camel!

The suggestion that, dealing with insane convicts, one or two things must occur, namely, that "you must make a prison of the hospital or a hospital of the prison," and that the latter alternative is wiser and more humane, is, we consider, more specious than sound. We think we have shown that the tendency of the prevailing system in this State is to "imprison" numbers of irresponsible insane, whose clear right it is to enjoy "hospital" care. Surely this should be reversed even at the inconvenience (if it need be and if it be such) to the hospital of caring for a few individuals who have been guilty of crime and have since become insane.

One of the strangest and most inhuman suggestions in regard to the insanity of convicts is, that it should be considered as "a part of their punishment." So far as their whole punishment is to be regarded as a divine infliction, the suggestion is entirely true and God's ways can undoubtedly be vindicated; but from this point of view the same is true of *all cases* of insanity; they are all visitations of Divine Providence and as such are just and are not to be murmured against. However great the suffering it is in every case a righteous infliction. But to say that insanity is any part of the punishment inflicted on convicts by the sentence of human law, is simply false. If it were true; if by the sentence of the law men were to be driven insane as a punishment for their crimes—some, and not others, without any "rhyme or reason" in making the distinction—it would be nothing short of the grossest and most detestable inhumanity as well as injustice. In the case of convicts insanity is no more a part of their punishment than any other disease. If a convict is seized with fever or small-pox, shall we say "it is a part of his punishment," and so leave him to its consequences? No! we are to give him such diet and care and medical treatment as will be likely *to insure his recovery in the shortest time.* This can be done in the prison hospital. All we ask is that the same be done in case the disease is insanity. If this can be done; if *the best* medical superintendence and care can be provided in connection with the prison, let it be done; we have no objection to make. But if not,—if better provision can be supplied for these purposes in connection with some established hospital and at vastly less cost,—then let this latter course be preferred and adopted.

The whole matter is narrowed to a question of expediency and expense. If the State is prepared to meet the expense of providing the appointments of a first-class hospital, expressly and exclusively for twenty or thirty "insane convicts," very well, let them be provided. But, if not, let some other *adequate* provision be made. At all events, *let not helpless lunatics be left incarcerated in the cells of prisons and poorhouses.*

We have said before, and we now say again, that neither insanity, nor the privation of proper treatment in case of insanity, is any part of the sentence imposed upon convicts by law; and if there are still any who maintain that insanity is to be regarded as "a part of the convict's punishment," we beg only to add that such views as these are not shared by the distinguished medical gentlemen nor by the eminent philanthropic citizens who have intelligently, and with full knowledge of the import of what they have done, set their hands to the accompanying memorials to the legislature, praying your honorable bodies to redress the wrongs, not merely or chiefly of insane convicts, but of the several classes of insane poor, upon whose defense we have entered, against not only the injurious insinuations of interested parties, but the actual personal injuries and sufferings which are continuously heaped upon them in defiance of every impulse of humanity as well as every sober and righteous conviction of reason and sound judgment.

To the Board of Public Charities of the State of Pennsylvania:

The undersigned, practicing physicians of the cities of Pittsburg and Allegheny, request your board to take action looking to the repeal or modification of some of the provisions of law in relation to the treatment of insane, more especially of those who have been acquitted on the ground of insanity or who have become insane while incarcerated in prison or penitentiary.

We understand that the laws of this State in reference to these unfortunates are such, that in some cases the courts are expressly forbidden to commit them to the hospitals unless they are deemed *speedily curable;* and that in cases where insane criminals or persons *acquitted* on the ground of insanity have been sent by the court to the hospital, the board of managers and superintendent or physician, if they deem them incurable, may send them back to the jail or penitentiary from which they came.

We are assured that such treatment of the insane, whether criminals or not, is inhuman; and knowing as we do that a prison or penitentiary is not and cannot be a fitting place for the treatment of human beings so sadly afflicted, whether incurable or not, we earnestly appeal to you, and through you to the legislature of our State, to have such a change made in the laws as will effectually prevent the exposure of the insane of any class to incarceration in our prisons, jails, or penitentiaries. Yours, &c.,

ANDREW FLEMING, M. D.,
GEO. D. BRUCE, M. D.,
H. T. COFFEY, M. D.,
F. LE MOYNE, M. D.,
W. J. ESTEP, M. D.,
J. N. DICKSON, M. D.,
THOS. W. SHAW, M. D.,
JOHN DICKSON, M. D.,
A. W. MCCOY, M. D.,
JOHN S. DICKSON, M. D.,
W. SNIVELY, M. D.,
A. M. POLLOCK, M. D.,
W. C. REITER, M. D.,
JULIAN ROGERS, M. D.,
R. B. MOWRY, M. D.,
C. B. KING, M. D.,
J. B. MURDOCH, M. D.,
W. R. HAMILTON, M. D.,
JAS. KING, M. D.,
JAS. MCCANN, M. D.,
T. C. RHOADS, M. D.,
JAMES MACFARLANE, M. D.

PITTSBURG, December, 1873.

PHILADELPHIA, December, 1873.

To the Legislature of Pennsylvania:

The undersigned, members of the medical profession, being aware of the sad condition of the "poor" and the "criminal insane," who are suffering cruel personal wrongs and constant deterioration of their mental and bodily condition in the jails and poor-houses of the State, respectfully appeal to your honorable bodies to provide such legislation as will effectually secure the admission and detention of these classes in the State hospitals for the insane so long as their malady requires it.

We believe that both humanity and public duty demand such legislation for the relief of wrongful suffering and for the restoration to health and usefulness of these afflicted and injured classes.

S. D. GROSS, M. D.,
JOSEPH PANCOAST, M. D.,
ALFRED STILLÉ, M. D.,
FRANCIS G. SMITH, M. D.,
S. WEIR MITCHELL, M. D.,
WILLIAM PEPPER, M. D.,
D. HAYES AGNEW, M. D.,
J. FORSYTH MEIGS, M. D.,
EDW. HARTSHORNE, M. D.,
CASPAR MORRIS, M. D.,
J. M. DA COSTA, M. D.,
HIRAM CORSON, M. D.,
HORATIO C. WOOD, M. D.,
JOHN H. PACKARD, M. D.,
F. F. MAURY, M. D.

To the Senate and House of Representatives of Pennsylvania:

We gladly unite our names with those of the eminent jurists, the distinguished physicians, the inspectors and wardens of the penitentiaries, and other noted personages, familiar with the subject, in the appeal of the Board of Public Charities to your honorable bodies to redress, by proper legislation, the wrongs of the "poor" and the "criminal" insane, who are now consigned to the jails and almshouses of the State, and who should, properly, be placed in the State hospitals for the insane, which were established by the public for their reception, their care, and remedial treatment.

JAMES J. BARCLAY,
JOSEPH R. CHANDLER,
MAHLON H. DICKINSON,
HENRY C. CAREY,
ISAAC LEA,
JOHN O. JAMES,
JAMES THOMPSON (late Chief Justice),
WM. BACON STEVENS,
JOHN WELSH,
CALEB COPE,
JOHN M. WHITALL,
WILLIAM BIGLER,
ASA WHITNEY,
M. SIMPSON, Bishop.

DECEMBER 1st, 1873.

After the fullest investigation of facts and the maturest reflection upon the case, we are constrained to declare that, in our clear conviction and judgment, every consideration of humanity, justice, propriety, and expediency is combined in favor of *placing the special hospital for the "criminal insane," so called, including, incidentally and temporarily, "insane convicts," on the grounds of some State hospital*, so as to be under a common superintendence therewith, rather than within the purlieus of any prison.

We, therefore, most earnestly renew our recommendation that such a separate hospital department be speedily provided, with the proper construction and arrangements for the purposes indicated, on the grounds of the Danville hospital.

We further feel constrained to suggest—and we do it with much hesitation and with sincere respect for all parties—that, in forming a judgment of this scheme, a preponderating weight ought not to be attached to the opinions of parties who may have any personal interest or convenience involved in the question, however respectable they may be, and even though they present themselves in the character of experts. The authority of experts is limited to their particular professional sphere. Their proper office is to serve as *witnesses* and not as *judges;* and any intelligent and disinterested layman, who, by personal observation and thorough study, has made himself acquainted with the condition of the insane in our penitentiaries, jails, poor-houses, and hospitals, is as well (perhaps better) qualified to judge as they are of the broad features of any plan proposed for ameliorating that condition;—to judge what is consistent with or demanded by the dictates of justice, humanity, and the public good.

We beg also to suggest that, for examining and determining what persons should be transferred from the prisons or poor-houses or other hospitals, to the separate hospital department above recommended, or therefrom to prison or the other hospitals, the law should provide that either the Board of Public Charities, by their general agent or some other commissioner or commissioners specially appointed,—who should make themselves thoroughly acquainted with the condition and wants of the insane throughout the Commonwealth (*i. e.*, of such as are kept under detention and restraint), who could be supposed to have no interest to subserve but those of justice, humanity, and the public good, and who could act systematically and on general and impartial principles,—should have the ultimate control, with such *advice* from the superintendents of the State hospitals and other experts as they may require; or as in the case of the New York law in this behalf, with the aid and advice of a commissioner of lunacy, specially appointed to aid the Board of Public Charities in their action.

If your honorable bodies should prefer the appointment of an independent commission, this board will, of course, be entirely satisfied.

In all this, we presume, of course, that the courts would, in the first instance, make such disposition of the insane, who come under their judicial cognizance, as they should by law be authorized or required to do. Provision might also be made for carrying up any decision of the aforesaid commission or of the general agent of this board which may be alleged to be erroneous or unjust, to some court, to be reviewed and either confirmed or reversed. It is remarkable that in the late convention of superintendents of the insane, to which reference has before been made, one of its members, having alluded to the provision of the New York law, empowering a judge to dispose, according to his discretion, of persons acquitted of murder and other crimes on the ground of insanity—sending them either to a convict hospital or some other, exclaimed, "Too great a sweep of power for one man!" And almost immediately after another member naïvely declared that "persons acquitted of a criminal act on the ground of insanity should be placed in the hospital for the insane, and the moment the superintendent considers him a fit subject for the asylum for convicts he should be sent there"!

The truth is, the very fact of the malady being obscure, and thus causing the general public to neglect its victims, excepting through mere curiosity, makes it important that the State, representing the community, should have a special agency whose duty it shall be to scrutinize the condition and needs of this class. Such a commission can understand these, as well as the physicians or attendants, and have no considerations of personal convenience to warp the judgment. The simple point of *diagnosis* of the particular phase of the malady is all in which it would necessarily be deficient.

It is the universal practice of governments which appoint commissions to constitute them of laymen.

We have said that the wrongs of the insane in prisons and poor-houses continue as they were when Miss Dix's "Memorial" caused the State to provide a hospital for their alleviation. We now say that, although every hospital built and projected has been recommended to the legislature with the same view, and seemingly with the same design, the system pursued has never extinguished and never will extinguish or even abate the evil. There are twelve hundred of these (outside of Philadelphia, where alone there are one thousand and fifty in the almshouse asylum) suffering incarceration and neglect. The *unnecessary costliness* of these hospital establishments for the indigent insáne, and the liberal admission into them of "*paying patients*," forbid the realization of the intentions and the desires of the legislature and the public.

In conclusion, we think we may assume the following as established principles or settled points :—

1. The State is bound to provide, not only for the safe-keeping, but for the proper care and treatment of all her insane poor.

2. Neither jails, penitentiaries, nor poor-houses are proper places for their detention or treatment, whatever may be the character of their insanity, or whether it be recent or of long standing—curable or incurable.

3. A person while insane can be guilty of no crime, and it is both unjust and inhuman to consign innocent men and women to the ignominious cells of jails and penitentiaries, or to the foul kennels of poor-houses, simply because, though insane and irresponsible, they are "dangerous to be at large."

4. Even insane convicts ought not to be retained in the cells of prisons, but transferred to some hospital where they may be both safely kept and receive appropriate medical treatment.

In view of the foregoing admitted facts and principles, this board begs to renew and repeat, by way of summary, the following recommendations, and most earnestly to urge them upon the attention of the legislature :—

1. That the law of April 8th, 1861, be repealed, or amended, in the points indicated in this report.

2. That the State should make prompt and adequate provision in general State hospitals *for all the insane poor* in the Commonwealth, determine by law how their expenses should be paid, require the several counties either to make equally suitable provisions in proper hospitals for their insane poor, or to send them to the State hospitals, and require the authorities of these hospitals to receive and retain them as long as they need hospital care.

3. That a separate wing or department of one of the State hospitals—to be under the charge of its superintendent—should be suitably constructed, arranged, and equipped for the reception, custody, and proper medical treatment (1) of those persons who continue insane after completing the period of their sentence for crime; (2) of those who, being charged with the commission of crime while sane, are adjudged insane before trial or sentence; (3) of those who are acquitted of certain crimes, as murder, arson, rape, burglary, &c., on the ground of insanity, and are adjudged too dangerous to be discharged, and, (4) perhaps, of other dangerous lunatics;—all these to be sent either to this department or to the ordinary hospitals, according to the discretion of the court or of the proper commission.

4. That all other insane persons who are brought up for the sentence of the courts should be sent to the ordinary hospitals, so that no insane persons in any case should be committed to prison.

5. That, *till an entirely separate hospital may be provided for their accommodation, "insane convicts" should*

be admitted to appropriate quarters in the above-mentioned special department,—their insanity to be ascertained and their transfer regulated according to provisions of law, and they themselves allowed as much or as little association with the inmates of this department as the superintendent of the hospital shall judge proper and expedient.

6. That a special commission, appointed for the purpose, or the Board of Public Charities of the Commonwealth, be authorized to transfer from the other State hospitals to the special department above proposed, and from that to the ordinary hospitals, such persons as upon due examination and inquiry shall be judged proper. Whether this same commission should have authority to remove insane persons from *prison* to the special hospital department, we leave without any expression of opinion. Definite provisions as to this might be prescribed by statute.

7. Inasmuch as there are strong and well-founded objections to condemning any person as *incurably insane* beforehand, and as the presence of incurables is no more disadvantageous to the curable, and often less so, than of some others who are curable, the board are not prepared to recommend their systematic separation, but, under the presumption that general hospitals will be provided for all the insane poor, leave them to be retained in the several hospitals and distributed in each as the superintendents may deem most advisable.

Such are our recommendations, and we present and urge them, not as theories, but as practical suggestions, looking to positive and immediate action.

We beg to call the particular attention of the members of the general assembly to the fact that most of these recommendations are supported and guaranteed, not by the MERE OPINION, BUT BY THE DIRECT TESTIMONY OF THIS BOARD AND ITS GENERAL AGENT; and not only so, but by both the opinions and the testimony of the present and former JUDGES OF OUR CRIMINAL COURTS, THE JUDGES OF THE SUPREME COURT, and by the INSPECTORS AND WARDENS OF OUR PENITENTIARIES, as well as by those of many superintendents of the insane, whose declarations on this behalf are embodied in this report; as also by those of LEARNED PHYSICIANS and INTELLIGENT PHILANTHROPISTS, who have made the facts of this case a subject of special examination and study; to which many other names might have been added from all parts of the State, if pains had been taken to secure them; and, finally, by the EXAMPLE AND EXPERIENCE OF OTHER STATES.

ADDENDUM TO PLEA.

PAYING PATIENTS IN STATE LUNATIC HOSPITALS FOR THE INSANE.

THE fact that so great a number of the poor and "criminal," though irresponsible, insane of this Commonwealth are now languishing in the county poorhouses or prisons, notwithstanding all the generous provision made for them in the State hospitals, is believed to be traceable, in a large degree, to another fact, that more than half of the inmates of some of these hospitals are and have been not *poor* but *paying* patients. This is especially the case with the hospital at Harrisburg. In behalf of this hospital, it has, indeed, been given out of late that, had not the superintendent sent the cases to Danville, the proportion of patients from the authorities of the counties would have been greater than those from friends. In answer, it is stated in the report of the Dixmont Hospital just issued (and this is a *private* institution, *aided* by the State), that, since the opening of that institution in 1862, one thousand two hundred and forty-nine of its patients have been sent by friends, and one thousand two hundred and eighty-eight by authorities in charge of the poor; while at Harrisburg the proportion has been two thousand two hundred and sixteen by friends, and one thousand two hundred and seventy-eight by the authorities.

This state of things is made a subject of grave complaint by the Board of Public Charities. But a serious attempt seems to be made (in some quarters) to defend this policy, even while it implies and necessitates the exclusion of so many of the insane poor.

We take leave to introduce here the statement made on this subject by this board in their report recently presented to the legislature, showing that they had viewed and grasped the question in all its bearings:—

"It may be said, and perhaps with truth, that in many cases the friends of insane patients who can furnish the smaller sum required at the State hospital for their support would not be able to meet the heavier charges of a private asylum; and that, therefore, such insane patients must be thus admitted at the hospital or sent to the poor-house. This idea seems highly plausible, and might at first receive favor from inconsiderate persons. But upon reflection it clearly appears unsound in theory; and upon experience it proves highly objectionable. If these patients are *poor*, why should precisely this class of poor patients have precedence of those who are still poorer? And if they are rich—as by the terms of the statute all "paying" patients are, then the law expressly gives the poor the precedence over them. Besides, all these middle measures of giving public aid to the poor are found in practice to be dangerous, and liable to great abuses on the part both of the recipients and the almoners of the public bounty. This case has proved itself, in our judgment, no exception to the general rule.

"It may be suggested that it has been thought well to have some *paying* patients in order to give respectability to the institution.

"We can scarcely listen to the suggestion with patience, or answer it with calmness. If all the poor were already provided for and accommodated, the suggestion might pass; although *we* should not make it. We should never propose that the State should tax herself to furnish hospital accommodations to the rich in any case, whether by way of gratuity or of profitable speculation. But this is not the case. The poor are not all enjoying the care and treatment of the hospitals; and shall they by the hundred and the thousand continue to languish into idiocy, or rave out their miserable lives in the cells of prisons, with malefactors and felons, or in the more wretched and hopeless receptacles of county poor-houses, in order that the hospital, which receives a few score of them, may be respectable, and its superintendent and officers may not find themselves in charge of an institution of mere paupers?"

The attempt is now made to defend the course pursued at the State hospitals, by exciting a special public sympathy in favor of the unfortunate class of "respectable" poor persons, who may have become insane,—persons having respectable connections and respectable antecedents, whose friends can now pay a moderate sum for their treatment in the hospital, instead of their being received—or rather rejected—as paupers; but who, if refused on those terms, could not have their expenses paid at a private institution, and would simply go to increase the number of the pauper insane who require to be supported and cared for at the public expense.

Now, we would not diminish one jot the public interest for this worthy class of unfortunate persons. We share it in its fullest extent. We rejoice that for them is found a special chord of sympathy in the susceptibilities of the public mind, and, for this very reason, we think they should not be received as paying patients, and that to the exclusion of the poor, in the State hospitals. These patients have friends and some means, and a strong hold upon personal sympathy; if they need aid, it is most properly to be afforded them through private and not through public channels; and we believe that in such cases it would be so afforded, and that they would generally be provided for at private institutions, if they were not received at the State hospitals. But who is to provide for those who have no friends and no means and no claim upon any man's sympathy except their helpless misery and the shocking repulsiveness of their squalid and abandoned condition? We simply maintain that it is these the State must provide for *first of all.* If, after having adequately provided for them, the State has still the means and the disposition to make public appropriations for eking out the scanty means of all her less fortunate citizens, who, though not strictly poor, are in comparatively reduced circumstances, we might or we might not object to her so doing; but for the State to undertake this sort of communistic charity now, to the neglect of the absolutely helpless poor, is, we maintain, simply preposterous. Moreover, we do not believe that the superintendent of a great public charity should be intrusted with this sort of discretion in selecting its recipients. He should not be exposed to the danger of abusing an enormous power of *personal patronage*, of consulting his personal convenience, or being influenced by the special solicitations of anybody's friends in dispensing the bounty of the State.

We may be permitted to refer to some cases of the misery of the insane poor which have fallen more or less directly under our own observation.

1. A young man at —— county poor-house, whose father had treated him with such uniform brutality, and exacting demands upon his ability to labor, as literally

to drive him crazy. The slightest sound startled him. He was afraid of the approach of the quietest step, even that of a cat. Night and day he was thus agitated by terror; and he found in the poor-house no possible care or treatment which could alleviate his *misery* or promise the least hope of recovery.

2. In the same place there was another young man, whose employer had abused him by stoning him in the field when his work was not satisfactory, striking head or body, as the case might be. This boy never removed his hand from his head at the part where the stone struck him last, and by which his mental health was broken down.

3. The old man who was starved to death in a poor-house the other day, medicine being *forced* into him, but food being considered unnecessary.

4. "The attractive young lady" driven to insanity by her seducer, and for the last twenty years occupying a cell of filthiness, with wet litter for a bed, resting like a beast upon her haunches, and so permanently cramped as to be capable of no movement but such as resembled that of a frog.

5. The patient in another poor-house, who exists perpetually chained by the wrists to the ceiling, lest he may tear his clothes.

6. The young girl in shackles at another poor-house, who, at the name of "mother," utters sobs whose pathos would touch the most callous heart.

7. And that other gentle-faced child, whose malady has been caused by religious over-excitement, seeking in vain for repose amid the shrieks of the intermingled inmates of the insane department of the poor-house.

8. "The splendid old man" in chains for forty years in —— poor-house, released by the general agent of this board, himself aiding in filing off his chains.

Add to the foregoing specimens the following, which we here reproduce from the report of the board:—

"In February last a visit was paid to this almshouse, and an insane inmate was seen—a young woman over twenty years of age—whose whole dress consisted of a thin chemise with short sleeves, a single skirt, and a pair of shoes. When brought before the visitors, a borrowed cloak was thrown over her shoulders. She was blue with cold, and utterly filthy in person. Her cell had the appearance of having undergone a recent hasty washing, but was pervaded with an odor loathsome in the extreme. On the day of this visit, the thermometer fell to fourteen degrees.

"In March another visit was paid to the institution by several gentlemen in a body. Only one portion of the building was visited, which is supposed to be devoted exclusively to women. In one cell was a young woman, the one already referred to. Her cell was without any furniture whatever; her bed consisted of one blanket; her clothing of a ragged chemise, open to her waist, and one scanty skirt and a pair of shoes. She was indescribably unclean, and alive with vermin. Her cell reeked with a sickening odor, the result of a total absence of all conveniences of cleanliness. She shivered with cold while in the presence of her visitors, the thermometer standing at the time several degrees below the freezing point.

"Opposite to the cell which we have very faintly described was another. The short day had already faded into dusk, and, as the light was thrown through a little aperture in the door, it fell upon two wretched women, both of whom were absolutely without a single garment to cover them. One of the poor creatures sat crouching in the corner, with a small blanket drawn across her shoulders, while the other was crawling on all-fours on the floor, without even this poor apology of any remnant of human decency. There was not a particle of furniture in the cell; and there, on this wintry March night, in an atmosphere which the witnesses declare to have been utterly horrible, were these two human beings, brought down far below the level of our domestic brutes.

"In an adjoining cell the visitors found a man lying on an old mattress, the only sign of furniture which they saw in either of the rooms inspected. They were informed that the inmate was a woman; but, upon one of the gentlemen calling to him, he sat up, and it was seen that it was a man. The attendant, with some confusion, explained that he must have been brought in while he was away.

"We found the female insane department in a shocking condition; so bad that it would be impossible to give a description of the place on paper. In some cells there were two or more women confined; some, without any clothing, lying on the floor without mattress, carpet, or anything else, except an old Government blanket. The place had a horrible, putrid odor.

"We examined one woman who was quite young. I was afraid to go near her, as she seemed covered with vermin. We were all much shocked by the visit, and I think I shall remember it as long as I live."

And the general agent reports the following amongst many like instances of abuses and neglect in similar establishments:—

"Insane, totally neglected—morally, physically, and medically; less attention is given to them than would be given to the lowest animals; four are incapable of self-care, confined in filthy cells; one a female, has great neighborhood notoriety, from sad incidents connected with her history. Known as an intelligent, esteemed, and attractive young lady, the daughter of a well-known inhabitant of the neighborhood, she fell a victim to the arts of the seducer. Insanity is alleged to be caused by her disappointment. This occurred twenty-one years ago. The sad case is rendered still more painful by her present forlorn condition. A bed of straw upon a damp, dirty floor, into which the external light can find no entrance, is the only furniture. A seat, a chair, or a bench, has apparently never been furnished; the consequence of which is that the muscles of the lower extremities, from the cramped position in which she was always found, have become permanently contracted, so that the only movement of which she is capable is one similar to that of a frog."

"An unusually large number of insane, many of chronic form, but quite a number of strongly marked cases, who are confined and had been chained to the floor until released by my direction. A young girl of seventeen years of age confined in a gloomy cell; since removed by my request to the State hospital, where she is gradually being restored."

"Twenty-two insane; twelve are kept in close confinement, some in chains; one always chained to the ceiling to prevent him from tearing his clothes; some entirely nude; at least six with straw litters; not one of the twelve was ever removed into the open air. All confined in apartments opposite each other, a narrow corridor extending between them. The effect of this close proximity was to make the day and night hideous with the distressing shrieks and yells of the wretched and maltreated madmen."

"Eight insane; one of whom hand-cuffed, one hoppled, one female confined to her room."

"One hundred and thirty-five inmates, four blind, one palsied, seven idiots; seven cells in the basement, with insane in each, in a revolting condition."

"Twenty insane; of these about eight were confined, not to their uncomfortable cells only, but restrained by iron fetters, long after the necessity had passed away. These were removed at my instigation, and the doors of their cells were opened, to give them the benefit of the open air and exercise, with decided improvement in their condition."

Now, all these cases, and others without number, have had their histories (histories as touching to human sensibilities as any which the more "respectable" poor can furnish), which should excite interest and sympathy, and should also command the efforts and influence of good men to create the needed revolution in the system now pursued at the State hospitals, to stop it at once and forever.

It is a fraud on the public to allow these wards of the State—and who alone of this class are strictly such—to go down to certain misery and death, while providing from the public resources for citizens who can be helped by their own means or the means of friends.

The poor, neglected and abused orphans and seamstresses and widows' sons and daughters, whom we meet under pauper care at the poor-houses, would not be treated even there as they are treated, if they had friends who would look after them and protect them. It is because they have no friends to help them that their condition is so forlorn.

When the State comes to take care of them, as she, *first of all*, should do, the other class—those who can pay from three dollars and fifty cents to five dollars or six dollars a week—will be provided for as they are elsewhere, and as others who are slightly above them in the scale of affluence. There are homes and hospitals for all of this latter class, for widows and orphans, for old men and children, whose support is, in part, paid for by themselves and friends, and the deficiency made up by private benevolence, often supplemented from the public coffers.

This should and would be the resource of the "paying patients" now in the State hospitals, if, by the personal system introduced there, the State had not been drawn away from her clear duty to enlist in a scheme of charity which is never recognized as the proper function or duty of the State—certainly not as her first duty. It would be just as reasonable to devote the almshouses proper to the maintenance of paying inmates and exclude the indigent, leaving them to perish. Just recur for a moment to the cases of wretchedness described above and imagine one of those poor creatures (if it were possible) to present himself at Harrisburg and implore admission to the State Lunatic Hospital and to receive for answer, "How much can your friends pay? Can you pay three dollars, four dollars, or five dollars per week for your treatment here? If not, if you have neither friends nor money, we have no room for you; we are already crowded, chiefly by those who can pay; this hospital was not established especially for such as you; those who can pay must have precedence over those who cannot; you must return to your poor-house or prison and die there."

What cooler mocking of humanity can be conceived of than this? Can such an answer be a true interpretation of the mind and purpose of the Commonwealth of Pennsylvania in founding her hospitals for the insane? Is the wretchedly poor, the absolutely naked and destitute lunatic, whose only claim is his misery, his helplessness, his friendlessness, to be met with the gentlemanly and supercilious questions:—"What is your social position? Where are your friends? Where is your money?" It is too outrageous to think of; there are no words whereby the enormity can be properly characterized.

Was ever an utterly friendless, helpless, destitute, naked, and starving pauper turned away from the doors of an almshouse in any Christian or civilized land, to wait outside till all (or any) of the more respectable poor, who could pay something for their food and clothing, should have their wants supplied? Was he ever told by the superintendent or managers of such an institution, "we have no room for such as you just now; you are too poor and friendless to find a lodging here; the sympathies of the public are, in the first place, for the more respectable class of indigent persons; you must give place to your betters; stay out in the cold and die as quietly as you can"? Has the State ever adopted, or is she ready to adopt, such principles as those in the administration of her bounty? We leave these questions for candid and thoughtful men to answer; protesting again that, for ourselves, we are not wanting in sympathy for the struggling sufferers of moderate or scanty means; we have no quarrel against them, or against any who, in their Christian benevolence, may be making personal efforts or sacrifices to afford them assistance or relief; we simply insist, that *the State should*, FIRST OF ALL, *make provision for the proper care of the absolutely destitute and friendless.*

In our judgment, the State cannot, at least now, afford to erect and maintain hospitals sufficient for the accommodation of both of these classes, viz., for the poor who can pay nothing, and for paying patients of scanty means; and, if she could, she should begin with the former. But under the present system of receiving into her hospitals even a larger number of the latter class than of the former, the State, with all her benevolent efforts and magnificent outlay in establishing hospitals for the insane, is making *no progress whatever towards relieving all of the former class.* There are now twice as many of the insane poor languishing in the dens and dungeons of the poor-houses and prisons of this Commonwealth as there were when Miss Dix first made her appeal for their relief, and the hospital at Harrisburg was built in response to her touching memorial.

No legerdemain in the cautious wording or adroit management of plausible propositions can annihilate that fact, or that other parallel fact, that, in the meantime, nearly two-thirds of the inmates of the Harrisburg hospital have been "paying patients." It matters not what excellent resolutions, purposes, petitions, or kind intentions are arrayed in defense against us. We make no personal charges of corrupt intentions, but rather of mistaken proceedings. We attack a system, not men nor motives.

If it be alleged that the presence of "paying patients" in the hospitals is *not the cause* of the exclusion or neglect of the poor, that there are now as many of the insane poor in the State hospitals as there would be if there were no "paying patients" in them; then it is evident, if that be true, that (the present system in other respects being retained) we need erect no more hospitals for the insane poor; we have already hospital accommodations for more than twice as many of them as require it. Is that so?

Should it be said that when application is made for the admission of the pauper insane at the State hospitals, no recent cases, only those of long standing or improbable cure, are rejected? The answer is, that among the "paying patients" cases of long standing and little likely to be cured are actually retained, and even admitted. If, by the contract made with friends, such cases might be removed from the hospital at the discretion of the superintendent, and are not, we do not see that it improves the case in any point of view. We have no doubt that these "paying patients" may be much more decent, quiet, gentlemanly, and agreeable inmates of the establishment, giving the superintendent much less distasteful and repulsive work and trouble, than those who might be brought to him from the foul dens of poor-houses or cells of prisons. All this we can understand; but this is no good ground in law or reason, or in the view of humanity, for preferring the former to the latter. Should it be alleged that neither the county authorities nor the criminal judges are ever deterred or hindered from sending insane persons to the hospitals by being told that it is already full or crowded; or should it be said that, though these officials are invited or encouraged by the hospital authorities to send the insane thither, they yet obstinately refuse or neglect to do so; then all we have to say is, the laws ought at once to be so amended as to *compel* those officials to send the lunatics who are at their disposal to the hospital at all events; and if then the poor do not come in, in such numbers as to displace the "paying patients," very well, we have no objection to make; but if they do, then we say the "paying patients" should give way to this other class.

We object to the present system. We demand a revolution. The scheme we would propose to substitute is easily understood. It is simply this:—(1) That, in all cases, the poor and friendless, those who cannot pay, should, in these State institutions, have precedence of the rich, of those who can pay; and (2) that, among the poor, recent cases should have the precedence of those of long standing, and so on, until as soon as possible all that need are provided for. For ourselves, we believe that such is the real intent of the laws as they now stand; but if that is not the case, and if the policy hitherto pursued by the State hospitals, and particularly by that at Harrisburg, has been, as is alleged by interested parties, in accordance with the existing laws of the State,—which we, however, on our part, emphatically deny,—then we ask that the laws be forthwith so amended as to secure the abandonment of that policy, and the inauguration of another, more just and more in conformity with the plain duty and proper functions of the State.

PROVISION FOR THE INSANE POOR.

In again presenting the claims of the insane poor to your honorable bodies, we are quite aware that the subject has already been made familiar by our frequent handling, and that we may labor under some disadvantage by urging the matter anew upon your attention. We believe, however, that, considering the subject as legislators, and aiming, as you will do, jointly to protect the interests of the State and of these, her recognized wards, the apprehension of importunity will not apply to yourselves, as may possibly be the case with such portion of the public as, from ignorance or indifference, are conscious of no responsibility in the matter. The majority of men, however humane their natures, prefer to give money as alms rather than care or consideration. They put their hands into their pockets for their share of the poor tax, and hold their account with the pauper portion of the community to be thereafter closed. They do not want to hear that their money has been misapplied, or to have their consciences or sympathies disturbed by any knowledge of the sufferings of the wretched creatures whom it should have relieved. It is only this strange but common union of benevolence and indifference in human proceedings which can explain the extraordinary spectacle that has for years been presented in this State, of magnificent hospitals on the one side, built and sustained at enormous cost by the tax-payers, for the benefit of the indigent insane, and, on the other, of the large majority of these very indigent insane, still held in almshouses, debarred from any reasonable chance of cure, and, in many cases, receiving treatment which would be an admitted cruelty if visited upon brutes; chained and naked, lodged in pens and cages unfit for the habitation of cattle; scantily and carelessly fed; without bedding or blanket or fire during the inclemency of winter; and all this in wealthy districts, filled with happy homes of cultured and Christian people.

We do not propose to detail again the sickening *minutiæ* of our investigations. Some of these, we thankfully announce to you, are buried in the dead past, never to be exhumed, as we believe, for a spectacle of sorrow and discredit to the communities which suffered them to exist. But we must submit, as briefly as we can, certain facts and deductions which, we trust, will have the force to settle your convictions as to the folly as well as cruelty of the past systems in this relation, if systems they may be called, and to settle and establish other and better ones, which will maintain the dignity and benevolence of our honorable State, as well as protect her financial interests from injudicious and unwise expenditures.

The number of indigent insane in the State hospitals, established primarily for the maintenance, cure, and treatment of this class, was seven hundred and sixty-four on September 30th, 1874, as reported by the authorities of these institutions; while the number of the same class in the poor-houses of the State and under other county provision, amounted to one thousand three hundred and fifty-two at the same date, exclusive of the insane department of the Philadelphia almshouse, which contained one thousand and seventy-five.

It is towards these latter—this great body of helpless beings—that we would direct your attention. We urge you to regard them critically in their actual condition, without any exaggerated sentiment or aid of the imagination. In every one of our county almshouses we find numbers of these unfortunates called "incurables," held and considered as a dead-weight upon society, in no wise differing from the lower animals in intellect or efficiency, to be lodged and fed as we lodge and feed the brute creation, with such scant measure of kindness and care as the temper of the superintendent may dictate. In most cases these officials are chosen either from political motives or because of their skill and experience in farming operations; and such considerations, we must admit, are not likely to insure a proper choice for the responsible position of caring for "minds diseased;" even if an almshouse was a place where such scientific ministering were practicable. The superintendent is expected to make the institution, *as nearly as possible*, self-supporting. The burden of his ability and his care-taking must be devoted to this preponderating effort. The insane inmate can give but little aid in this paramount undertaking, and he is therefore a clog and a hindrance, and pays the penalty of his helplessness in partial or absolute neglect. No consideration is given to the phase of his malady; no effort is made to discover whether it is curable or incurable; and it is the grand exception when the insane inmate of a poor-house issues therefrom clothed in his right mind.

The more accurate and detailed have been our investigations into the condition of this class, the more are we convinced that none of God's creatures call upon us more urgently for help and pity than the insane man, whom we have thrust ought of sight into our county poor-houses and left there unnoticed for years. There is laid upon him every one of those forms of suffering which Christianity calls upon us to seek out and relieve; he is a stranger among strangers; a terrible background of poverty and wretchedness lies behind his advent into the place; for, as we all know, so general is the perhaps irrational but natural prejudice against these institutions, that nothing but utter friendlessness or the extremity of want can account for his entrance into it. He is in prison and sick; sick with a deeper disease than those which only kill the body; the man himself has lost the place, rights, and well-nigh the existence of a man; his body goes to and fro, performing its natural functions as an animal, but the living creature within, which made him human for good or evil ends, which gave him the chance to be the faithful husband and father, the useful citizen, the God-fearing, honest helper of his fellow-men, is struck with death, answers not to any call or summons. Surely this poor wretch, beyond any other man, might echo the cry of Job, "Have pity upon me, for the hand of God hath touched me."

To act humanely, or even intelligently, toward any class, it is necessary that we should, in some degree, comprehend its peculiar character and needs, and its individual idiosyncrasies. This is not difficult to do in the present case.

In the records kept by the State and other insane hospitals, one or two curious facts have been elicited, bearing strongly, by inference, on the condition of the same class in almshouses.

First.—Subtracting the number whose profession or business is unknown, more than one-fourth of the whole remainder of male insane patients are farmers or farm laborers, and a large proportion of the female insane patients are the wives and daughters of the same class. The fact that the population of the State is largely agricultural does not altogether explain this result, almost the same disproportion being found in the statistics of the insane in other States and countries.

The solitude, the lack of intercourse with other

minds, the increasingly restricted routine of ideas year after year, all undoubtedly tend to make the agricultural life one tending to foster any disposition to melancholy mania. Other causes will readily suggest themselves to any one familiar with the habits and modes of thought of the population of our agricultural districts. The small farmer or farm laborer and his wife lead lives of hard manual toil; however pure or wholesome the mental atmosphere about them may be, it is one of exceptional narrowness and seclusion, where the same small subjects of thought are iterated and reiterated with a steady monotony.

More than the dwellers in cities, they build on the good opinion of their neighbors the social rank they are able to hold in the small community, the members of which, shut out from the outside world, watch each other from generation to generation with exaggerated interest. Petty debts and petty savings assume an incredible magnitude in their morbid anxiety. Many a man and woman give their whole lives to hard drudging and to small, biting economies in order to send a boy to college, or to free their few acres from mortgage. In such a solitary, narrow life, a disappointment or grief or physical ailment which touches the brain has leisure to canker and do its deadly work, which, in a life of less circumscribed ambitions or scope of outlook, would healthfully disappear by sheer force of friction.

The deadly work at last is done; the man is pronounced insane; he is a helpless burden on the State; his family sink into misery and poverty. Now, what would humanity and common sense dictate to the State as the proper course to pursue? Doubtless, to cure the man, if possible; restore him to his place as a working citizen and the supporter of his family, and relieve herself of the actual burden which he has become, and of the impending burden of his family. The State hospitals ought to afford skilled medical treatment for his case, and that wholesome change of daily life, that cheerfulness, consciousness of protection and friendly care essential to his cure.

What does the State do with him? Sends him to the county almshouse, within sight of his own home;—it may be to the almshouse which he has been taught to dread from his childhood as the receptacle of all that is degraded and vile; forces upon him, with every hour, his own damning disgrace in the eyes of his neighbors (the only world he knows); teaches the poor, luckless being, sometimes through inhuman cruelty, to regard himself thenceforth as cast out and accursed from human brotherhood, as the lepers that in old times stood without the gates, crying unclean! unclean! For no guilt but that of his misfortune, he is visited with punishment more terrible to him than death,—a punishment which, from the previous habits of thought and life which we have tried to portray, is certain to fasten his malady upon him irrevocably.

We have regarded this question, so far, from the side of the insane pauper, in the light of humanity. We shall now look upon it from the stand-point of public interest, and hope to be able to show that the confinement of this large body of useless dependents in a position where "cure" is impossible, is no less disadvantageous to the State than to the wretched victims.

First.—It is an uncontroverted fact, established by the authoritative statements of the highest medical experts, without dissent, that insanity is a physical disease and as readily curable as other bodily maladies.

Secondly.—The number of recent cases (cases where the disease has not existed over three months) cured under scientific hospital treatment is about seventy-five in every hundred, in the first six months' time. It has also been shown, by the same authority, that not over seven in every hundred of the insane confined in the ordinary almshouses leave them restored to health. Our own reports state that eighty per cent. of the insane in the State are held as incurable.

Now, if seventy-five per cent. are curable (as they are, according to scientific computation, tested by experience), and that percentage has actually been cured in our own hospitals, the only explanation of this terrible majority of incurables in Pennsylvania is their confinement in almshouses.

We would point out as matter for your consideration, in passing, the different modes of treatment of this class of unfortunates in the almshouses and hospitals, both exercised under the authority of the State; for the State makes the laws which control the action of the counties.

The almshouse system is based upon the old theory by which the mind was held to be absolutely apart from the body. The insane man was held by the ancients to be possessed by a god or a demon, and was either treated with reverential homage, and his maniac utterances received as divine oracles, or he was driven out, as a thing accursed, from human habitations. Among ourselves, but a generation ago, insanity was regarded with awe and dislike, as an inscrutable malediction of Providence, belonging to the emotional or religious life of man. It was accounted for (as sudden deaths were then disposed of by coroners' juries) as coming "by the visitation of God." The almshouse system is, as we said, still based upon this theory. The unhappy wretch, cursed by this visitation of God, is given a straw litter, food and drink, and is locked in a cell covered with vermin, to wait until the same mysterious dispensation of power shall cure or kill him. We need but cite as proof the condition of the Philadelphia Almshouse Hospital (as favorable an example as exists in the State, judiciously governed by a skillful and humane physician), where, owing to overcrowding, it is necessary to place two or three patients in one cell, and hand-cuff them to prevent their injuring each other, and where, notwithstanding the hourly visits of attendants, the danger of murder from this forced, unwholesome contact, is reported by the medical superintendent as imminent, and where it has actually occurred on several occasions. Five hundred more patients are received into this institution than its capacity warrants. Yet this is our model almshouse, under the care of a skilled physician. What chance of cure is there here for the lunatic, hand-cuffed to keep him from killing or being killed?

The common sense and higher religious intelligence of mankind have fortunately discovered that in this case, as in every other, God works through secondary causes,—that insanity, as well as scrofula or tetanus, can be traced to physical laws and their violation. The material brain which is the mouth-piece of the immaterial mind, is found to be subject to the same chemical changes, the same hygienic influences, as the liver or the stomach. It needs medicine, rest, certain kinds of food as much or more than they. A guilty man who drops dead is not now supposed to be smitten by the suddenly-outstretched hand of an angry God. "After death it is found that the cerebral tissue is torn by an effusion of blood into substance." When this mouth-piece—this mechanical organ—is out of order, it necessarily misrepresents the mind. "The organic affections of the brain," says an eminent medical authority, "necessarily modify the mental conditions, not only by destroying the efficiency of a certain portion of the tissue, but by interfering with the due performance of organic changes in other parts." The researches into the path of knowledge, of which this is but the starting point, have been vigorous and accurate. Not only is it a matter of certainty how far and in what manner disorders of the mind may affect the material organs, but also the reflex action of the diseased body upon the thinking power is at last subject to plain, practical rules, and may be controlled and to a certain extent hindered. The scientific physician can not only decide how far the unhealthy action of the mind of a morbid or visionary man is due to lack of oxygen, or surplus of bile in the blood, but he can trace, by reasons founded on the solid basis of statistics, the great majority of cases of insanity and idiocy to tangible causes. Cretinism in certain European countries is distinctly traceable to the argillaceous soil and enormous deposits of gypsum in the hillsides; a singular form of melancholy mania prevalent among the inhabitants of La Bresse is produced by the malarious air of the marshes. M. Esquirol says that one-half the cases of insanity among the higher classes in France, and one-third among the lower, have been inherited from parents or ancestors. Seventy-seven per cent. of the cases at the Bicêtre were hereditary. Epilepsy, chorea, all neural diseases, and consumption in the parents, manifest themselves in insanity in the children. In a still larger degree chronic alcoholism in one generation adds, in the next, this crowning, most terrible, calamity to its deadly fruit.

The point and force of these statements lie in the truth that insanity, thus traced by the clear eye of science to its physical causes, is, like any other malady primary in the body, open to cure by scientific means. We have thus reached the cause of the fact that while seventy-five per cent. of "recent cases," receiving scientific treatment in our hospitals, are curable, eighty per cent. of the insane in Pennsylvania are pronounced incurable, owing to their detention in poor-houses.

How does this fact affect the economy of the State?

Putting the question of humanity aside, it may seem at first view cheaper to suffer these thousands of helpless human beings to become inmates of almshouses, than to subject them to the more costly treatment of the hospitals. The answer is a matter of figures, not sentiment, and we will now endeavor to show conclusively that the truest economy will be secured by making the well-managed hospital the sole recipient of every insane man, woman, and child in the Commonwealth, and by making such legislative provision as will furnish accommodations for at least every recent case which may hereafter occur.

Whatever errors may have occurred in the census of 1870 in the enumeration of the insane in some of the States, so far as it relates to the number in the State of Pennsylvania it may be taken as sufficiently correct for all practical purposes. We do not assume that it is perfect, for that, with the machinery existing under present laws, is impossible; but it is entitled to confidence as regards the numbers of the "unfortunate classes," particularly the insane, until disproved by facts gathered under a more systematic agency. In a previous report made to your honorable bodies, we stated that, "by the returns on file in this office, the number of insane maintained in institutions, or by authorities making reports to the Board of Public Charities, on September 30th, 1873, was three thousand eight hundred and forty-two. It is estimated that there are in addition about six hundred, who comprise the increase in county institutions since the above date, those who are retained under family care and those who wander about as outcasts, making a total of four thousand four hundred and forty-two." In the census, the number of insane on June 30th, 1870, was three thousand eight hundred and ninety-five; allowing for the increase of the same, on September 30th, 1873, they would number four thousand three hundred and sixty-eight, being a difference of but seventy-four. A more remarkable evidence of the accuracy of the census is furnished by the investigation of the Board of State Commissioners of Public Charities of New York, in regard to the number of this afflicted class in that State. The prosecution of the inquiry involved the addressing of nearly seven thousand written and printed communications to physicians and officers of institutions. The result of the investigation showed that there were living on December 31st, 1871, according to the reports, six thousand seven hundred and seventy-five. The census of June 30th, 1870, enumerated six thousand three hundred and fifty-three, to which if added the number obtained from the rate of increase, as shown by the census of 1870, would, on December 31st, 1871, give, as the number living, six thousand seven hundred and thirty-three, or only forty-two less than the number ascertained by the investigation of the Commissioners of the State Board of Public Charities of New York. We make these statements as confirmatory of our view as regards Pennsylvania, in which the enumeration of this afflicted class is sufficiently accurate to furnish a basis for any legislation for their proper care and remedial treatment.

In the third report of this board, we stated that it may be expected that one in one thousand six hundred and ninety persons in Pennsylvania will yearly become insane. This statement, emanating from the high official authority of medical experts on the subject, was believed at the time to be correct; but an examination of the returns of the hospitals for the insane, in regard to their admissions, and the number discharged therefrom as restored or died, has, in connection with our proved practical accuracy of enumeration of this class of unfortunates, given us reasons for believing that about one in three thousand nine hundred and eighty-six of the population of Pennsylvania annually becomes insane; that one in one thousand six hundred and ninety *does not*, is clearly shown, thus:—

On June 30th, 1863, there were in Pennsylvania, according to the annual increase, as shown by the census, three thousand and sixty-seven insane persons. Upon the basis that one in one thousand six hundred and ninety of the population becomes insane annually, there would be developed from 1864 to 1873 twenty thousand two hundred and seventy-five cases of insanity, which, added to the number remaining from the preceding year, would give twenty-three thousand three hundred and forty-two cases in ten years.

If this was true, what became of them? From the returns of the State Lunatic Hospital at Harrisburg, Western Pennsylvania Hospital at Dixmont, Friends' Asylum at Frankford, Pennsylvania Hospital (Kirkbride's), and the Philadelphia Hospital, there were restored in these five institutions three thousand four hundred and ninety-four, and one thousand nine hundred and eighty-one died within the same period, viz., 1864 to 1873, leaving a balance of seventeen thousand eight hundred and sixty-seven cases, according to the above computation, to be accounted for. Of this number, we know from our returns and investigations that there were not four thousand four hundred and forty-two living on September 30th, 1873, leaving a balance to have died, or been cured in almshouses or families, of thirteen thousand four hundred and twenty-five. This statement alone is sufficient to show how mistaken is the estimate that one in one thousand six hundred and ninety of the population becomes insane.

[We note in passing, in regard to the hospitals for the insane, that the low percentage of cures is due to the fact that but one-half of the patients received had the disease for less than one year prior to their admission.]

In illustration of our theory as to the probable percentage of new cases of insanity, we present the following table, giving the population and number who should have become annually insane upon the basis of one to one thousand six hundred and ninety, during the decade from 1864 to 1875, inclusive :—

YEARS.	Population.	Will become insane annually on the basis of 1 in 1690.	RESTORED OR DIED IN FIVE HOSPITALS.		
			Restored.	Died.	Total.
1864, ...	3,138,385	1,857	335	215	550
1865, ...	3,199,270	1,893	380	223	603
1866, ...	3,261,336	1,929	301	204	505
1867, ...	3,324,606	1,967	351	216	567
1868, ...	3,389,103	2,005	395	190	585
1869, ...	3,454,852	2,044	339	210	549
1870, ...	3,521,951	2,084	347	157	504
1871, ...	3,590,277	2,124	381	207	588
1872, ...	3,659,928	2,165	366	200	566
1873, ...	3,730,931	2,207	299	159	458
Number become insane in ten years,		20,275	3,494	1,981	5,475
Add number remaining insane from 1863, ...		3,067			
Insane population for ten years, .		23, 42			
Deduct restored and died in hospitals, ...		5,475			
		17,867			
There were not *over* this number living September 30th, 1873, . .		4,442			
Leaving as restored or died in almshouses and private families,		13,425			

As we have already stated, it may be assumed, as near an approximation to the truth as can possibly be now obtained, that one in three thousand nine hundred and eighty-six of the population of Pennsylvania annually becomes insane. In verification of this estimate we present the following table, exhibiting the number of cases developed annually, with the aggregate insane population from the year 1864 to 1873:—

YEARS.	Population.	Number will become insane annually on the basis of 1 in 3986.	Aggregate insane population.
1864,	3,138,385	787	3,854
1865,	3,199,270	802	3,976
1866,	3,261,336	818	4,103
1867,	3,324,606	834	4,234
1868,	3,389,103	850	4,369
1869,	3,454,852	867	4,509
1870,	3,521,951	884	4,653
1871,	3,599,277	901	4,796
1872,	3,659,928	918	4,949
1873,	3,730,931	936	5,108
Will become insane in ten years,		8,597	

If to the eight thousand five hundred and ninety-seven who, in consonance with our computation, became insane in ten years, we add three thousand and sixty-seven as the number remaining from the year 1863, it will give a total of eleven thousand six hundred and sixty-four as the insane population for ten years.

It is important for us now to inquire how many were restored, how many died, and the probable number remaining at the end of the decade. The next table will show these facts, thus :—

YEARS.	Aggregate insane population.	IN HOSPITALS.		OUT OF HOSPITALS.		Total of restored and died.	Number remaining insane.
		Restored.	Died.	Restored.	Died.		
1864, . .	3,854	299	159	120	102	680	3,174
1865, . .	3,976	366	200	67	58	691	3,285
1866. . .	4,103	381	207	62	53	703	3,400
1867, . .	4,234	347	157	114	97	715	3,519
1868, . .	4,369	339	210	96	82	727	3,642
1869, . .	4,509	395	190	84	71	740	3,769
1870, . .	4,653	351	216	103	88	758	3,895
1871, . .	4,796	301	204	140	120	765	4,031
1872, . .	4,949	380	223	94	80	777	4,172
1873, . .	5,108	335	215	130	110	790	4,318

Here we learn that of the eleven thousand six hundred and sixty-four insane, four thousand five hundred and four—38.51 per cent.—were restored, and two thousand eight hundred and forty-two, or 24.36 per cent., died, leaving four thousand three hundred and eighteen insane on June 30th, 1873. The number based upon our own returns would be four thousand three hundred and ninety-two.

We now inquire whether any additional accommodations in the form of hospitals are needed. The increase of the *insane* population of 1873 over that of 1864 was 36.04 per cent., while the increase of the *sane* population, for the same period, was only 18.88 per cent.:—

	1864.	Increase.	1873.
Sane population, ...	3,138,385	18.88 per cent.	3,730,931
Insane population, . .	3,174	36.04 "	4,318

Although such is the fact, it would be erroneous to infer that all the recent cases are sent to the hospitals and the balance of the admissions made up of chronic cases.

The following table will show to what extent recent and chronic cases are admitted into the hospitals :—

YEARS.	Number resident in the hospitals at beginning of year.	Duration of disease before admission of those received during the year.			Per cent. on admissions of those whose disease was under twelve months.	Annual population of insane in the hospitals.
		Under twelve months.	Above twelve months.	Total.		
1864, . . .	1,293	360	451	811	44.4	2,104
1865, . . .	1,346	412	472	884	46.6	2,230
1866, . . .	1,442	473	503	976	48.5	2,418
1867, . . .	1,453	489	532	1,021	47.9	2,474
1868, . . .	1,616	514	508	1,022	50.3	2,638
1869, . . .	1,719	503	560	1,063	47.3	2,782
1870, . . .	1,835	537	572	1,109	48.4	2,944
1871, . . .	1,996	578	521	1,099	52.6	3,095
1872, . . .	2,166	591	613	1,204	49.1	3,370
1873, . . .	2,274	520	595	1,115	46.6	3,389
Totals, .	. . .	4,977	5,327	10,304	48.3	

Thus we see how our hospitals are rapidly filled with unfortunate patients whose duration of disease was of one, two, three, four, five years and upwards, who cannot but become a lifelong expense to the public. We have, for the purpose of this paper, in the above table, considered as "recent" cases those whose disease before admission was under twelve months, compared with others existing over twelve months.

It is but proper to state that many experts in the treatment of this disease limit the term of "recent" cases to the class in which the malady existed for only six months or less. The highest authorities, as Tuke, Esquirol, Pinel, and others, agree that the average time in which a chance of cure may be expected is less than one year, and after the third year the probability of cure is at the rate of about one-eighth of one per cent.

We now inquire what has been the result of treatment in our hospitals?

YEARS.	Annual population of insane in the five hospitals.	Per cent. on the whole number treated who were discharged as—			Total number discharged.	Number remaining at the end of the year.
		Restored.	Died.	Improved and unimproved.		
1864, . . .	2,104	14.21	7.56	14.26	758	1,346
1865, . . .	2,230	16.41	8.97	9.96	788	1,442
1866, . . .	2,418	15.76	8.56	15.59	965	1,453
1867, . . .	2,474	14.02	6.35	14.31	858	1,616
1868, . . .	2,638	12.85	9.96	14.03	919	1,719
1869, . .	2,782	14.20	6.83	13.01	947	1,835
1870, . . .	2,944	11.92	7.34	12.94	948	1,996
1871, . . .	3,095	9.72	6.60	13.70	929	2,166
1872, . . .	3,370	11.28	6.62	14.60	1,096	2,274
1873, . . .	3,389	9.88	6.35	13.60	1,011	2,378
Totals, .	. . .	13.03	7.31	13.60	9,219	

The result of the neglect of early treatment is strikingly exhibited in the above table, which shows that of the population or number annually treated, an average of only 13.03 were restored, 7.31 per cent. died, and 13.60 per cent. discharged as improved and unimproved. This population, as we have shown, is largely composed of chronic insane; eighteen to twenty per cent. of the annual admissions are re-admissions, and in only 48.3 per cent. the disease had existed for one year or less. It cannot be doubted that much better results under more favorable auspices would be obtained. All diseases in their incipient stages are readily manageable, and insanity is not an exception.

In the Journal of Insanity, 1870, page 379, it is stated, "that when patients are subject to early and judicious treatment in the first stages of this disease, from eighty to ninety per cent. will recover." We have cautiously stated in a previous report that "about seventy-five per cent. of recent cases of insanity will be cured in the first six or twelve months, if placed under proper and skillful treatment in our best hospitals," while "in poor-houses not more than seven per cent. will be cured in twelve months." This, we believe, is a fact admitted without a dissenting voice. What then would have been the result had there been ample accommodation for the reception of all the insane for the period named, viz., 1864 to 1873, with a compulsory law requiring that these hospitals should be used, or equally adequate measures for their restoration? Take the case of the 8597, which, as we have shown on page 411, is the probable number who would have become insane from 1863 to 1874, and assume that seventy-five per cent. or 6447 would recover; at an expense of three dollars per week for twenty-six weeks (the average term of treatment), it would amount to $502,866

The remainder, 2150 incurables, to be provided for, during an insane life of eighteen years, at a cost of $3 per week, would make, ... 6,037,200

Total cost of hospital treatment of 8597 insane persons, . . . $6,540,066

On the other hand, supposing these 8597 insane persons had been disposed of in the poor-houses, seven per cent., or 602, would recover in twelve months. At the rate of $1.50 each per week, the cost of maintenance would be . . $46,952

Leaving the remainder, 7995, as chronic insane, to be supported for say eighteen years, at $1.50 per week, which would amount to 11,224,980

Total cost of poor-house or no treatment, ... $11,271,932

This shows a clear saving of $4,731,866. Furthermore, as it costs the community or State to rear one of its members from birth, to the time when he earns more than he consumes, the sum of $500, then the first cost of the seven thousand nine hundred and ninety-five chronic insane was $3,997,500, and if we assume that they would have earned, if they had continued sane, on an average one hundred dollars per annum in excess of what they would have consumed, supposing they had lived eighteen years, it would have amounted to $14,391,000, which would have added so much to the wealth of the State. This constructive loss added to the first cost, amounts to $18,288,500. But under hospital treatment, supposing that only two thousand one hundred and fifty should remain incurable, there would be, by the same calculation, a loss or cost to the State of $4,945,000, which added to the amount saved by hospital treatment makes an aggregate of $9,676,-866, or a gain of that much to the wealth and power of the community, which has to a large extent (we may safely say one-half) been lost to the State for want of ample hospital accommodations, where the insane could have received adequate and skillful treatment. For we find that instead of eight thousand five hundred and ninety-seven being sent to the hospitals as soon as the disease was developed, there were of those whose disease had existed for twelve months or less, only four thousand nine hundred and seventy-seven admitted, and from the crowded condition of the hospitals, preventing the proper classification of the patients, and greatly retarding their treatment, but a very small percentage, as we have shown, were cured. We urge a very careful attention to and also criticism of the above demonstration.

If this same state of things continues, we may well inquire what will be the result in the next decade, or from 1874 to 1883?

The following table will show the estimated population, the number that will probably become insane the aggregate insane population, with the number that will probably remain in the middle of each year:—

YEARS.	Population.	Number will become insane annually on the basis of 1 in 3986.	Aggregate insane population.	Estimated will remain insane in middle of each year.
1874, ...	3,803,311	954	5,272	4,469
1875, ...	3,877,095	972	5,441	4,625
1876, ...	3,952,311	992	5,617	4,787
1877, ...	4,028,986	1,011	5,798	4,955
1878, ...	4,107,148	1,030	5,985	5,128
1879, ...	4,186,827	1,050	6,178	5,307
1880, ...	4,268,051	1,071	6,378	5,493
1881, ...	4,350,851	1,092	6,585	5,685
1882, ...	4,435,258	1,113	6,798	5,884
1883, ...	4,521,302	1,134	7,018	6,090

Estimated number who will become insane in ten years, . .	10,419
Add number remaining insane in 1873, ...	4,318
Total, ...	14,737

The population of the State, and of the insane in the above table, are estimated upon the ratio of increase as shown by the census of 1870, and exhibits some important facts for the consideration of philanthropists. Upon the basis that one in three thousand nine hundred and eighty-six become insane annually, there will be developed in ten years, from 1874 to 1883, ten thousand four hundred and nineteen cases of insanity. These, added to the number remaining insane from 1873, viz., four thousand three hundred and eighteen, will make a total of fourteen thousand seven hundred and thirty-seven. Of this number we estimate that, including the hospital at Danville, which went into operation in 1873 (the number restored outside of the hospitals being in proportion about the same as in the preceding decade), five thousand and sixty-four will be restored, and three thousand five hundred and eighty-three will die, leaving in the middle of the year 1883 six thousand and ninety insane persons living. It will thus be observed that the insane population would be increased from four thousand four hundred and sixty-nine, in 1874, to six thousand and ninety at the end of the decade, under the system of treatment now in operation.

This growing burden upon the resources of the Commonwealth imperatively demands that immediate measures be taken to lessen the number of these unfortunates. In other words, that the current system respecting them be revolutionized by proper legislation.

It is the interest of the State, as well as the demand of humanity, that this should be effected. Dr. Jarvis has stated in the fifth report of the Board of Health of Massachusetts, page 382:—"*If the persons who are attacked with this disorder are as promptly cared for as others when attacked with fever, dysentery, pneumonia, eighty or ninety per cent. can be restored to health and usefulness; but, if neglected, the disease tends rapidly to fix itself upon the brain, and becomes more and more difficult to remove. If allowed to remain one year, the chance of restoration is materially diminished. In two years this hope is reduced more than half; and after five years' duration few are restored, and even then it is due to some unexpected turn of the disease, rather than the result of healing remedies.*"

It is thus clearly demonstrable that the economic interests of the State are largely concerned in uprooting the past and re-establishing a future for this class of dependents, which shall not only restore them to the power of self-support and family support, but also shall gladden many lives upon which gloom and misery now perpetually lower and depress. It is a most discouraging task to undertake the proposed revolution. We estimate that there are now in this Commonwealth four thousand four hundred and sixty-nine insane persons, and that of these three thousand five hundred and seventy-six are incurable. The discouragement which is felt in contemplating such a state of things is simply overwhelming. It exceeds even that which one feels in regarding the increase of the criminal or the pauper class; and we are less insensible to it only because the former are regarded as further beyond the pale of human consideration than the selected few who are their keepers. The public interest and the active public sympathy decline, because of the false notion which exists, that these stricken members of the community are doomed to desertion by the "mysterious" malady which has overpowered and obscured their reason, while it happens that every day we are enjoying domestic comfort, sharing business enterprises, or taking counsel with many, who have at some time been members of the very class who, by a false public impression, become as estranged from public care and thought as are the mummies in the Egyptian catacombs.

Having proved conclusively, as we think, that some other method than that heretofore used by the State must be tried (unless we accept the alternative, which plainly confronts us, of a great and increasing aggregate of unrelieved suffering and disease, and a corresponding expenditure of public funds for the maintenance of their victims), we turn to the suggestion of a plan by which we believe the remedy may be applied with benefit to the treasury of the people, as well as to the stricken and helpless beings whose sad woes appeal to every heart, not only for sympathy, but for sure and permanent relief.

Past experience has demonstrated that the legislature will not build costly hospitals fast enough to receive the gathering increase of the insane, and especially for the reception of the population of the various poor-houses, who are so imperfectly cared for in the best conditions of such houses of detention. Outlays for these structures have come to be of magnificent proportions; so much so, that the legislature of 1872 felt constrained, by economical considerations, to refuse, for that year, all pecuniary aid towards the completion of the Danville Hospital, although the needs of the insane for hospital accommodation were sore and pressing.

This is not surprising when we discover that the cost of such infirmaries for the sick poor are so enormous, and the length of time required for their construction so great. Patience becomes exhausted, and liberality receives a natural check.

But if the legislature becomes informed of the real condition of its helpless wards, by frank and honest statement concerning them; if, knowing their needs, it is shown a reasonable plan for their relief, quick in application and attainable without extravagance, the question of its readiness to accept and carry out such a measure without delay cannot, we think, be doubted.

Such a scheme we are now prepared to recommend, after full deliberation. It consists in the establishment, on the grounds of each of the State hospitals for the insane, detached buildings, near enough to the main institutions for convenience, for the accommodation of say two hundred of each sex of the chronic, and for the most part quiet, patients, whose number is always largely in excess in all of our hospitals.

These houses can be built substantially, and in perfect adaptation to their uses (and in accord, also, if necessary, with the architectural character of the main building), for $500 per patient, including furniture and every appliance and appurtenance demanded for their proper administration. They might consist of a single structure for each department, to accommodate two hundred patients, or, as in the case of the Willard Asylum for the Insane, in the State of New York, of groups of buildings for each department, with accommodations for fifty patients each; which is preferred by the managers of that institution and its most able and efficient medical superintendent, Dr. John B. Chapin. These extensions would be, of course, under the controlling authority of the physician-in-chief, but they would be directly managed by a superintendent and matron, and ordinarily visited by an assistant physician of the institution. The cost of "living" accommodations for these four hundred patients by our proposed plan would be $200,000. The average estimated cost of the Danville Hospital, *by builders*, was $1,200,000, with the originally intended provision for five hundred inmates, and without furniture. Its actual cost and its ultimate extent cannot be accurately estimated.

It will not be difficult, moreover, to compute the saving in the expense of maintenance and treatment of the inmates under the proposed management. The present weekly cost, as stated in the reports of the medical superintendents, is about four dollars and eighty-five cents *per caput.* We estimate the cost, under the system we now respectfully submit to your honorable bodies, not to exceed three dollars and fifty cents *per caput.* As to the ability of the chief to conduct an institution of such capacity as is herein indicated, we need only point to the hospital for the insane connected with the Philadelphia almshouse, in which are maintained over eleven hundred patients: as large a proportion of the curable class as in the State hospital, and with a want of almost every desirable feature for convenient or successful administration.

We quote here some passages from the last report of the Willard Asylum for the Insane, bearing most pertinently upon this very important question:—

"The number of insane persons in the asylum on the twentieth day of November, 1874, was nine hundred. The number of patients occupying single rooms was two hundred and ten; the remainder occupied associated dormitories. No casualty occurred during the night, and in my observation injuries are inflicted by the insane more frequently in the day-time. We record the experience of another year in confirmation of the opinion entertained that a large proportion of the chronic insane may be cared for in this manner without disturbance or danger to each other: the noise and turbulence of the insane being due principally to the presence of acute cases. We have passed through the wards, and about the buildings at night, without hearing more than one or two voices, and frequently entire quiet prevails.

"A number of cases have been brought here during the year, and forever released from the restraint of chains and noisome cells. A single case, that of an unknown foreigner, deserves a passing mention from the fact that he bears the marks of former respectability and intelligence, who was released from the heavy chains which he had worn about his legs for a period of nineteen years—a fate which rarely falls to the lot of the most hardened felons in countries less civilized than ours. Since the admission of this person he has occupied a room with others, and is harmless. We could record many similar cases, and fear that other instances exist in the State. We have speculated upon the causes which have led to the imposition of such painful restraint upon these wretched persons over long periods, and infer it has, perhaps, followed a single outbreak of maniacal violence, which is handed down among the traditions of the establishment and neighborhood to excite an apprehension of repetition. These facts should be commended to journalists, and engage the attention of others who are in the habit of arousing the public mind to the abuses and wrongs of the insane.

"Dr. Hoyt, secretary of the State Board of Public Charities, informs me, in a recent letter, that he 'found two hundred and thirteen insane locked in cells or chained (in an insane population of one thousand five hundred and twenty-eight) in the county poor-houses, when visited by me (him) in 1868. Most of these, it was said, had been so restrained for a long time, and many of them for several years. They were generally filthy, violent, and destructive, and several were entirely nude.'

"'The number of insane at present in the county poor-houses is nearly as large as in 1868, but they are in a much better condition. During the present year I have visited about forty of these institutions. I found several insane in some form of restraint, but observed none in chains, and but few locked in cells.'

"'I attribute this improvement in the condition of the insane under local care, to the removal of the more violent and disturbed cases to the Willard Asylum. There is still urgent need for more accommodation for the chronic insane.'

"We are gratified to be able to present this official statement, indicative of an improved public sentiment toward this unfortunate class. We trust it can soon be announced that this practice of caring for the insane has been effectually abolished throughout the State.

"One very serious objection heretofore made against our public buildings for charitable purposes has been their cost, hence the satisfaction we feel in presenting the actual facts and successful operations of these less expensive, yet substantial and comfortable, buildings for the care of the insane. Their reasonable cost obviates the objection, for, when good homes can be provided for the pauper insane of the State, at $500 *per capita*, who will complain or object? And when to this is added their support in comfort and safety, at an actual cost of three dollars per week, who will not commend the system which has led to such a result, and rejoice in a charity which has rescued so many from the ill-provided poor-houses of the State? One great object aimed at by the establishment of this asylum, and by connecting with it the cottage system of buildings, was to reduce the expense both of building and care. The result has fully met our expectations, and has, we think, assured the complete success of the great and humane enterprise of providing better homes for the chronic pauper insane than the poor-houses and the jails of the counties where necessity had compelled their confinement.

"By centralizing at the main asylum the general management, and by doing at the same place the baking and laundry-work for all the buildings, much expense is avoided, and more vigorous supervision and accountability secured. To this fact we attribute much of the success here, and upon it we base our confident expectations for the future, that we can extend without the heavy outlays for additional offices and for laundry and other purposes. The matter is reduced down to the simple cost of building, heating, and furnishing, and these, as has been demonstrated, may be brought to $500 per patient hereafter. We dwell upon this subject, because, in our judgment, it affords the real solution of the great question, what can be done with this most helpless and unfortunate class of our people? We assume that it is the duty of the State to look after, protect, provide for, and secure this class. They are homeless, friendless, irresponsible, dangerous, incapable of self-protection, and yet are citizens, part and parcel of the body politic; assuredly they are, and should be wards of the State. In the establishment of this asylum, the State has assumed to provide them a home, and has made provision for their proper care. It is quite evident that this humane purpose would have been greatly retarded, if not entirely defeated, without devising less expensive buildings than had heretofore been erected for the care of the insane. The class to be received here being chronic, can be provided for in cheaper buildings, with less expense than more recent and excited cases. Keeping these ends in view, we have proceeded with our system, planned our buildings, and now propose to extend on a scale that will give more room and better accommodations for less money than was supposed by many to be possible.

"In submitting to the legislature the result of another year's observation and experience in the management of this asylum, we would say we are more and more confirmed in our estimate of its importance and its peculiar adaptation to its purpose and aims. It was a great problem, 'How can the chronic insane be cared for?' and, most of all, how can this helpless, hopeless class, who are literally homeless, and to a large extent friendless and reduced to pauperism, be provided for? This question, involving so largely a just benevolence and becoming humanity, this institution is surely and wisely solving. Necessity compelled the use of the jail and the poor-houses; but neither jail nor poor-house is or can be made fit or proper places for insane people. In them, in addition to the mental disturbance, of necessity was added physical restraint and suffering. The safety of others demanded chains, shackles, and confinement. The want of convenience forced the shameful herding together of the sexes, when the animal passions had survived the loss of mental control. To remedy these great and crying evils this asylum was instituted, and for four years has been working its great, humane, Christian purpose. It has unshackled from the limbs of many of both sexes chains that long had bound them. It has taken from damp, cold, loathsome cells many more who had hardly seen the light of day for years. It has furnished to such, and hundreds of old, infirm, hopelessly insane, and demented ones, a good, warm, comfortable, and safe home. To do all this, it has burdened no one to any great extent. In addition, it has demonstrated that the great problem is easy of solution, and hence the earnestness with which we urge this subject so persistently upon your attention. We certainly can so extend the substantial, cheap buildings here on lands belonging to the State as to relieve all the poor-houses of the State from the presence of the insane now therein, or who will be liable hereafter to be sent there. Aside from the great good to the unfortunate insane, this result would greatly add to the efficiency and comfort of the almshouses for their legitimate work. We are assured that the work of this asylum has greatly improved many of the almshouses from which the insane have been removed. In every aspect in which the question has been viewed, the demand comes with constant and increasing force to go on until all the pauper insane are provided for outside of jails and poor-houses; to go on until all of this helpless, pitiable class are provided with safe and becoming homes, here or elsewhere, by the State."

It has been made perfectly clear by the facts we have set forth, by the authorities of the highest medical character which we have cited, by the gathered results of our own painful experience, and by the like experience of other similar commissions, that poor-houses are not proper places for the reception, care, or treatment of the insane. It is adverse not only to the interests of humanity, but to reason and common sense. The riches of benevolence are squandered thereby, as well as the substantial and tangible wealth of the community. We think that we have demonstrated this problem clearly and accurately to every unprejudiced, unselfish, thinking mind. We submit, then, that it is time at least to begin to close up this inhuman and destructive system. We have presented a plan which will effect this object, and which, we believe, will in time reverse the respective ratios of the curable and incurable insane within our State. If the cost of maintenance at our State hospitals for the insane is brought down to three dollars and fifteen cents, as at the Willard Institution, or rather to three dollars and fifty cents, per week per inmate, as at the Massachusetts State Hospital at Northampton, under the medical direction of Dr. Pliny Earle (a synopsis of whose very definite and detailed account of the system and its results is hereto appended), as we think it should be, and, as we believe, the worthy superintendents of our hospitals will succesfully endeavor to make it, the State can afford to allow the same ratio of reduction on the diminished, as she does upon the present cost, in the admissions of the indigent insane from the county authorities; which would remove the only existing obstruction to the reception of this class into the State hospitals. The cost, then, to the counties, would not exceed two dollars and fifty cents per week for each patient; and no county could fairly claim that it was more economical to keep her insane poor at home. Even now, when the interest upon property, the cost of wear and tear, and the proper proportion of the expense of supervision are charged, the real cost of each inmate of the insane department of an almshouse cannot be less and is often more than the sum we have suggested as the weekly charge by the State hospitals. And when we consider how insufficient in all respects is the almshouse treatment, and how the public mind demands and will further demand a higher standard and more effective system of care and treatment in these county establishments, if they continue to receive this class of the sick poor, it cannot be questioned that the pecuniary interest of the counties will be served by remitting entirely to the care of the State all of their insane who are not provided for in private hospitals. And we trust that the State will make provision to receive them, as she should do, for every reason that humanity and even self-interest can suggest.

SYNOPSIS OF REPORT FROM DR. PLINY EARLE, OF THE MASSACHUSETTS STATE HOSPITAL FOR THE INSANE AT NORTHAMPTON.

Total cost of hospital to the State was $373,000, of which sum $19,000 was for boilers, alterations in heating, new water-tanks, &c., several years after the hospital was opened. Deducting this sum from the $373,000, leaves the original cost to the State as $354,000.

From the year 1861 the entire appropriations which have been made to the hospital by the State amount to only $5000, which sum is included in the $19,000 previously mentioned.

As an offset to the $5000, the hospital has paid for additional land to the amount of $7425. The State has thus been overpaid for its bonus the sum of $2425.

The amount paid by the hospital for repairs and improvements during the nine years, from September, 1865, to 1874, is $95,318.91. The cash assets now on hand exceed the amount in 1865 by $18,526.43. The value of purchased provisions and supplies, including fuel and stored clothing on hand and paid for, is estimated at $12,381.98 increase over the amount on hand in 1865. The household furniture is estimated at least $8000 greater than in 1865. These various sums together make the total of $136,652.32 as the amount of debit of the State to the hospital.

The necessary current repairs of the buildings are estimated at $3000, which, for nine years, would make $27,000; deducting this sum from the $136,652.32, there is a remainder of $109,652.32 as being the amount which the hospital has itself expended for necessaries, which are usually paid for by direct appropriation from the public treasury.

These expenditures have been made from revenue derived from patients. We will take, for example, one year, as follows:—The weekly average number of patients for the year ending September 30th, 1874, was, of State paupers, $284\frac{48}{100}$; town paupers, $102\frac{88}{100}$; private patients, $82\frac{6}{100}$; total, $469\frac{42}{100}$. Their cost of maintenance was, for State paupers, three dollars and fifty cents per week for full support, including clothing; for town paupers, three dollars and fifty cents per week, exclusive of clothing; for private patients, at various prices, none over ten dollars per week, and averaging only five dollars and forty-three cents per week for each. Such were the sources of income for the year. The expenditures for the same period were as follows:—Expenses of repairs and improvements, $10,720.13; increase of cash assets during the year, $1,182.01; increase of purchased and paid for supplies, $2,224.66; an orchard of about fifteen acres of land, $4000. Total of self-betterments of the hospital during the year, $18,126.80.

CONCLUDING CHAPTER.

THE COMMONWEALTH OF PENNSYLVANIA ADOPTS THE PRINCIPLE OF PROVIDING HOSPITAL ACCOMMODATIONS FOR ALL HER INSANE POOR, RECOGNIZING THEM AS THE WARDS OF THE STATE.

THIS was one of my earliest thoughts and wishes in regard to the care of the insane; and the most persistent efforts of the administration of the Board of Public Charities were made to secure its adoption and execution.

As a preliminary step in this direction, the following action was taken by the board in relation to the insane department of the Philadelphia almshouse, as reported in 1870 to the legislature:—

At a stated meeting of the Board of Public Charities, held at the capitol on June 1st, 1870, Mr. Harrison offered the following preamble and resolution, which were unanimously adopted:—

WHEREAS, The insufficient and unsuitable accommodations for the inmates of the department for the insane of the Philadelphia almshouse, render it impossible not only to employ proper remedial measures for their recovery, but even to secure their personal comfort and safety; therefore,

Resolved, That this board respectfully request the Guardians of the Poor of Philadelphia County to take early action on this subject, and to adopt and persevere in the most effective measures to have these accommodations enlarged and improved.

Mr. Clymer offered the following resolution, which was adopted:—

Resolved, That the committee of this board for the district, in conjunction with the general agent, be instructed to present the above preamble and resolution to the proper authorities, both of the almshouse and the city of Philadelphia, and to express the views of the Board of Public Charities on this subject.

Stated Meeting, September 7th, 1870.

Mr. Harrison, on behalf of the committee on the Philadelphia almshouse, made a report and read extracts from several newspapers, expressing their approbation of the action of the Board of Public Charities in reference to the Philadelphia almshouse.

Report.

The committee appointed to communicate with the proper authorities in reference to the crowded condition of the insane department of the Philadelphia almshouse, respectfully report—

That shortly after the adjournment of the board, we presented the resolutions of the board on this subject to the Guardians of the Poor and the Councils of the City of Philadelphia, accompanied by a communication to Councils, hereto annexed, intended to impress them with the urgent necessity of affording immediate relief to the inmates of the above institution; that these papers having been appropriately referred, conferences were held with the committees, and other members of Councils; that a plan was devised to extend the accommodations for the insane, in the simplest and least expensive way that would secure proper wards for remedial treatment; that the information obtained was imparted to Councils, with a request for an application of $70,000, the sum needed to accomplish the work, which was granted by both branches, by a unanimous vote. Full plans and specifications have been prepared, after consultation with expert physicians, and a contract awarded, and preparation made for beginning the work.

The following communication was addressed to the Select and Common Councils of the City of Philadelphia:—

GENTLEMEN:—The undersigned, who have been intrusted with the duty of presenting to the authorities of the city of Philadelphia the accompanying preamble and resolutions of the Board of Public Charities, respectfully beg leave to state that we have endeavored to make ourselves thoroughly familiar with the condition of the insane department of the Philadelphia almshouse; and that we have done so, after large observation of similar institutions in various parts of the State. That while we observe, with unqualified satisfaction, that this institution is under the superintendence of an able and faithful physician,—an advantage too seldom enjoyed by county asylums,—we are constrained to recognize the painful fact that the contracted accommodations for so large a population, and the almost entire absence of needful resources for the application of scientific remedies, render a physician's skill almost useless, unless to repair the bodily harm which the inmates suffer, either from self-infliction or the violence of their companions, excited to frenzy by a mutually reacting irritation, which is the outgrowth alone of their crowded and unclassified condition. We are well aware that this communication would be an appropriate one to the board of guardians, and we should not fulfill our duty without urging upon them the necessity of instant attention to the subject; but, as legislation by yourselves is needed to enable that board to reach any practical result, we address you, also, as the more important authority in the premises.

We might easily set forth to you the clear right of this dependent and afflicted class of our citizens, not only on the ground of humanity, but of law and justice, to liberal care and guardianship from the city of Philadelphia. We might expose in detail their condition of constant retrogression, instead of advance, in mental and physical health; we might give our views as to what extension is needed to secure effectually the personal safety of the inmates, or, what is better, so to classify them as to give them the advantages of hospital treatment; but we forbear to occupy your attention at this time, further than to say, in behalf of the Board of Public Charities, that we should deprecate any reliance upon the prospective relief to this department of the almshouse, which may be anticipated from the establishment of a house of correction;* but that, with our present convictions, we have confidence only

* The thought was encouraged by some of the officials of the city government, that the contemplated house of correction would so relieve the almshouse as to afford the needed room for the insane inmates.

in the prompt enlargement of the department for the insane, upon the premises where it is now located.

GEO. L. HARRISON,
HIESTER CLYMER,
Committee.
WILMER WORTHINGTON,
Secretary and General Agent.

STATED MEETING, DECEMBER 7TH, 1870.

Mr. Harrison reported further proceedings in reference to the insane department of the Philadelphia almshouse.

The following communication was addressed to the Councils of Philadelphia on October 31st:—

GENTLEMEN:—The undersigned, members of the Board of Public Charities, who have especial supervision of the institutions in that district of the State in which Philadelphia is located, beg leave to make the following statement to your honorable bodies:—We look back with the most grateful feelings at your recent action in behalf of the insane department of the almshouse, and anticipate with confident hope that the condition of its inmates will be benefited to their own great improvement and the consequent credit and economic advantage of the city; but in order to realize full success, we earnestly ask your attention to a few points bearing most influentially upon the management of that institution. We take it for granted that suitable provision will be made for heating, lighting, ventilating, &c. the projected extension, which will be moderate in cost, but which should be obviously arranged for *now*, to prevent damage to the buildings and to save expense from its introduction after they are completed.

Another important consideration is the compensation of the medical superintendent, and the character and qualifications of his assistants. It is entirely undeniable that a servant, conscious of unfair treatment, whether as to recompense or otherwise, is unable to meet fully the requisitions of his service, whatever may be the degree of his conscientiousness; and, for *this reason*, we fear that, should it become certain that the present appropriation for salary of that officer at our almshouse will not be considerably increased, the deep interest which is now manifested must necessarily decline; and it is quite sure that no suitable successor can be engaged on such terms. We feel confident that the physician of seven hundred and fifty insane inmates, with a salary of $1350 a year and perquisites of residence and vegetables, which would not increase this sum by $150, cannot, however devoted to his work, enjoy that satisfaction and that freedom from care for his domestic interests, which are essential to his full efficiency. We hope, therefore, that in the interests of the institution and the public, as also in justice to whoever may be the incumbent of that office, a more reasonable salary will be appropriated. We beg, in this relation, to adduce a few examples of the salaries paid to the physicians of similar institutions. At Colney Hatch, England, John Welsh writes that the "physicians receive equal to $3000 in gold, with house, fuel, light, butter, milk, and vegetables."

At the New York State Lunatic Asylum, with six hundred inmates, the appropriations for 1869 were "$10,000 for officers;" for "attendants, engineer, apothecary, butcher, tailor, farmer, bookkeeper, clerk, &c., $37,983.49." The physician has three assistants. At the hospital for the insane at Flatbush, Long Island, the salary is $2000, with residence and full support, including the convenience of a horse and carriage. The number of inmates there is six hundred. There are two assistants at $800 each. At the institution on Blackwell's Island, New York City, the salary is $2500, with dwelling apartments commodious and convenient, and partial subsistence. There are three assistants, the salary of the first being $1000. In our own State, Dr. Reed, of Dixmont, near Pittsburg, receives $3000, with dwelling and subsistence. He has four hundred patients, with, at present, one assistant at $900 salary, another being promised. Dr. Curwen, of the Harrisburg institution, receives $2500, with two assistants at $800 each; also, commodious apartments in the institution, subsistence, and other liberal provision. Number of inmates, four hundred. We are not aware of any similar institution of any magnitude where the compensation is so inadequate as at our own, and where there is no paid assistant. We therefore respectfully suggest that the salary of the medical superintendent of the insane department of the almshouse be increased; that a suitable dwelling-place for his family be provided, and that he be furnished with at least one paid assistant; for we must not fail to bear in mind that an insane asylum is not merely a place of detention, requiring only men of bone and muscle as "keepers," but a hospital, where scientific and experienced skill is required, with anxious care by night as well as day, for remedial treatment. In this connection we would also suggest that a moderate appropriation be made for the employment of *paid attendants*, the paupers who are detailed for this work being wholly unfit, and generally, from want of feeling and want of principle, practising cruelty or neglect, subversive of the first essentials towards relief or cure of this peculiar malady. With these improvements in the affairs of the almshouse asylum of this city, we are confident that, when the extension is completed, so evident an amelioration of the condition of that afflicted class of our citizens will be apparent, and so evident an advantage to the community from the speedy restoration of many of the inmates, as will lead us all to rejoice in the benevolent liberality which Councils have manifested in their behalf.

GEO. L. HARRISON,
HIESTER CLYMER,
Committee.
WILMER WORTHINGTON,
Secretary and General Agent.

This communication was referred to the Finance Committee of Councils, who reported favorably on its recommendations, and, thereupon, Councils made the requisite appropriations to carry them out.

Thus was taken up the best, and at the same time the most conspicuous example of an insane department in an almshouse with medical superintendence, but without suitable hospital accommodations for either sex. The appeal prepared by me, as chairman of the committee on this subject, was recognized by Councils, the grant was made without dissent; and extensions of the male and female departments were built as suggested. For the first time, up to this date, was full opportunity given, in a county almshouse, to the impoverished and helpless insane to enjoy the benefits which are derived from hospital accommodations, and hospital care and supervision.

Subsequently, in accordance with the further suggestions made in a second appeal to the Councils of Philadelphia, the medical superintendent was more adequately compensated, a paid assistant was given him, better nourishment was allowed to the patients, and the plan of "working the department in the cheapest way"—not the most economical—was abandoned. The efforts in this first movement were thus crowned with success; and while communicating with many members of Councils in relation to the matter, the expectation was announced that the State herself would at length assume the obligation and adopt the policy of providing hospital care and maintenance for the insane poor of Philadelphia, as well as of the rest of the Commonwealth; thus making her policy, in this regard, uniform and universal. The belief further was expressed that she would be prepared for the recognition of this humane and generous duty within the period of five years; and, for this end, incessant efforts were put forth to inform the intelligence and stir up the humanity of leading citizens to aid and sustain the board in the accomplishment of this great and cherished object.

The day after my report to the board in the Philadelphia case, recited above, the following record is made of its proceedings:—

MEETING HELD AT HARRISBURG, DECEMBER 8TH, 1870.

Mr. Harrison offered the following resolutions, which were adopted:—

Resolved, That the Board of Public Charities, having witnessed the evils which result from the connection of insane asylums with almshouses, and believing that a wrong is done to the insane by classing them with paupers, hindering the public from estimating aright their claims to sympathy and remedial treatment, disapprove of such an alliance, and believe that the best interests of this afflicted class of her people, and the duty of the State, concur in the establishment by the State, within a reasonable time, of sufficient accommodations for the maintenance and treatment of all the insane who may not be cared for in private hospitals.

Resolved, That, in the judgment of the board, all superintendents of hospitals for the insane should be members of the medical profession.

The effort thus inaugurated in 1870 being earnestly followed up from year to year,—as the preceding pages will show,—resulted, in the winter of 1875, in my framing a bill for carrying into effect the desired object. Being unable to remain in Harrisburg during that session of the legislature, the measure, though reported to that body, was not pressed for enactment; but the legislature of 1876 passed the bill, providing for the purchase of two hundred acres of ground and the erection thereon of a State hospital for the accommodation of the insane poor of Philadelphia and some contiguous counties.

Though deeply regretting that the pressure of other engagements prevented me from accepting the place of chairman of the commission for carrying this act into effect,—to which I was appointed by the Governor of the State,—I close this little volume with the expression of my hearty joy and thanksgiving that the erection of this hospital, with the completion of others now being built, will enable the State to perform her recognized duty of supplying hospital accommodations for all the insane poor within her bounds; so that none need hereafter be left in prisons or in almshouses. The Harrisburg hospital will provide for the central portions of the State; the hospital at Dixmont for the south-western part; that at Warren, when completed according to its plans, will amply suffice, for many years to come, for the north-west; the hospital at Danville, when finished in like manner, will furnish abundant accommodation for the north-eastern portion; and, finally, the South-eastern Hospital, for the building of which the whole sum needed has been appropriated by the legislature, will be made to provide for Philadelphia and the adjoining counties, namely, for that district of the State which is designated by its title.

Thus will a great sum of money have been expended; but thus, also, will one of the most imperative duties of the Commonwealth have been fulfilled.

INDEX.

www.ingramcontent.com/pod-product-compliance
Lightning Source LLC
LaVergne TN
LVHW021128110826
845150LV00005B/964

* 9 7 8 1 4 2 5 5 5 0 1 9 6 *